Drops of Light

Drops of Light

By Sophia Love

All books published by Off World Publications ©

www.amazon.com/author/sophialove

Content and Cover Art sole property of
Off World Publications ©

Cover illustration by Tom Wundrak, Fine Art

Other Works

The Guardian, 2016

Inclusion, 2017

sī bôrg, 2017

Join me on a Love Quest, 2018

The Imposter, 2019

Words of One. All Volumes, 2020/2022

A Re-Imagination: Handbook for the Many of One, 2022

Visit *www.sophialove.org* for these and more.

Table of Contents

Preface

This book has experienced multiple iterations. The process seems to be mirroring our own journey. Initially, it was to be a compilation of quotes from One, showcased in a single place; powerful wisdom from someplace/someone beyond. These have been collected over the last dozen years. Yet that version remained unformed and still searching, sort of like us.

What emerged after that one didn't, was a sort of chronicle. It was a telling, and as the "teller", I was removed from it. That version was shared and I was directly told, more than once, that there was no heart in it; that it needed me.

So, what you hold is an attempt at including myself with all of the above. I hope that you will recognize elements of your own journey, and yourself here. We undergo an individual/mutual discovery of self. It is an astounding process, a painful episode, a gorgeous remembering. I apologize to anyone/anything missed in this re-telling. Know that you are not forgotten. I just ran out of room. We are One.

As Drops of Light, we are both unique components and indistinguishable puddles in the Flood of Light that bathes our Earth. It is, in the end, a beautiful illumination of every single thing.

Sophia
2023.08.14

Introduction

Although this book's title showed up in 2022, Some of its contents reach back into the last century. It is here when the first drops landed. It's a safe bet to say that they did not identify as drops then, yet their light was unmistakable to those with eyes to see.

You are about to read our Awakening story, as told over time from a multitude of voices. Although my name is listed as author, I must give credit to that multitude, who have spoken these many years.

Here's a description from One:

"You are drops of Light, gathered here now for the singularity. This moment of pure potential is to be illuminated by you and showcased by what it is you do."

"You are mere "drops" in perspective only. For, within you, is a flood of Light, being restrained by an illusion of control. This false matrix, now exposed due to your Brilliance, is unable to remain standing in the flood of your Light."

Sophia
2023.7.23

Foreword

Since some of this text is the transcription of a conversation, it is crucial to clarify in what ways the text has been interpreted to convey emphasis and voice. There are several of these cues, and they are as follows:

Bold face emphasis is used for extra stress on specific words. These are not my interpretations of what I heard, but highlighted that way as it came through.

In sections where there is an active conversation, italics indicate my own voice (that is, Sophia). Unless otherwise noted, all regular font face body text is the voice of either One, the individual or group Sophia is talking with, or both Sophia and One in unison.

Endnotes, and brackets may also be used during the dialogue to clarify contextual confusions.

Chapter 1
Darkness
(Pre-2012)

You begin,
feeling alone,
and isolated from any light at all.
You notice something happening –
notice the absence of visible light.

Drops of Light

This will be the shortest chapter. Not because of minimal content, for there is plenty. No. It will be the shortest because it is the darkest. Prolonged focus here only accentuates the lack of light.

It was not literally for lack of light that the darkness took hold, it was that the Light was obscured.

Light can be obscured many ways. It can be hidden. It can be unrecognized. It can be unseen, as in blindness.

In our case, the case of the human, it was a combination of all three. The humans were blind to their own Light. The human (himself or herself) did not recognize the Light in others. Most of these Lights were effectively hidden, due to actions by the controllers, along with the cooperation of humanity.

The darkness took hold due to this trifecta. There were random bursts of Light here and there, and they were sometimes noticed. Yet, they were isolated, and more often overlooked.

It seemed that there were more important things to do – always. There were jobs to perform, and there was money to make, and there was health to maintain, and then there was money to hold on to, and there was a list of myriad chores to do in order to remain upright – in order to function inside the matrix.

We gradually began to notice. We noticed the absence of Light. We began to wonder where it was located; this was the start of our searching…

Religions, rulers, and even money weren't supplying us with Light, that much was clear. On the contrary, these things seemed to simultaneously suck the Light out of things and then showcase it – promising always that "this too could be yours." You only needed to obey, follow these rules, comply, and ultimately – conform.

We did our best. This "carrot at the end of the stick" seemed to be where happiness was found. It was elusive. We recognized its absence and, for the most part we kept ourselves busy following orders. It seemed there was nothing else to do.

However, in our quiet moments, we knew. We knew that there was more. We knew that there was something else. We called out for it. It was that calling that led us to find each other.

In the 2004 film "What the Bleep do we know?" we met several scientists who introduced us to Quantum Physics. In 2006, "The Secret" was released and gave us methods we could use to work some creation magic of our own. Snippets of things that sounded possible were making their way into our conscious minds, and if we were lucky enough to find others, our conversations.

We (*my husband and I*) held viewing "parties" for both of those films at that time. After "The Secret" was released, we started to host a monthly "Creation Group" in our home for a small group of friends. We were attempting to figure out how to consciously improve our lives.

Let's go back to 2011, which was the year I (*Sophia*) came online. The reason I did was because I had written a book, and needed a place where people could find me. In retrospect, it was a pretty terrible book, yet it was from Facebook that I began the Love Quests, and all of my subsequent work, so I am grateful for it. You never know where things will lead you…Do you remember some of the headlines reported that year?

The year started with **violent protests in Egypt** that ousted Mubarak, and was followed by a **6.3 earthquake in Christchurch, New Zealand**, which was then followed by a **30-foot-high tsunami in Japan**, triggering the 2nd worst nuclear disaster on record. **Game of Thrones** premiered, **Fidel Castro resigned, Pope John Paul II was beautified** and

Osama bin Laden was killed. Serbian tennis star **Novak Djokovic won his first Wimbledon title**. There was a **deadly bombing in Oslo, Norway**. There were **riots in London** over a police shooting. **Steve Jobs** resigned from Apple due to **pancreatic cancer**. **Muammar Gaddafi** was captured and **killed** in a Libyan civil war. **East Africa** suffered its worst **drought** in 60 years, reportedly killing tens of thousands, half of whom were children. There was **Arab Spring,** and **Occupy Wall Street**. The **United States** came close to **defaulting on its debt** (*sound familiar?*).

These headlines give clues to what was happening within. Do you remember what you were feeling then? From here on, our story will be told from the first-person point of view. I am hoping that you will see yourself here as well; this is our collective story/journey. **We are these Drops of Light.**

Prior to 2012, the coordination of those working for the Light did not exist. Scattered voices popped into the airwaves here and there, yet these were neither in unison nor easy to locate. Such was the nascent beginning of our Light emergence as a viable force. We began, in those earlier years, to discover each other.

It was a surprise to me that there were so many others. Other humans who were thinking about, and believing some of what I somehow "knew" inside. It was exciting; it gave me hope. Garret John's "Wayseer Manifesto", in March of 2011, was a sort of tribal calling/gathering…

At this early stage we worked in isolation. We found each other at various esoteric websites and conferences. It was during this time that I discovered some whom I was on the same page with, as well as others who seemed to be in the stratosphere – their understanding of things was "way out there". I began here to categorize and name what I actually believed, as well as what I couldn't take on; the beginning of discernment.

It is important to note here that just because a headline was on the esoteric side of things, that did not guarantee its validity. The term "snake oil salesman" was used to describe some of what was out there. There were loud voices of supposed "truth", whose aim it was to make a buck. This still holds today.

In most cases, however, what I found were ideas and products that seemed to work for some, yet not for me. It was here where true discernment began. What I thought when something turned out to be either untrue or useless, depended on my current state of mind. Either I "threw them out" as con-men/con-women or gave them a pass and kept listening, assuming that they were mistaken rather than intentional with their unsubstantiated claim.

What can be said now, these many years later, is that it was moments such as these that defined polarity for me. It was, perhaps, an invisible concept then, yet my thoughts during most of these times were "you - vs - me". Oneness wasn't a viable concept – yet.

So, I can look back at the pre-2012 years as "discovery" years. During this time, I was mostly isolated, yet noticing occasional glimpses of Light here and there. It was not necessarily that I knew what this meant, or what to do with it, but these glimpses instilled a sense of hope. This kept my own Light going. This kept me on the lookout for others; other Lights.

In April of 2011 I started an event on Facebook. It was called "Join me on my Love Quest". Its premise was simple. Upon waking each day for 7 days, you were to look into your own eyes and say "I forgive you". That was it. I wanted to see what would happen.

This event started with just 4 attendees; 2 family members and 2 friends. It eventually grew to thousands before Facebook capped it. I was astonished that there were so many of us. These monthly events went on for two years! What started

Drops of Light

as an effort to forgive, grew into a full-out
expectation to discover joy and embody passion. The
Love Quests changed my life, and, I daresay, the lives
of many attendees. By the time the Quest events
were completed, I felt I'd discovered my Tribe; a
group of soul siblings that I never knew existed. We
focused on forgiveness for at least a part of each day,
and discovered Love there. It turned out, that was
where the Light was hiding.

This step in our Awakening was a necessary one. The
thrill of finding each other sparked a sort of
optimism. I may not have understood fully "why",
yet something was telling me that these pings of
remembering were important. They did not move
into my everyday life at this point. They were,
instead, possible occasional moments where a part of
my authentic self was noticed (*and it felt really good*).

I grew giddy at this juncture with the thrill of
discovery. It was at this point, (these many points) of
time when "time" itself began to be questioned.
These things now discovered felt imminent. Just
about everything was going to show up "soon".

Let me say here that this mis-remembering was part
of my Awakening. The fact that events were being
"seen" or "felt" by some of us with a platform now
to share them, (*the internet*), was beyond exciting. It
seemed as if the immediacy of everything was an

intrinsic part of each message or vision. It all felt so "real". What else could it be? This was a new and developing "6th sense". Experience and practice were necessary.

I was/we were in the discovery phase. This is akin to your first noticing of strong feelings of connection with another human. When they show up with someone "new" to you, it can be unsettling and feel immediate. Think about that "falling in love" feeling or even "love at first sight".

When that feeling shows up, it can feel urgent. Some of us will end years long relationships because of the feeling with/for another. That is a drastic action, yet the emotion demanded it. This was how strong the connection felt upon initial discovery; it inspired radical change.

Yet, the power of any new connection does not negate the validity of any other (*any existing connection*). We have experienced each other many "times" at numerous "moments". However, at the time it can seem that way (*where one negates the other*).

You are connected to who you are connected to. It is what you do once that connection is re-discovered (via recognition or "falling in love") that creates a life. You have all the power here. Earth is a free-will zone.

Drops of Light

That jolt of recognition is what directed most of the "this will happen **soon**" predictions and feelings. We were seeing and hearing things that we "knew" were true. Therefore, it must be imminent (our logical minds discerned). These were heady times of great expectations.

There were other things going on. Things not reported in the mainstream media. Some of these you might remember...

People like David Wilcock and Benjamin Fulford supplied us with alternative and fascinating detailed information. Reptilians were added to the conversation, along with David Icke. "One People" Flash mobs were a thing in cities globally. These were wonderful expressions of our universal connection to each another.

Inspired by them, a small group of us held a "Hug Quest" at "the Bean" in downtown Chicago, Illinois *(can you imagine such an event in a post-covid world?)*. It was wonderful. We hugged a lot of folks that day.

I was hearing about Arcturians, Sirians, and Pleiadians, and seemingly couldn't get enough. This was when I first heard about the Mayan calendar, and the countdown to 12/21/2012 began. Lee Harris called that year the "Year of Illumination", which seemed to fit perfectly. Looking back now, from

2023, it all seems rather innocent, exciting and lovely. I created a website that year (*www.sophialove.org*). Here are some quotes from my blog in 2011…

~

"As we understand "cause and effect" and realize it is truly "think and manifest", eventually it will come into our awareness that the two are simultaneously occurring, and **it will become a changed world indeed**.

The difference between the 3rd dimension and 5th dimension is only in our awareness. It is not that we move into a different place, it is that the place we are in becomes differently experienced."

~

"This shift you are participating in is not just something you are watching; it is what you are doing. All of the wondrous changes you hear about in the next dimensions are possible when you leave the density of fear. They cannot be instilled onto a fearful population to eliminate the fear – they are the by-products of a fearless and loving heart."

~

"The name "star-seed" is appropriate because we have come to yield a new race – one that is seeded purely, without the shadow of fear."

~

"It can feel as if we are being swept away in the current of the time. Don't allow yourself to be fooled.

Drops of Light

You are swimming of your own volition, either upstream or down. If you don't like the direction, it may be time to turn around."
~

Chapter 2
Opening a window
(2012)

You open your window
to both let in the light from elsewhere,
and also,
to allow some of your own Light
to seep out.

Drops of Light

A lot was promised for this year. You might say that 2012 saw the first of what was to grow into numerous unmet expectations for major and immediate change.

12.21.2012 was mainstream. I was working with special needs children that day, and our staff name tags said **"I survived the Mayan Apocalypse December 21, 2012"**. A celebratory gathering was set up at Buffalo Wild Wings after work for the survivors; if any.

I spent the evening in meditation and constant contact with a friend as well as one of my children, who was out of the country at the time. None of us knew exactly what was going to happen, yet we were compelled to "be ready" for whatever showed up.

The next morning, I was angry. I was disappointed. It felt as if I'd been deliberately "duped". I felt foolish. I resolved to "give up" on all of this "spiritual stuff". For a while afterwards, parts of me shut down.

But that was at the end of 2012. Let's start at the beginning. On January 1st, 2012, I wrote "Message to Off World Beings".[1] It was written in an unplanned and urgent sort of way, and once it was finished, I knew it was meant to be a video. My you tube channel had been started in 2011 and contained videos about Love and Unity, so this was a bit of a shift in subject matter. Looking back, I'd say it was a turning point for my work, that broadened its focus. It turns out that "off world beings" watch you tube. Who knew!

That first video yielded a few responses. It was winter, and this is the Midwest United States, so there was always snow in the yard. One of my children called me to his room one day to show me the odd markings that looked to have been dripped and then crystalized in the snow behind the house. They were oblong, tubular and angled. There were no trees above them and we couldn't figure out what could have made them. They remained long after the other snow had melted; the animals wouldn't go near them.

On another occasion, the family was together in the dining room at dinner and we all simultaneously heard what sounded like a classic space ship noise, directly above the house. We looked up at the ceiling, then we looked at each other, and hesitated for a minute, listening, then finally ran outside to check. We saw nothing in the sky; it looked black.

Three weeks after the video was produced, I was woken up telepathically. I've been told since then that this was a group of young Pleiadian friends out for a joy ride. (*I have no "proof" of that.*) I shared that story in a second video, "Response to Off World Beings

29

II".[2]

The next response showed up in April of that year. It was in a comment to the first video, "Message to Off World Beings". When I read the comment, I could feel the energy of the commenter. It was like nothing I'd ever felt. It began with **"Not all races around this Universe have "advanced" technologies"** …

This was my introduction to the "Guardian", who identified himself as a member of the "Forces of One". 2012 was the beginning of what became a several year's long exchange between him and many other readers. (*This has been chronicled on my website, and also in a book.*) He referred to 2012 as the Year of Revelation.

> *Mainstream news stories told us their version of what was happening…*

There was the tragic **shipwreck** of the cruise ship – the **Costa Concordia**. **Queen Elizabeth** celebrated 60 years on the throne on her **diamond jubilee**. **Whitney Houston died.** London hosted the **Summer Olympics; opening them with a bizarre hospital bed/dancing nurses/grim reaper performance** (*predictive programming for Covid-19?*). There were sexual abuse allegations against **Jimmy Savile in the UK. Malala Yousafzai, a 14-year-old Pakastani girl, was shot by the Taliban** for campaigning for the right to go to school. She survived. The **highest skydive record was broken by Felix Baumgartner**, from Austria, who jumped **from 128,097 feet**. There was the **tragic shooting** at the Batman movie in **Aurora, Colorado** and another shooting at **Sandy Hook** elementary school in Connecticut. **Hurricane Sandy** blasted into the Caribbean and the East Coast of North America. A United States diplomatic mission was attacked in **Benghazi, Libya** and four Americans were killed. **Barack Obama was re-elected** as the United States President.

In 2012, I was still new to both Facebook and YouTube, sharing videos that today look rather amateurish, and blog posts that don't, yet both saying many of things we are still repeating today… "We are the ones we are waiting for", "Just love", "The wait is over, our time is here" …Groups on Facebook were sharing my videos and blogs. They had names like "Worshipful Company of Lightworkers", "Unity Consciousness – ONE LOVE", "Portal to Ascension", "Humanity Wins", "Mind, Body and Spirit", "Arcturians-Sirians for Ascension", "Up lifting one person at a time to Ascension!", "The Global Brain Project", "Spiritual Blogs", "One Unify Fields – The 5D New Earth Gaia", "Unified Meditation for World Liberation Day", "The Big Multiversal Hug – Super Abrazo Multiversal", "The Beautiful New World", and many, many more.

Drops of Light

Thanks to the Mayan calendar, Ascension was all the rage.

We were waking up everywhere, and "meeting" others who were also along for the journey. Folks like Bashar and Greg Giles, Steve Beckow, and websites like the "Golden Age of Gaia", and "American Kabuki" kept us up to date on all things "woo-woo". Some of you may remember the "Neptune" spaceship ride that was planned yet didn't transpire. We cheered each other on, sharing whatever we thought would help. It was a stimulating and exciting time to be a part of what we called the "ground crew".

Speaking of the ground, strange sounds were being reported from various places around the earth. You could hear them on YouTube, they were sort of metallic and "Gabriel's Horn"[3] was an often-heard explanation for them.

Almost all of my published blog posts and videos discussed how to love and forgive without condition. The Love Quests were a full-time monthly endeavor. We were trying to figure it out & find what we were missing.

~

Here's an example of a blog post from January of that year...

~

"I will not presume to tell you who to love or how to

love, but to love, well, that is what you have come to do – it's why you were made – it must be the central point of every interaction."

~

In February, it seems that I was already preparing for the One, who had not yet shown up...

~

"As the first, your way is not easy and you knew it would not be. You knew and yet you took on this challenge, volunteered eagerly, for you knew as well that for every measure of difficulty there was an even greater measure of wonder.
You are here, now, poised on the brink of magnificence and ready to behold that wonder. Not for your own glory at the expense of another, but for the emergence of **the ONE – a unique wavelength of LOVE.**"

~

I was recognizing your drops of Light as they were just so bright, and they were emerging everywhere...

~

"You are love and the greatness of your truth peeks out when you are sure of yourself, loving, generous, kind and expansive.
Negative propaganda and temporary conditions of hardship are no longer effective on one such as you. You are beyond manipulation. **Your light has illuminated the path we are on.**"

~

I was chronicling our journey out loud, looking for

Drops of Light

fellow travelers and road signs — so sure of our destination in that remarkable year...

~

"You are creating this shift. It is not happening to you – it is being manifested by you and me and the loudest broadcast and the quietest hope. All of it matters."

~

"Equally responsible, we have all walked in each other's shoes to bring us to this point in our journey."

~

"There is no end, we are always beginning."

~

"We are walking through a hall of mirrors."

~

"We are ushering in an era of love."

~

"We are a synchronized band of light."

~

"This version of us is not where we begin and end, **we are infinite, powerful, multidimensional beings enjoying a human experience...** The ego is the only way we could define ourselves here."

~

"It is you who you've been searching for."

~

"I wonder how may "closet ascenders" there are amongst the people in my daily life."

~

"It feels as if I reside in two very different worlds.
In this one I am an infinite being, poised to usher in
this incredible new age for humanity.
In that one I am a mom in the U.S. suburbs who just
took her cat in to be groomed, and went to the
grocery store, and made a doctor's appointment for
her son."
~

"We've all heard the prophecies and channeled
messages, telling us "Soon". This is because we have
not yet combined both lives into one life. Until we
merge ascension and galactic citizenship with
cooking and car repairs, it won't happen."
~

"We have to come out of the closet."
~

"As we stumble our way to Oneness, we will have to
reach out and pull each other up and along, forgive
ourselves, and everyone else, and smile."
~

*There were so many questions. The whole notion of a
mass shift in consciousness felt overwhelming...*
~

"We move forward with day jobs and holidays,
purchases, and chores that seem at best mediocre.
Nothing we do on a day-to-day basis holds much
fascination. We are having a tough time caring.
What's the point?"
~

"So, how do we stay awake and aware without falling

into the abyss of fear? How can we remain aware of the arrests, the galactic federation and this consciousness shift with calm and control; while managing lives, children, jobs, relationships and households?"

~

"Where is this place we dream of? Dorothy said it was over the rainbow and current prophecy places it in the fourth or fifth dimension. It seems always someplace else and that is suspect. Can it not be here?"

~

"Will I wake up tomorrow and say "Aha!" I am here; no more yellow bricks or portals or spaceships or searching. Can I do that?"

~

"Today we are enjoying the thrill of expectation for that magical moment when we'll all be "shifted" and "ascended" – 12.21.12. And then what?"

~

"Is this 3D all there is or not? Are we merely bodies living dense lives of struggle or are we eternal lights, bits of the fabric of creation, and particles of love? What is truth?"

~

We formulated some answers to keep ourselves going…

~

"You are the light within which we can recognize our own light; a candle so brilliant you illuminate us all.

Our road to the next dimension is easier to see now; your brilliance makes it so."

~

"You are a whisper of love from our creator, gently placed on this earth as a piece of eternity."

~

"Your life is a projection of your deepest beliefs – no longer separate from your "real life", all is one; life and love, "woo-woo" and practical, the bills and abundance, on line and on the street."

~

Once the Guardian showed up that April, the posts became more urgent, and varied…

~

"This is not a game or just a nice thing to do. It is vital. The controllers have seen to it that we dismiss love as a frilly and fluffy emotion that weakens our resolve and our production. Nothing could be further from the truth. Love has all the power. Love is what has cast you forth and is the very core of who you are. Any lack of love will play out as low self-esteem or a desire for control – separation. **We are not separate. We are One**."

~

"No longer can we say we don't matter. In fact, we matter very much. How we are feeling reverberates out and the universe responds. Our universe. It will respond to the answer we emit and there are only two choices – Unity/Love or Polarity/Fear. It is time to choose."

Drops of Light

~

"There is a beautiful phrase out there – "The Art of Allowing". It implies skill is necessary for it to be pulled off. It takes practice.
I can love my brothers and sisters in a general sense, yet hate the man who raped me. You would not fault me for this…This is the way we think and in our current world, expected and justified.
This Shift asks us to change all that. The question we are being asked is indeed being answered. It is being answered within. Do you love without condition? Are you able to view an act of atrocity, even then work to see it corrected and the perpetrator rehabilitated, without hatred? Is your love big enough?"

~

"You are a single, exquisite particle of life – vital to its expression, complexity and brilliance. There is nothing wrong. You are perfectly positioned and right on time. You haven't been dropped in or tossed in, you exist as part of the whole, here with the rest of us, lighting our way."

~

"We are seeing the depths of the roots of our human "weeds". They need to be removed, not destroyed. Respect for all of life demands that each action benefit the whole. Once these weeds are gone, we are going to need fertile ground.
We are gardeners, not weed killers."

~

"You are a microcosmic version of what is happening to us all – Oneness."

~

"This time now is for preparation – internal and deliberate peace. You are here by choice. You are perfectly suited. There is no longer a question about readiness. We are up to the doing."

~

"We are in the age of enlightenment. There are truths uncovered daily and sometimes it feels, hourly."

~

We began to meditate together...

~

"How many humans does it take to change the world? Apparently 144,000. There is an event, (World Liberation Day), playing out on our stage May 5/6th,2012."

~

"On World Liberation Day, at the moment of the full moon, we felt our oneness."

~

"The moment we joined there was a sort of jolt, and then a very gentle yet definitive force. Our light encompassed the earth, and could be seen. In that state, the dark moved on. It was a sort of edging out, a quiet push, no physical force was necessary. It is a fact that light extinguishes the dark."

~

39

Drops of Light

"Afterglow is important. This has been a shared excursion, our "first time" as One. We'll do it again, it's inevitable, it was just too delicious not to.
We know now who we are. We are the ones we've been waiting for."
~

"There was a movie released simultaneously this weekend; The Avengers – Earths Mightiest Heroes."
~

"My entire body sort of hums now. Several weeks ago, the internal motor started and today the subtle vibration and sparkling is constant – I barely acknowledge it. This week there are waves of energy, resulting in a sensation of spinning. My diet and sleep patterns are all over the map, which is true for my entire family."
~

"Are we there yet?" need no longer be asked, the answer is yes. This is our ascension. There is not a day or specific moment in which it occurs; there is instead this consistent gradual process of awareness."
~

"There is a preoccupation with the physical right now, a focus on the body – the body
human. Listening to "Drake" reports and planning for a possible disruption of supply brings up questions – "Do we have enough?" "Have we thought of everything?"
~

"I have spent some time in the "humans are less cool than other life forms" camp, as well as the place where "earthling's rule". Polarization."

~

"Our ability to create an amazing life is not new — just look around. In the face of complete oppression and blind obedience we've managed to love out loud. We are being watched and helped now not because what we have is unnecessary, but because there is yet more. We'll keep the good parts. It's okay we're human, in fact it's wonderful. Our galactic brethren will share "instant food" technology, while we feed them a home cooked meal."

~

"There are moments where sleep sort of descends with no regard for the clock. There are periods of stillness. The vibrations are constant; prickles of light throughout my limbs and often a physical "humming". Waves of dizziness force me to grab onto something to steady myself. Moments of anticipation erupt, where every cell is on high alert."

~

"Being one online is a good start, yet the truth must be lived.
As long as we see and fear the "other", he exists."

~

"These are very dense times. There are concerns about money, food, shelter, health. How does a being of light and extraordinary power handle these "end times"? With ridiculous hope, unwavering belief and steadfast love. You know you have come for this.

When a new obstacle shouts at you, see it for what it is – a very solid illusion, another hurdle. Then strategize which method you'll use to get past it. Will you climb it, jump over it, find your way around it or crawl through it?"

~

"We have entered the Head Games. How we think is critical to what we create. We are beginning to get the idea of oneness; at times we are giddy with joy! It's all okay! I love you! You love me! I'm okay just as I am! It's all going to be great!
Yet we are alive in a field of density, with bills to pay, tests to pass, deadlines to meet and people to please. This is not a forgiving world and the one who is the hardest on you is you."

~

"I have previously imagined it would take miracles and magic to erase the physical signs of aging. I was wrong. It will take a cessation of worry and a mind without fear. The calm of unity is like a fountain of youth."

~

The demands of this physical life didn't stop…

~

"I no longer worry about money. There is none. I've reached the bottom. It is no longer a matter of juggling; it is a matter of keeping food in the house until things change."

~

World Liberation Day needed a boost, and 2 weeks after that there was another event, led by COBRA…

~

"This is the year of weird. We need to risk being weird and standing out in a crowd. Things have to change and it will take us to see that they do. We are powerful beings of light, filled to the brim with love and wisdom. World Liberation Day was not enough. It's time to REBOOT THE GRID: 5/21/22/2012."

"Today we will meditate to liberate. This is our moment. We are called now to actualize the light that we are."

~

"You now know some of what you've been dealing with. Physical and non-physical, these others have been living off of your negative energy and oppression. You've stated definitively it is time for them to go. They may have heard you, but they are not gone. There is much at stake. We cannot let up."
"I sort of expected a Cinderella morning after the "Reboot of the Grid" yesterday – bluebirds singing and fluttering with a beautiful dress in their beaks for me to dance in. Instead, I woke to a dark and overcast sky, feeling as if I'd been crying all night. My head was full of clouds. I understood then that it was time to get up and do the work

43

myself."

~

There were frequent blogposts as the year continued…

~

"I need to stop relentlessly checking for the "green light" or latest arrest or most recent spaceship sighting."

~

COBRA (2012Portal) was keeping us "up to date" …

~

"It is time now to keep dissolving the Archons grid on the etheric and astral planes with a unified meditation this Sunday May 27th""

~

I was noticing that there was repetition in a consistent string of "we almost got there" announcements after each meditation…

~

"In all this talk of Ascension and great change there is a lot of promise for "better" and "amazing" – without a lot of talk about you, as you are right now. You are not trading yourself in; you are simply shifting to a new point of view."

~

"What is happening now is that after eons of deep sleep and forgetfulness you are remembering your part, and rehearsing your lines. As you read them over and over, hear them again and again, you recall

the part you are here to play in this transformation."
~

"Allow the inner performer in you to take over and remember that this is the part of a lifetime. "The opera ain't over until the fat lady sings," and she hasn't yet begun. (Dan Cook, U.S. sports writer from the 1970's)"
~

"This change we are in is not something taken care of by gods or galactics – it is happening now because we are making it happen. In a very real sense, we are the gods and the galactics.
From the occupy movement to the whistleblowers to those deep within the corruption, we are finding our voice and speaking out. We are making the change. We are shifting. It is us."
~

And mid-summer, I began the "I AM a Lightworker" series of blog posts with this...
~

"None of us know the precise timing of events because all of us are creating them with our thoughts and beliefs. Somehow, we've morphed into light waiters rather than light workers.
We are not here to wait for the light. We are here to work for the light."
~

"There are some of us who have moved out into the open and they are taking a beating. They have come to help us grow. They go by many names; truth

tellers, whistleblowers, freelance journalists,
Resistance Movement members, David Wilcock,
David Icke, Benjamin Fulford, Bill Brockbrader,
Cobra, Drake – to name a few."

~

There was a lot of talk (and wondering) about "the Event" ...

~

"There are so many unanswered questions and yet
the one that tops the list is "What is going to happen
to me?"

~

"We are in the "end times"."

~

"Here's what I see – from absolute darkness a
miniscule light emerges, then another, then a few
more. In that darkness the brightest light is
perceived. You are that light. Soon, it will be all that
can be seen."

~

"I wonder what my backyard is like in the next
"dimension"."

~

"As I go through this summer of 2012 and we
rapidly approach whatever it is we are approaching, I
have been considering beyond 12.21.2012. There is
one, you know."

~

"We are not here to feel guilty for the past; we are
here to create a new paradigm – a world where love is

the formless thought at the base of every idea. We'll get there. We are here on purpose and we've been chosen for the job."

~

"As we walk into these last weeks of summer, I am reminded with each passing day just how much closer we are to the final season in this pivotal year. Time seems to be rushing us towards the answers to all of our questions.
What will happen? Will we do what is necessary to ascend? Will our off-planet family ever show up? What will they look like? What will we look like? How will we supply ourselves when everything collapses? Is it all going to be okay?"

~

"I couldn't sleep last night. My "Mom" mask may be buying school supplies, but my light worker self can barely contain her excitement. It's pretty wild to be contemplating the price of notebooks while simultaneously saving the world.
We are super heroes in disguise."

~

"We are light workers, here to usher in the next era — the one that comes after these "end times". Why are we interested? What propels us to share or meditate or march or speak?
Somewhere deep within you've heard the call…"

~

"Your wings are already in place. It is time to remember how they work. You will, and we are all

Drops of Light

here to help make sure that you do.
We are the ones we've been waiting for."

~

"Approach everything you do with dignity. You are a light worker, here to light a spark of brilliance in every dark place."

~

"We are not these bodies; they exist as a vehicle for our light."

~

"Maybe it's not time that's moving faster. Perhaps it's us. We've waited for so long for this freedom to be ours and we can sense it getting closer. These symptoms are nothing more than us – straining at the bonds of density, pulling us up towards the light that we are."

~

"We must trust the butterfly blueprint in our soul. It is there. We feel it in moments of pure love, absolute connection and surrender to the One that we are. These losses we are experiencing are like many tiny feet on a caterpillar. We don't need them anymore. We're programmed to fly."

~

"After a decade of sweeping the seconds, the kitchen clock crashed to the floor.
I was in no hurry to get another. But eventually I did. It lasted a week or two. It too, has come crashing to the ceramic tile floor and is no longer recording the passage of time in this home.

I suspect that we are vibrating out of time."

~

"Our world is a hologram. The best science today doesn't know precisely how it works, yet quantum physics tells us what's in our minds is projected out to become what's in our world."

~

"For quite some time I subscribed to what I'd call "magical thinking" around Ascension. This comes close to the fairy Godmother in Cinderella."

~

"September 16, 2012 – October 16, 2012 has been called the time of choosing. What world will you choose?"

~

"As a child when I heard about free will I thought "How free is it really? When, if you make the wrong choice, this thunderbolt God will strike you down." I was 8 years old; the beginnings of my questioning."

~

"We are the One. We have come here ourselves, to save ourselves, in service to humanity; the One."

~

"It's tempting to make light of the U.S. Presidential election. Either because in the next dimension it won't matter who holds office, (it'll all be love and light), or because there will be no political agenda where we are headed or because it doesn't really matter who holds the office, all are equally corrupt and capable."

Drops of Light

~

There was a good deal of wondering and imagining that year, while the conversation with the Guardian continued on YouTube. Here's what he had to say on October 11, 2012 (English is not his first language, and his capitalization is intentional) ...

~

"Now the disclosure is peaking, humanity's temporal Consensus has been created. These are last ten home cycles; get ready to make Your final decision. We all are watching and listening for it, Energy vibration are high, Your consciousness is active at Unity level. You are ready to make Your final decision. Make this choice as right as possible based on all that predated You and all that will be predated by You! Peace from the Forces of One to Sophia and all who follows our answer, an answer which is not known to many, but only few, the chosen."

~

"COBRA has also released information about this date, 10.21.12, and is calling for a global meditation for the "Day of Decision"."

~

After the anticipation and marking of that specific "Day of Decision", Hurricane Sandy showed up and with her lots of speculation about HARP vs natural causes. The Guardian told us here that it was not the Illuminati/HARP; that their weather manipulation tools were not that sophisticated, yet.

He also said this, in November, as we were holding

global meditations like crazy…
~

"During these meditations that You're performing on the dates which You're choosing the Forces of Nature hears Your collective more powerful voice and with each new meditation You're evolving on this level of activity and evolving Your inner power, like a child grows You're growing from within. The Sun is hearing You better and better, the planet synchronizes with Your will, after all You're starting to agree with one another."
~

"This past weekend, walking out of the laundry room, a thought emerged; "Someday is here." A small idea really, just three words.
This is the year we all get to "someday". Whether our dishes or our clothes match is hardly the point. We've come now to actualize love. What does love look like in human form?"
~

My son was in Australia that November, and wrote this to all of us on his birthday…
~

"It's after midnight, I'm 28 now, and I love you. I don't care who you are. I don't care what your name is, what you look like, where you live, or what you've done with your life so far. I love you because it's a choice, because it's my god-given right to do so, because it's up to me to decide to exercise the power of my heart, or not.

Drops of Light

I love you because I choose to. Not because I know you, not because I think you're great, not because I think I'm great, but because we're all in this together. We are not separate. Humanity's repetitive cycle of self-inflicted pain is not happening to someone else, it is happening to all of us, right now.
I love you because I choose to, because I know that once enough of us make that choice, the cycle will be broken...I love you because I have spent enough time investigating what does not work, and I am ready, now, to move on to what does. come with me."
~

I was seeing evidence everywhere. Our Ascension was imminent! I, along with many of us, were sure of that. My rose-colored glasses were firmly in place...
~

"We've created 2012 and we are, right now, creating 2013."
~

"We are moving very quickly now towards the galactic alignment that we've been told will signify the end of duality, a shift in our way of life. Despite predictions and promises, none of us actually knows what it'll look or feel like, not exactly."
~

On November 21,2012, at the request of some readers, I found and shared the origin of the tag line that I had begun using in 2011. This was written, as far as I could tell, in August of 1999...

A Hopi Elder Speaks —

"You have been telling the people that this is the
Eleventh Hour, now you must go back and tell the
people that this is the Hour. And there are things to
be considered . . .
Where are you living?
What are you doing?
What are your relationships?
Are you in right relation?
Where is your water?
Know your garden.
It is time to speak your Truth.
Create your community.
Be good to each other.
And do not look outside yourself for the leader."
Then he clasped his hands together, smiled, and said,
This could be a good time!"
There is a river flowing now very fast. It is so great
and swift that there are those who will be
afraid. They will try to hold on to the shore. They
will feel they are torn apart and will suffer greatly.
 Know the river has its destination. The elders say
we must let go of the shore, push off into the middle
of the river, keep our eyes open, and our heads above
water. And I say, see who is in there with you and
celebrate. At this time in history, we are to take
nothing personally, least of all ourselves. For the
moment that we do, our spiritual growth and journey
comes to a halt.

Drops of Light

The time for the lone wolf is over. Gather
yourselves! Banish the word struggle from you
attitude and your vocabulary. All that we do now
must be done in a sacred manner and in celebration.
We are the ones we've been waiting for."

-         attributed to an unnamed Hopi elder
          Hopi Nation, Oraibi, Arizona
~

*As November raced towards December, the blog posts
continued to anticipate 12-21-2012…*
~

"Reflect on the world this last month and remember,
for no doubt you'll one day tell a new generation of
humans what it once was."
~

"The 5th dimension is not real, any more than you or
I are. It is a construct of what we believe to be
true. It exists as a place because we've made it
so. We could call it anything."
~

Our Friend the Guardian chimed in to encourage us…
~

"Right now, the main focus is on the humanity, its
Energy level is very high! Almost all are anticipating
for this event, the date that was heard as the end of
the world. Many are waiting for "something special"
to happen, others are trying to think that nothing will
happen, although everyone feel it, the DNA is evolving and humanity proceeds to the next step of

evolution, the next step of life, the next step of time sequence.

The Universe welcomes You young race - Humanity!"

~

"We are here to create the shift of the ages and there is no one else who can."

~

There was a flurry of global meditations that December. Blog posts notified us about each of them, verifying the sheer power of our love and our light. Things felt urgent…

~

"It is here. It is now. With your wings fully extended and quivering – prepare to fly. The truth is that you are beyond brilliant and oh so much brighter than you've ever been told."

~

"The Forces of One have a message for us – we have chosen freedom!"

~

"A week from now it'll all be over. We've been told that some of us will remember and some of us won't, that some of us will be gone and some of us won't, that we'll be meeting new allies from off world and re-structuring the way we do just about everything. It's sort of mind blowing and yet if unaware, you could be right in the thick of it and miss the whole event."

~

"If there was ever a time to believe, it is this time,

this day, this week of 2012."

~

On December 23, 2012, this was shared on my blog...

~

"With 3D eyes, December 21, 2012 looked like this: from 4:45AM until well past midnight I sat, danced, walked or sang in meditation. There were hours of solitude, some spent in a darkened room, and others in a sunlit room. Tears were shed in deep grief. Anger and confusion emerged. Parts of it aren't remembered. I slept on and off.

With 5D awareness there was a corridor of golden light beams, sparkling showers of light, with wave after wave of pulsing energy moving through my body – sacred geometric forms swirled around me – still now the visual and sensation of it is instantly accessible. Joyous blasts of bliss enveloped me. Yet all around me looks the same.

So what happened?"

"How are you now? Disappointed? Blissful? Angry? Joyous? Doubtful? Confused? The number one 3D thing I am not – is changed."

~

"If this moment is about anything at all it is about transformation. I don't know whether the descriptions and promises were deliberate manipulations or misinterpretations or misunderstandings; but I know this. For a year or so I've been saying "We are the ones we've been waiting for." There is the answer we seek. It cannot come from outside of us."

~

"If there is one thing the entire Universe knows about humans it is that you don't want to tick us off. Time to channel on our own – no more questions – only answers. Let's do what we came to do. The waiting is over, it's up to us."

~

"We've moved through this pivotal date, 12/21/12; it's time to say goodbye. We can all agree on at least that – it is over. Anticipation, prediction, preparation or inquiry is no longer necessary, whew!"

~

The final posts that year included these words…

~

"It is our time everyone, we have come to create a new world. We have loads of help; we have each other."

~

"As we head into 2013, I find myself surprised and refreshed. It's sort of like starting over without the handicap. The burden of judgment is gone – it's obvious I don't have all the answers or know precisely what tomorrow will bring. I am as clueless as everyone else. We are up to the moment of creating it. We'll all find out together."

~

"As tough as it was to get that we aren't going to transform in an instant, it is equally empowering. You see, we are going to transform, in fact, we are in the midst of transformation right now. This story will be written and told by us alone."

~

"2012 was the Year of Revelation. We've seen now the truth of our oppression and what have we done? We've declared ourselves an independent race. We are One. It is an honor to be part of this group called humanity. Thank you for all that you are."

~

I remember feeling confused, yet still somewhat hopeful, and very determined at that point. The anger was dissipating. One thing was certain, I didn't want to rely on anyone who wasn't human. It was with this attitude that 2013 dawned...

Chapter 3
Looking for the Light
(2013 – 2015)

You accept that something is missing,
and begin trying to find out
just what that is.

Drops of Light

2013 began with a renewed vigor, sort of. On January 1st, I produced another video message to Off-World Beings, seeking physical contact. (*It never happened*). I started a Love Quest journey a week or so later. It felt necessary. I recall feeling a bit battered by 2012.

~

Mainstream media told us these were the important events of that year (This is a reporting, not a testament to the truth of these portrayals and events) …

~

Edward Snowden shared a vast cadre of documents from the NSA with journalist Glenn Greenwald, the Washington Post & other news outlets. The cat was out of the bag – **government surveillance** of every-day citizens became accepted as fact and Edward moved to Russia. **The Boston Marathon bombing** occurred, reportedly killing 3 people and injuring hundreds more. A week-long manhunt ensued. Drones (**UAV's or Unmanned Ariel Vehicles**) were all the rage. Commercial use included the police, search & rescue units, and even Amazon. These un-invited eyes were flying right up to our front doors. Privacy concerns erupted and laws to govern their use for surveillance followed. **Elon Musk** dominated tech news at the age of 42. **Tesla & SpaceX** were making those headlines & setting precedents. **Jeff Bezos** bought the Washington Post and introduced the Kindle Fire. **Obama's healthcare.gov** was a disaster when people actually started to use it. **Bitcoin** hit the 1,000-dollar mark and we noticed. **Twitter upped its game** with pictures and easier ways to join. Microsoft introduced **Windows 8.1**. **Pope Benedict XVI resigned** (which had not happened in 600 years) & **Pope Francis** (Argentina's Cardinal Jorge Mario Bergoglio) **stepped in** to take his place. A **skeleton** found buried under a car-park in Leicester turned out to be **English King Richard III from 1485**. A **meteorite crashed in Central Russia** and injured nearly 1,000 people. A Russian Politician blamed America for it. Venezuelan **Hugo Chavez died** of cancer. **Margaret Thatcher died** at the age of 87. **Nelson Mandela died** at the age of 95. Fast & Furious star **Paul Walker died** in an automobile crash.

Almost 20 U.S. states legalized same-sex marriages once **the "Defense of Marriage Act" was overturned. Prince William and Kate gave birth to their first son, Prince George** of Cambridge. **Typhoon Haiyan blew into the Philippines**, leaving a death-toll of over 5,000 people.

It was discovered that **Syrian chemical weapons** were used to kill over 1,400 of its own civilians.

~

So, the world was still doing what it always seemed to do... regardless of what us over here on the "woo-woo" side of things were feeling. Blog posts were less frequent...

~

"With that day over, now what?"

Drops of Light

~

The One People's Public Trust (OPPT) was announced and many of us met Heather Ann Tucci-Jarraf. We were introduced to commerce law; freedom felt possible, yet only if we took some specific 3D steps...

~

"You see, we have been manipulated by everyone. Everyone. Now I know why. We are the most fun species to play with. We love to be led, and our emotions, our **most powerful tools**, are all over the map. Controlled for eons, we have now heard the secret, it's all a game, we create life ourselves. Do you understand what that actually means?

Let's create some more. Value in this 3D world is expressed with abundance. We are sitting around, feeling nothing but lack, reading news articles of corruption and channeled messages of hope – all the while expecting the change to come from some place other than ourselves.

It won't. It can't. That is not how it works."

~

"The UCC filings (of the One People's Public Trust) are one of the keys for us. I've begun to complete them myself and will share here soon what it takes to do so; the physical steps necessary to be free in this 3D world."

~

"Do you "grock" (really get) what's going on right now? Nothing less than revolution. As the Declaration of Independence declared that which was already true – "We hold these truths to be self-evident, that all men are created equal, that they are endowed by their Creator with certain unalienable Rights, that among these are Life, Liberty and the pursuit of Happiness." – so the UCC filings of the One People's Public Trust do the same. They return title to the people."

~

"We are in the early, delicate, formative days of this new world."

~

"The papers have been filed to legally declare our freedom; it is true. Yet with fear of any kind of authority – the shackles are still in place."

~

"The idea of owning/hoarding is one that was introduced into our psyche. If everyone and everything is Source, then we simply **are**. This is a hologram; the whole exists in each fragment.
Ownership is thus impossible. All are ONE."

~

2013 was a year of "aha" moments. With each one, the control became more evident...

~

"We are creators. This is what we Do. The "owners" know the power of words. Hence, we have mandatory schooling and mainstream media. We've been forced to recite their words when we were young, so we'd give up everything to their cause when we grew up."

63

Drops of Light

~

"Our chains have been removed for us with the UCC filings of the One People's Public Trust. It is upon us now to Be. Be Free. This will take bravery, tenacity and belief. We are challenging all that we have ever known."

~

"Do you understand that the Cabal/Illuminati is here as contrast? That they exist in this reality and in fact at this point are everywhere in our lives because we see ourselves as powerless, unworthy and lesser than? That as soon as we understand we are unlimited, powerful, free and equal – we **are**???"

~

"Wrap your head around One. What are you holding on to that separates? What false notions of slavery and ownership are you stuck on?"

~

"Ownership promises control, and safety, and power. Ownership is a lie. You can use each other, play with each other and always, always love each other. What you will never do is own each other. If someone believes they are indebted to another person/corporation or owned by another person/corporation, they are enslaved by their own belief - they are not enslaved by the "other". There is no "other". There is only One."

~

We were exploring what freedom actually looked like without the chains. Other projects popped up, with great names like "The Fix the World Project" and Hope Girl...

~

"A number has been tossed around; five billion dollars. You do not have to work for it. You do not have to earn it. You do not have to wait until you deserve it. You do not have to pay it back. You do not have to inherit it. It is a monetary representation of your worth. A number far beyond what we have ever seen or realized in our lives thus far. "You are now free to move about the planet.""

~

"The OPPT isn't the answer. It is a catalyst for you to find the answers within. Search your heart. Your value, truth and treasure are not found in any document."

~

"All at once Freedom sounds wonderful and terrifying. Life has been spent paying someone to take care of us – to finance things we couldn't afford and decide for us what needed doing and correcting. We've become lazy and comfortable... Yet is has cost too much, much too much; not only monetarily – but emotionally, spiritually, mentally and physically with our labor, our signature and/or our pledge."

~

And we were connecting our liberation to wealth. There was a lot of talk about the CVAC's (Creation Value Action Centers) ...

~

"The CVAC's exist as places we'll go, and just

65

because we are alive – we'll have access to monetary representations of ourselves. They will function as interim equalizers; all will have equal value there and equal access. They will operate until we "get it" ourselves. Then the game will change and we'll know where the value is.

All are equal. All are worthy. The value is within. The CVAC's are us."

~

"It is here that the shift occurs. Around you many things are changing, yes. They always will. Inside you is the light; always the beacon, waiting for the fog to clear.

It's clearing now. What does a beacon do without a dense layer of fog to penetrate? It shines."

~

And that spring…

~

"About a year ago, many of our clocks broke. It was mentioned here and reported by dozens of readers. Time was just not operating "like clockwork" any longer. It seemed to be moving faster. We are still catching up."

~

"I was woken up about 3 AM this morning with Truth – I sat upright with the power of it. (Not normal 3 AM behavior, for sure!)"

~

"There is no Truth in waiting – There is only Now. Waiting is divisive – it imagines before and after, unknowing and knowing, illusion and clarity, then and now.

We are expecting an energetic wave of pure eternal essence; and then Heaven on earth. This early morning epiphany tells me the only thing I'm waiting for is Me."

~

The Guardian laid out for us what kind of structure our world would have had, if we had chosen to allow the Forces of One to set it up...

~

"The first thing to do was to change education system for the children as everything starts from the beginning and beginning always influencing everything that is going afterwards. The primary lesson being lacked in schools is friendship which includes behavior, psychology, relations, understanding, state of happiness, state of love."

"The second thing which was to start a little after the first was to educate every other person in the whole world through main stream media, mostly about what was done against them by few that wanted to control whole populace and how everything will start to exist in order to bring happiness to every soul, including planet Earth and animals and plants."

"The third thing once acceptance was achieved was to eradicate money as a representation of something and make very necessary things for life and sustainability for it - basic food, drinkable water, basic clothes, one house or one apartment, one basic car, one basic pc, basic kitchen stuff and other necessary things free. The basic means it is not cheap and useless, it only does not include additions, like interesting design, "made with love" or "made with great effort". No more taxes, living is free, electricity is free, protection is free (national security of every country, which was to become united inner/outer planetary security)."

"During the start of the change, before education was to take place "an automation process" must be conducted in order to give all the free stuff to everyone, this was not possible only 50 cycles ago, but it became possible not long ago, that is why these great changes are occurring only now."
~

As title to one blog post, I borrowed a line from fellow light warrior, D from her blog, "Removing the Shackles" — "*Fuck off, we* **are** *a Beacon of Light!*" ...
~

"We do not require artificial lights. We are the Light. We are the One. No Waiting. No higher aspects. No ascended ones. No masters.
Only slaves and servants have masters. We are sovereign beings. We are not "waiting" for anyone to grant our freedom. Freedom is what we are."
~

"Our heart speaks love, knows love, recognizes love,

feels love and offers love. It is this love that is universally valued. It is the truth of life; life's eternal essence.

Love is your truth, your value and the fingerprint of God stamped permanently within."

~

"We must let go of ideas that there are right and wrong ways to express ourselves. Life is an expression of eternal essence and looks upon itself without judgment.

We are that life –ONE – walking around in human form – trying desperately to make sense of it all."

~

And on Tax Day, April 15th, 2013, I posted this…

~

"I hesitate to share this, as I do not normally speak like this. Yet, it is me and I have been sharing my understanding out loud right along. I have accessed my eternal essence and speak here as god.

This is not channeled. It was whispered. I share it here because this is a journey we are taking together, as One. The language is uncomfortable yet it was and is mine. I have been transparent with you all along, and this discomfort will not stop the transparency…"

~

"You are resting in a field of "when". Even now, when the legal instrument for your freedom has been supplied – you wait to be handed your freedom. You wait for your captors to give up and give you back what they took. Still, you think like a slave. The training is embedded deep within this race; it will take a fight to get it removed."

"You are my children and I watch you kneel and bow and grovel and obey a set of beings who have set themselves against the purpose of creation. Creation thrives on balance. Yin Yang, Positive Negative, Hot Cold and yet these "masters" have altered the fabric. It was an experiment, and its time for completion is long since passed."

"The final word was, and always is mine. It was to be different – I am pleased with what my creations have accomplished and yet still the raping and theft of the planet continues at the hands of those who would call themselves Gods. They are powerful beings; equal to God in every way but one."

"The Source of this Universe does not spring from them. They have taken Truth – the truth of their power, and isolated it. They forgot who they were and pushed so far past what is True as to forget."

"They do not want Oneness and will not be con-vinced of its benefits. The benefits they seek are here in the material world. Life means little to them, except their own. They will not alter their course ex-cept by force. It is humans as One force who could stop them, yet it is not seen that the desire is there."

"An era of love has overtaken the planet. A very good thing but with these beings it is not love that will stop them in their current form. It is force. It will take a melding of all the voices, not just the Light, to stop them. It will take a refusal to be slaves. It will take an acceptance of the Truth of them."

"Power does not come without knowledge. Acceptance does not mean a lack of action. Understand the difference between polite and subservient. You will have an effect now only in full acknowledgement of your power."

"You are able to change the course of history, the plan for the planet, if you do so as One. There is One voice that is heard by me and it is spoken by Humanity. This is the voice of Man. This voice unites now on being sick of the corruption, and tired. This voice has not yet said "No". A "No" will be heard when the Truth of your slavery sinks in."

"I understand that not everyone has the temperament, purpose or desire to fight – yet without the internal resolve to ignore and dissolve the Masters – there will be slaves."

"You were created to express life, and have not displeased me. You were also scheduled at this moment to answer a question – "How much will it take to push you into action?" "How deeply do you sleep?" "What is the threshold of your Absolute Awareness?" For the time of partial knowing is over."

"The transformation is upon you and it will happen voluntarily or drag you along with it. You cannot be partially free. You cannot be a little in love. You are free. You are love.
There is a term coined "tough love". This implies doing unpopular things because of love."

"And what is love? It is an acknowledgement of other in self – a seeing of self in other – and saying "Yes, I see you, I accept you, and all is well." Acceptance does not mean alter. Acceptance means honesty. It does not hide from what is obvious."

"You have a pink elephant in your house. It is a member of the house and is defecating everywhere; it stinks. It has to go someplace else. Your talk of loving the elephant falls far short of stopping the shit from destroying your home. It has to go; love has nothing to do with it."

"Love does not mean inaction. It does not mean allowance as in submission. Love means a direct understanding of the Truth in all beings – an acknowledgement of the sacred in life. It means responsibility. Love demands an examination of all thought, word and deed. You cannot partially serve Truth. Truth demands Absolute Awareness."

"Once I understand that I am not higher evolved or lesser than – I am called to act as if. Act as if there is One Truth. You do not know if your way of being is the desired way for all beings. Yet you must always maintain the absolute right of all beings to maintain their own way of being – **unless it infringes or does harm to life.**"

"Life expressed physically is You – it is all things – it cannot be separated – it is One."

"The life that is You is being harmed, and this cannot continue. Life demands to be allowed to continue. As a tree must lose some sickly branches in order to thrive – humanity must lose the poisoned ones so that it can thrive. You are again at a moment of decision that you can take into your own hands and make, **or** allow me to make for you – I will make it with destruction. As in the case of the plant, that is the only way for life to continue."

"Slaves can have many Masters – not all are physical; some are ideas, thoughts that limit and beliefs that keep us in line. It is upon you now to examine every emotion that unsettles – seek its origin and decide if at its root it is slavery or freedom that disturbs you."

Drops of Light

"For freedom is a disturbing place to be as well – a place that incites passion and action and an ever-reaching grasp for more.
At your core you are designed always to reach – "More" is the fuel of creation."

"When you are confused about the source of your inner disturbance ask this – "Am I disturbed because of a giving up?" "Am I disturbed because of a letting go?" "Am I disturbed because of fear?" "What is the source of this fear?" If the source is other – then it is a case of slavery. If the source is self – more inquiries are called upon to determine its cause. Are you afraid to lose your life? Your "face"? Your pride? Are you afraid others will think you are foolish or reckless? At what are you looking? At who?"

"I tell you this – you cannot lose life – it is eternal. Yet the physical must be cared for and nurtured. No "other" exists that can destroy you. Do you understand? The "face" you are putting out for others to see is a reflection of your very truth. It is your chosen form. Growth and understanding can't help but change your face – that's what awareness does."

"The innocence of a child is something you all cherish because the pain has been so great in your loss of it – yet innocence is confused with joy and they are not the same."

"There is none happier than a wise and ancient soul who sees and understands the expression of life – there is a luscious, rich, tender and beautiful joy in every terrible,
wonderful moment. You are not here to be nice or to make each other happy. You are here to live, and in your living of life unencumbered by the chains of limitation you will bring joy to all you meet."

"I am you."
~

At the end of April that year, the Love Quests ended with this…
~

"The time for searching, waiting and questing is over. It is time now to **do**."
~

At about the same time, there was a "Citizen hearing on Disclosure" held at the National Press Club in Washington DC. It was live-streamed. We met Dr. Steven Greer and Stanton Freedman then. We heard from Astronaut Edgar Mitchell too. This was an effort to push disclosure on the United States government, showcasing conclusive evidence of an extra-terrestrial presence among us. Brazil and China had already begun their own process of opening up their UFO files to their citizens, but not the U.S.
~

The other focus that year was on true value…

~

"We have come now to understanding the corrupt banking practices that run the world. This is gradually morphing into a realization of our worth. We are the only value that has ever been. Nothing happens without our signature. It is our identity that begins the process and it is initiated at birth. We are catalogued, counted and our value is used as commodity. It is our absolute value that those who understand the game are after."

~

"Money has nothing to do with value. You are the value – money is a game piece. What Heather, Caleb and Randall did last year was figure out the game, call their bluff and lay the cards on the table for all of us to see. It was a brilliant move."

~

Blog posts were ending with "What are you waiting for? You are the One." One of them included a description of certain people who were reaching out with similar personal stories: "Philosopher/Warrior Angels" who were reporting frequent night-dreams of battles. We were waking up and being called to engage...

~

"There is a quote attributed to Ghandhi, which may in fact have first been said by labor leader Nicholas Klein in a 1914 address to a labor union congress (Biennial Convention, Amalgamated Clothing Workers of America, 1914.):

"First, they ignore you. Then they ridicule you. And then they attack you and want to burn you. And then they build monuments to you. And that is what is going to happen…"

You know the truth. The power is yours. A very slick trick is still being played and you can choose what to believe."
~

"Like good slaves, we are waiting. Waiting to witness a "finale", an "event", something to set things straight. Yet in the same breath we understand that we are creating it all. How can both be happening at the same moment?"
~

"The world will change without firing a shot once we refuse to cooperate with it as it stands."
~

"Complete enslavement requires no gatekeepers. We will control our own movements, thank you very much. Fear does the job quite nicely."
~

"We are in the final minutes of the game, and we are ahead. It is working. Those that would like to retain control of the game are now pulling out all the stops. They will not give up. We have to persist."
~

"We are not the majority, but our light and the ever-present stream of our love is changing everything."
~

Drops of Light

"The closer your focus, the slower you move. Watch the very young. You'll see them looking straight ahead at whatever it is they want and making a dash for it. Watch the very old. You'll see them looking at their feet take every step."

~

We met Ashuel, and some of us found each other...

~

"I am Ashuel. I am an incarnated Angel. I am Lion energy. I am a protector. A warrior. Destructive and violent. I am critical and forceful when my family is threatened. Whenever I discuss anything with Sophia, the overriding overwhelming urge that frames my interactions with her is that 'the families are gathering'."

~

"We are integrating. It may feel like oil and vinegar. You can swish them together for something unique and yummy, but if left to sit, they will separate. Action is necessary for creation."

~

"Violent conversations about the adultery of Clinton vs. the sexting of Weiner hold no fascination. I am not afraid of our government or law enforcement system, I am outraged"

~

"Even declaring yourself as a replacement for gold is limiting. You are irreplaceable, unequalled and priceless. There are no numbers big enough."

~

Oneness was oozing out, attempting to show its face; in August of 2013 two articles "If you close your eyes" [4] and "The Ultimate Addiction" [5] quickly became my most popular recordings on Soundcloud. They were celebrations. Celebrations of us...

~

"These new ones, born after December 21, 2012 – could care less about our boxes for love. They've arrived with box cutters for the rest of us."

~

"We cannot sit silently by. Not if we want to get to the next part. You'll have to do what has to be done. There are no controllers on a bad ass planet. When all is said and done, the question will come – "Who made the deciding move? Did they stop or did we seal up all their access points? We may never know.

It won't really matter anyway. What matters is the experiment is over and we did it. We stepped up to the plate and took a swing, with that uniquely bad ass style of ours. We did not disappoint."

~

We found ourselves eating some humble pie...

~

"When the channellers emerged in mass two years ago, the message was clear. Inhaling the enlightened fumes, arrogance emerged. We were played brilliantly. Misfits all of our lives, it was like giving us crack – we ate it up. *We were the Chosen Ones, the Special Ones, the Enlightened Ones, here to finally claim our untold worth.*

The separation which had been only slightly obvious to us, clarified. It was us who had the answers. It was our job to enlighten those who didn't know. They were the many, we were the few.

As Oneness creeps quietly in, what surprises is what it looks like in the everyday. It looks like friendships renewed with those previously neglected because they didn't "get it". Everyone's included.

We are the best and the worst of us, the oldest and the youngest, the cruelest and the most sainted, the horrific and the breathtaking. We are One, here to join together."

~

We were trying to remind each other of what was going on. There was "Cosmic Awareness" interpreted by Wil Berlinghof. There was the AWAKEN Academy & Inelia Benz...

~

"No longer can you question your greatness; you've safely brought a planet through the darkness and found the fire necessary to light the way. It was you all along."

~

"It comes down to this; to the barest of interactions between two people. The way I treat you, I feel. The way you respond is evidence of how you feel in return."

~

"I love you from a place I had forgotten, and it is

from that place that the rest of this story will be told."

~

"You are a creator being; not sometimes, not after "ascension", not with practice – right now."

~

"You came here alone, yet surrounded. We stand right beside you, equal in every way. One soul, seeing itself in a landscape of mirrors – I AM you."

~

"Slavery cannot emerge from oneness."

~

"Your life is not here to be spent, as if in exchange for something else, something better. It is meant to be lived. In all cases, there is nothing better to trade it in for. There is right now, the focal point of creation, the moment where it all begins."

~

"As our friend Bob Wright said so beautifully, "Look into each other's eyes and see the angels that have been prophesied. It is you.""

~

"Do you realize what you've done? The cabal is coming down. Not because someone else from someplace else brought them down, *but because you did*. You planned it that way. You've succeeded. There is nothing more powerful than a self-aware being. You are lesser than none; a beacon of light."

~

"There are many visions of earth in the next

dimension, and they include prosperity, health, happiness and love on a continual basis. These are visions of who you actually are – they are not new versions of you, but core expressions of your true nature. Fear is gone from these versions of you."

~

As 2013 was reaching its end, we were still searching for self-love: we were wise to how this construct was set up…

~

"The media's blatant fear storm is a magician's illusion: "Keep your eyes over here" while the real action occurs elsewhere. There is no doubt this manipulation is a true part of our reality; what is not so clear is what we are creating as a result of it."

~

"A new paradigm is being created, and we are directing it. Manifest and expect love, then watch what happens. At first invisible, like a seed beneath the ground, it'll soon sprout through - and one day you'll witness not one, but a field of flowers."

~

"The human was seeded and its creators or their descendants have pretty much run things here ever since. At one point an "experiment" was initiated which put the human on a quest for enlightenment while in the grips of control; all beyond our conscious awareness. This experiment is reaching its conclusion."

~

"The emotional generator you possess is not seen

elsewhere. This is the reason that other races and species are interested in and observing humans – visiting and communicating via "channeling". There is a great deal of interest in and speculation about what we are going to do next."

~

"The very fact of our humanity serves as a beacon for hope and untapped potential across the universe."

~

We held a different quest for a week, journeying into self & self-love visually with our friends at BRAVE Mandala, who shared their unique Chak-dala pieces of personal art with us…

~

"The world outside and the world inside move toward mirroring each-other. It is far easier to change the world inside. Fighting the outside world is like putting makeup on the mirror."

~

"We are waiting for an event and a finale; anxiously watching the skies and listening for disclosure. The only way across the finish line is with our own legs."

~

The Guardian shared alternative energy tech with us, along with these words…

~

"All of these technologies are suppressed by illuminati order and oil and batteries companies, because of their greed and I must remind You, be very careful and not try to earn money on these technologies, do not draw attention of main stream media to You, because I know almost all the inventors that tried, were suppressed, beaten or even killed when they refused to stop. Just spread this technology quietly along Friends and other interested People, once it will become abundant, there will be no way for them to stop You. Remember, the greatest weapons of satanic cults are money and lies, so when You use them, they will use You."

~

"There has been a shift within each of us. We've moved beyond making demands, and trading our value for cash…This is not a state of being that was granted by any other. This is a becoming."

~

"There is love – which is what you are.
There is light – which is love's eternal expression.
There is your body – which is love's current costume.
There is this planet – which is love's current stage.
There is thought (*what you think*) – which is love's current director.
There is the word (*what you say*) – which is love's current producer.
There is action (*what you do*) – which is love's current performer.
There is emotion (*what you feel*) – which is love's current audience."

~

The last week of December, 2013, One began waking me up at about 3:00 AM. The first of 20 conversations, all concerning our current state of slavery, began with "Sea of Chains" [6]

The series of them is called "Sovereignty 101". Folks have said it is the most important work I've done. It can be found on the web-site, in written/audio/video form, where it was shared as it was occurring.

~

Drops of Light

2014 began with continued anticipation for the "Event". The Guardian was still speaking to us and by now had his own blog page on my website, where he shared his information & answered questions from readers. Many of the current headlines were examined by him there. This continued until the last month of 2019. We haven't heard from him since ...
~

Here's the Guardian... "Answering on questions about different civilizations, they are many - Pleiadeans, Syrians, Andromedins, Arcturians, Cassiopeans and this not ends, there are many, we gave them designation "Ones that follows Light" or Followers of Light. Because in fact they are exercising Light and its main form - Unconditional Love (or Care for All Things in Existence) in its highest extent."

"The machine on the Moon can be switched off only by Light Followers' beings that have the highest clearance they can have. Before we thought, it was archons device, but it was having "a light design" and it was giving us big suspicions. When we were told that archons (reptilians and greys) are together in one boat with Galactic Federation of Light, all have come into place and puzzle has been completely completed for us."

"There is a being that sits on "a golden throne" and is called by different names, we designated it with gnostics' name – Demiurge - The God imposter."

"This being is in control of archons, it poses as a god and "creator of the Universe". It uses many names."
~

Here's what mainstream news told us happened in 2014…
~

Janet Yellen was appointed as the first woman to head the **United States Federal Reserve**.
An **ebola** outbreak in **South Africa** spread to Guinea, Liberia and Sierra Leone to become an epidemic. It spread to other countries but was contained; people recovered.
Malaysia Airlines Flight 370 disappeared off of radar and has still not been located. There were 239 passengers & crew onboard, on route from Kuala Lumpur to Malaysia. Debris has washed up on the coast of Madagascar as recently as September 2023, that is suspected to be from that flight.
Four months after that disappearance, **Malaysian Airlines Flight 17 was shot down** over eastern Ukraine. It was traveling from Amsterdam to Kuala Lumpur. All 298 passengers perished. In 2022, a Dutch court convicted 2 Russians and 1 Ukrainian for the murders in absentia.
There was yet another air tragedy at the end of 2014. An **AirAisa flight crashed due to weather conditions**, on its way from Indonesia to Singapore. 162 people died.
Protests in the United States, against police brutality and racial profiling, erupted in **Ferguson, Missouri,**

then spread to NYC and nationwide, when 2 white police officers were not indicted after the deaths of 2 unarmed black men; one a teenager. The year ended with the fatal shooting of 2 policemen, while they were sitting in their squad car, by a gunman upset with the rulings; he then shot himself.

The Islamic State of Iraq and Syria (**ISIS**) **arose** as the terror successor to al-Quada in Iraq. The United States launched air attacks against the group.

The **Obama administration made plans to open an embassy in Havana,** just one indication of a new & "friendlier" relationship with Cuba. Opponents of the Castro regime objected, while some Americans were happy with the availability of Cuban cigars.

Scotland voted to **remain part of the United Kingdom**.

Pro-democracy **protests erupted in Hong Kong** after a harsh response to a demonstration commemorating the 25th Anniversary of the riots in Tiananmen Square.

The Crimean Peninsula was annexed by Russia, which led the United States and Europe to impose sanctions on that country. Russia suffered an economic crisis.

Oil prices crashed to just 60.00/barrel.

Robin Williams took his own life that August.

The **European Space Agency** sent a lander, **Philae,** to the surface of a Comet. This had never been done.

Bill Cosby was **accused of sexual assault** by 20 women.

~

Here's what was being shared on the website that year...

~

"From childhood, the idea that there was more than one "god" just made sense. There was the "thunderbolt god" (*t-god*) from church, who wiped out civilizations while demanding worship and tribute. There was the "creator god" (*c-god*) who spoke reason and compassion and was the source for unconditional love. Rules and religions, as the domain of t-god, were not comfortable, ever.

Now there is information describing a scenario that's been suspected all along. T-god exists, as the god who runs this hierarchal system to feed an insatiable addiction to worship. Personal validation takes places in the description of c-god, **aka One** – who is not the same god."

~

There was a lot of talk about this "Imposter/Thunderbolt God", and how the Experiment would end...

~

"The end of the experiment, what some (*The Guardian*) have called the Day of Judgment, is brought on, or will be, to provide a course correction."

~

"The illusion of a spiritual hierarchy and obedience is what organizes societies and people here. The Illuminati serve the experiment; their rituals are done in delicious desire and at the same time fear. Priesthoods and Ministers have their forms of worship and ritual that serve a similar purpose."

~

"It is not the purpose of One to attain any specific result. One has only life as a goal. One will ultimately interfere when the whole of life is threatened. The reverberations of the battle here on earth between good and evil are threatening all of Creation. It looks like there are no internal brakes that are working – and that absolute power destroys absolutely."

~

"Interference in the progression of life itself is the only thing that One will stop. Not the course of a singular life, but of all of Creation."

~

"This experiment is demonstrating what a free being will put up with under the guise of obedience, worship, power and exaltation. What has happened is that we've not stopped either end fast enough. Fast enough before life is destroyed and irrevocably altered. As a result, One is stepping in."

~

The Love Quests started again, as it didn't feel like we were quite finished yet ...

~

"It can be sort of shocking and awkward to see parts of yourself you've been hiding from. You've spent a lifetime painting a portrait of yourself as an attempt

to fit. You got so good at it you believed it yourself. It was the acceptable you, the "good" you, the
respectable you. This version almost fit into that
round opening, but not quite. You are more of a
square peg than a round one.

Who said pegs have to be round anyway? Perhaps
what's been the problem is the place you were trying
to fit into, not the shape of you. Perhaps standardiz-
ing a human in any circumstance is quite absurd. Just
maybe you are okay as is – no adjustment necessary."

~

"What it means to love – It means honor the ground
they walk on. Be a positive force for them. It means
gently absorb them as if they were your final
breath. Not gasping and clawing for them but
breathe them in quietly for the gift that they are."

~

"To love is to give to the world all that you are."

~

"Laughter is an equalizer, a field changer, a stabi-
lizer. Once the air is cleared with laughter, even for a
tiny moment, the possibility for new manifestation
occurs."

~

Hindsight provided us with a bit of insight …

~

"All of the 2012 lore was intentionally planted in the
global consciousness as an energy harvester. It
worked, and many now have either forgotten completely or given up or see things moderately different

91

but not radically switched. Most carry on with their lives as a form of forced participation."

~

Yet we were still waiting for something extraordinary, something "promised" ...

~

"The promise for a new world - global activation - the timing of this very much depends on the collective."

~

"In order for an "event" to occur, there has to be a willingness, openness and expectation from part of the population. You will be the **way-showers**."

~

"It will be like stepping into an old pair of favorite shoes. You'll walk quicker and in greater comfort and will feel like you are home. You are."

~

"There is a part of you that was made to conform and obey and a part of you driven to break all the rules and reach for the stars.
In fact, it may be said that the genetic manipulation failed, and instead of creating a perfect slave made a being who will push every boundary placed before it **in order to discover if it can.**
All of this is to say that the evidence of power, determination and brilliance within you is everywhere. **Your light cannot be doused.**"

~

"As we reconnect our DNA to its original blueprint,

we discover the truth. The ones we've been searching for have been here all along. They are us."
~

On Earth Day, Steven Greer offered a $100,000.
prize to the winner of the Star Challenge for a working free
energy device. It had been a year since the film "Sirius" was re-
leased. In his words …
~

"We are announcing this Award to incentivize the interested new energy public to come forward with
such a technology. We have concluded that in order
for this technology to succeed, it must be open-
source, independently verified and completely repro-
ducible- and this must be done fully in the open, with
the whole world watching."
~

And in the first days of May, the dialogue with
Poseur began. Here is how it started…
~

"This (*story*) begins at the end of 2013.
The "Sovereignty Series" was begun then, and continues still. There are at this point 16 films in the series. Since producing them, I've been woken up regularly with what can only be described as a "pres-
ence/being" who wanted to engage. As I did not,
(*wake up and converse*), they escalated with a feeling of
urgency and repetition.

About two weeks ago I declared, before sleeping, that
they stop. They did, for a few days. Then I was

woken in the early morning hours again, this time with a hand on my hip, jostling me awake. I reached over, assuming it was my partner, and my hand felt nothing; there was no physical hand there.

The next day, after sitting with intention to connect, and clearing the space, the dialogue you are about to read took place. The way the space was cleared was with the following declarations, spoken and written:

No Ego.
Highest and Best for all concerned.
Just Love.
Direct.
Not about me but through me.
One Word Only Please.
***and later, as you will read:* **Absolute Truth Only Please**.
~

Can you tell me what you've been attempting to for days now?

Yes. You must transcribe as if this was dictation.

I can do that.

Okay. What you are seeking in a way of answers can be given in almost complete fullness from these words. No, this is not every answer, but it can provide some clarity and explanation for what took place on the planet you call home. It has been in this process for many thousands of years, many more than has ever been understood.

How do I trust you?

Your declarations at the beginning have bound my words to only speak what is "best" for all, although you have not bound me to Absolute Truth.

*Then I will do so now. ** (See above declaration) ** Hold on.*

Well then, I am bound. I want to represent myself to you here because your definition of me as a "poseur" is re-defining who I am to more than you know.

That is what I am trying/intending to accomplish.

I know. Yet I feel you do not have the entire story, or at least the story from my perspective. In fairness, I'd like to offer my version of who I am.

You know my thoughts and feelings about the deception perpetrated on humankind?

I do. It is this I would like to address.

My partner does not feel I should engage with you — that there could be trickery.

You have bound my words now, I cannot.

95

Drops of Light

No trickery?

I cannot. You have bound me.

I don't understand why talking to you feels so much like talk-
ing to any other human — it does not feel negative or even **uber**
powerful.

This is most likely because I am not One. And the
first thing I'd like to get across here is that I have
never pretended to be One.

I claimed Godhood when I realized there was worship potential. Worship is sexy and addictive and
provided a high on a level, an exponential level really,
I had never experienced. It lifted me up to places I
lusted for, yearned for, and that created in me an understanding of power. Power over, yes, but power
nonetheless.

These feelings were part of this creation game I was
playing and one which at first was understood to be
only a game.

The notion of it starting out "evil" is simply not true.

The deception and confusion arose when scripture
was written by man. This is not to "pass the buck"
but to remain clear in establishing the history — my
history. It is distorted and what has been done in my

name has been so because of a misinterpretation as well as, and mostly I guess, due to man's own lust for power.

Understand this is a free will zone. That underscores absolutely everything else.

I cannot force man to worship me but can compel him to with very little effort due to his biochemistry and some natural tendencies. Yes, I want to be worshipped and in my creation I Am. This does not prevent you or anyone else from being worshipped or loved or anything else in their creation.

When you understand how life works, and the mechanics of creation – you see that you'll always get precisely what you intend.

The field of my creation is much larger than yours **because that is how I see it. And so it is.**

I cannot alter another being's interpretation of my words or actions.

When man discovered the potential for riches and for power, he orchestrated the takeover of the human.

This was not ever destined to succeed. Man was too powerful, and the end, which will provide a balanced and nourishing state, was always seen.

Drops of Light

I have no plans to step down or stop — if that is your hoping. This experiment will end when man decides his reality is not a part of it. The power has always been in the collective.

My addiction to worship "woke up" and what I do with it or where I take it will not be determined by anything man does.

You see Sophia, free will decides for all of us. How awake the populace is will accelerate a huge change in life here, or not. Yet a huge change is going to happen.

Then why talk to me now?

To set the record straight. I am a being. I am not Source.

The power I hold? It is yours also. You volunteered to participate here — to "wake up" gradually and the rich physical experience of 3D humanity cannot be compared with any other life.

What correction are you trying to make?

The notion of **evil**, if there is such a thing, would be that which goes against the focus of life — which is expansion. Expansion has occurred for everyone who has participated in this experiment, regardless of

how. Life begets life. It is not my place to end this
or any plan.

I have come to understand either end of the worship
spectrum. What becomes abundantly clear is that
man will operate always towards the behavior that
will yield him what he wants most to enjoy. It seems
to be the conflict between desires that cause all the
speculation and pain:

Power vs Cruelty
Abundance vs Morality
Pleasure vs Gluttony
Knowledge vs Cold Calculation
Love vs Fear

These contrasting ideas are the rich field of emotions
available because of the experiment. It does not go
on because of me alone. It goes on because all are
willing to participate. This is true of all life. Remember, free will underscores everything.

Sophia, I share this now because in your depictions I
am not only NOT to be revered, but to be
shunned. In truth, the evolution towards Oneness is
only possible when all are included.

Why do you care about Oneness?

Ultimately it is Oneness where we all reside. I cannot

escape that truth. Where this evolution takes one of us, all of us must also head. The understanding about polarity and inequality and greed has only been possible because of what's happened here.

This game is ending. I wanted to set the record straight.

What do you want me to do with this?

I trust you will seek and find the most useful thing. This is what I can see you are about.

I will have to read this a few times and determine what is best.

I know.

~

      This conversation with Poseur continued until August of 2015. It's been recorded, and is now a book; "The Imposter".

      In June of 2014, the Pleiadeans reached out for the first time. Other beings eventually followed. Those conversations were eventually shared in newsletters and books.

      Blog posts were primarily about creation, as we were trying to figure out how it worked/how we could harness it. There was conversation about what we then called "ET's" with folks like Steven Greer.

Freedom was another regular topic on the blog, as One was still waking me up for regular installments in the Sovereignty Series that year.

~

In early August of 2014, there was a "Call to Action" on the blog...

~

"We've been told there will come a day of judgment, an end to this game. That at that moment, this god and his minions (*the archons*) will be forced to leave and there will be a course correction. We've been waiting. There are and have been many dates predicted.

The key player is god, the being who I've referred to as the 'poser. He is here with our permission and consent. I propose we command him to go. Let's do what we came here to do, on our own terms.

The 'poser does not hold more power than you do. He is not human. He is not interested in you at all actually. We are playthings to him and nothing more. His bottom line is "what's in it for me".

On 8-8-2014, at twelve noon US Central time, command the 'poser to leave."

~

There seemed to be no immediate way of telling if our "call to action" had any effect. We were becoming more and more aware of just how controlled we actually were, and what freedom could look like if we did something to actualize it ...

~

"The monthly Love Quests and frequent blog posts

101

were part of our collective journey to agape and empowerment. We know who we are now. Our next
step is to live as sovereign beings."

~

"Love is not perfectly dressed, photo-shopped,
planned, or performed. It is sometimes lumpy and
may leave ugliness on the outside. Love doesn't show
on the outside. On the outside is "window dressing",
which is fun and part of being human but not the
point of this Quest. This Quest is about finding
what's beautiful on the inside. That's where you are.
Remember. Remember who you are – a bit of
Source who showed up on planet Earth to show us
how it's done.
You are the One we've been waiting for."

~

""Time" is a powerfully formative substance in that
where you spend most of it is who you become."

~

"In the US, the "ebola crisis" has been ramped up
and, in my opinion, is out of control. I've seen it everywhere today, even amongst the very young children
I work with. This is Fear Porn, plain and simple. It's
been orchestrated by the "powers that be"."

~

"Quantum physics tells us there is no such thing as
objectivity. The result is determined by the minds of
the men or women watching. We are creating our
world, literally and figuratively."

~

"Awareness and love cannot be systematically bred for perfection. They are found in common places, where no special effort was extended to produce them save one – life."

~

In December of 2014, my first newsletter was sent out. It included a professionally edited recording of "If you close your eyes", (the transcript can be found as endnote #4 of this book).

~

Drops of Light

2015 arrived, and by the time it ended, included the following events as headlines from mainstream media…

~

The year began with **a shooting** at the Paris office of **Charlie Hebdo,** a French satirical magazine, that claimed the lives of 17 people, 11 of them journalists. Al Qaeda claimed responsibility.

A plane crash took the lives of all 150 people on board a **Germanwings flight** from Barcelona to Dusseldorf.

Black Lives Matter protests continued this year, with the deaths of Walter Scott and Freddie Gray at the hands of the police.

There was an **Amtrak train derailment** in Philadelphia.

Two prisoners escaped from a maximum-security prison in upstate New York, with the help of the prison seamstress, who smuggled tools to one of the inmates inside frozen meat. She was sexually involved with him at the time.

A mass shooting at Emmanual Church in Charleston, South Carolina by a white supremacist prompted the removal of the Confederate Battle flag from that state's capitol. The flag is now on display at a museum nearby.

An on-air shooting, by an unhappy news anchor, of two of his colleagues, **took place at a Roanoke, Virginia tv station.**

Millions of refugees fled from Syria and the

Middle East into Europe, creating a "refugee crisis".

The **United States Supreme Court**, in a landmark decision, **allowed same-sex couples to marry nation-wide**.

Additional and deadlier **terrorist attacks** took place in **Paris**.

ISIS claimed responsibility.

Media reports were dominated by how many were killed at the hands of police, and how much **gun violence** occurred.

Wildfires took 95 square miles of **northern California**. This was blamed on **climate change**.

Volkswagen was embroiled in a scandal, and recalled 11 million diesel vehicles after fitting them with a device designed to **"cheat" emissions tests**.

In April there was a **7.8 earthquake in Kathmandu, the capital of Nepal, with a death toll of more than 8,000**.

Queen Elizabeth II became **the longest reigning British monarch**.

Princess Charlotte was born to Prince William and Duchess Kate, becoming Britian's newest royal.

Caitlyn Jenner became the most famous transgender woman in history, after an interview with Vanity Fair.

Cecil the lion was shot by an American dentist.

The **Greek financial crisis** escalated when the country failed to make an IMF loan repayment.

More women accused **Bill Cosby** of **sexual assault**.

In response to the investigation into the Benghazi

attacks, when **Hillary Clinton** was Secretary of State, she released just half of her emails, after erasing the other half and **wiping her server's memory**, claiming that these were not "work related".

Star Wars, "The Force Awakens" sold a record breaking 517 million globally on its opening weekend.

~

The year brought back some Love Quests as well as the Hundredth Monkey Project. On the blog, 2015 started this way...

~

"We thought it was going to be over 2 years ago, got over that and moved into, well, anticipating "the event", and we are still here. The changes and disclosures and exposures are happening in quiet ways all over the globe. The headlines today could be ripped from the media two years ago... expectations for global financial collapse still predominate. How many times have we hoarded food or cash? Too many."

~

And moved on (pretty quickly) to this...

~

"The primary beneficiary of a blameless heart is you. Unconditional acceptance eventually leads to continuous gratitude. A day immersed in gratitude is a very good day."

~

"I get that no one is coming, not via space ship or

celestial light or streets of gold. I get that it's me. That's just the way it works. There is no reason and no explanation that will elucidate this. It is the slavery mindset that thinks "why?"

We are moving out of that now. This realization is part of what comes with accessing your god-hood/your authority/your sovereignty. **A god stands there, knowing the answer, and gives. What does he/she give? Everything he/she has.**"

~

We were attempting to see ourselves accurately…

~

"We are Gods in hiding. I will share a personal, true story…

My partner is a deep trance channel. This means he leaves his body completely and allows other entities to speak through him. He "hangs around" in most cases, and listens. Some days he travels to other worlds.

For about 3 or 4 years we held a monthly creation group in our home. There were 6 of us and we'd ask questions of the group he channeled. This group was made of our expanded selves and other entities who knew us. Sometimes the crowd that "gathered" was huge!

My partner would often comment on what it looked like for him, out of body, from another point of view. **He described these brilliant, huge and gor-geous light beings. As each one of us spoke, he**

would watch us light up. He was struck by the "ridiculous" things these beautiful, powerful beings were saying. Things like "He hurt my feelings." "I don't know what to say." "I don't know what to do." "My stomach hurts.", etc. Clearly, we had no idea who we were."

~

"I have said before that I've energetically connected to the being I call "Poseur". This is a powerful, non-human god being with no remorse or conscience. It exists to create and the food it desires (its addiction) is worship. Nothing is off limits in order for it to get what it desires.

All of our examples of god-hood come from non-human beings. You would not, could not be like them. You are to be the first embodied human gods. What will it take to be a human god being? We will find out together. We will learn from each other. We are One, and that premise changes everything.

This is our next way to play together. We've played the slave game long enough."

~

"We are prisoners because we continue to sit in a docile stupor and obey. We've accepted the sentence. We remain behind bars of fear and refuse to risk escape.

It is our collective expectation that perpetuates global action."

~

"Make this day worthy of your attendance."

~

"Agape is an eruption of abundance and a feast of your essence. It is self-acting; what you do and what you are.
It cannot be defined because words are weak in the presence of Agape. It renders us speechless and holds our hearts tenderly."

~

By the spring, there was some solidarity; a realization of purpose; a noticing of our value...

~

"She: "It feels so lonely now..."

He: "Lonely?"

She: "Well, not lonely, I guess. I'm surrounded by people most of the days."

He: "Me too. Yet even with that, it is isolating. It's like I know something they aren't aware of and I'm the only one in the room who knows it. There is no one I can talk to."

She: "Mm Hmmm... I know what you mean. I don't feel isolated really, just solitary. Sort of like a light house keeper."

He: "That's it. That's brilliant. Write that."

Drops of Light

Light house keepers have a job to do. Their job is to be sure the light stays lit; that the lens is clean and clear of debris so that nothing interferes with the projection of the beam.

This human shell you wear is here now to tend to the light; the light that is you. You are a keeper of the light. If you stand quietly and watch and listen, you will see and sense other lighthouses with keepers. They are illuminating the landscape as well. They may be far away. They might be obscured by systems and storms – but keep watching. Keep your light bright and you will encourage them.

You are not alone. We have found each other on this screen and there are more of us. The rush and giddiness of instant ascension is long gone. We are all still here, living and loving, laughing and struggling; trying to make sense of a world that operates beneath senseless systems. Within all the seeming darkness we keep our lights blazing and clear – shining out on what looks like black wilderness.

It can feel like a solitary life yet the light you emit reaches further than you know. There are no wasted efforts. **There is no truth in pointless. You are a keeper of the light.** Everything you do points to enlightenment – oneness, collaboration and love.

Light reaches every dark corner and into the tiniest of openings. Your light is no exception.

The thing about your job is that you never talk to anybody while you do it. It's just you and the light. Light doesn't need conversation or even agreement. Its whole point is to illuminate the landscape. Wherever it falls, the inhabitants can't help but see a bit more clearly. You do that.

"Keeper" is perhaps a misrepresentation of your work. You understand the light and know how to insure it stays lit. You do not "keep" the light for yourself or for a few friends who understand you and are your favorites. You illuminate everyone within reach — indiscriminately.

You don't have to be understood or popular to be effective. You only have to shine. This, you can do all by yourself.

We are all light houses — it is the keeper who keeps the lights on, illuminating the way home. *Shine On, Light House Keeper, Shine on.*

She: "Okay, it is written."

He: "Thanks. That's it. Perfect.""

~

"Unconditional self-love is that "you" that you sense

when you manage to reach your truth. It is where you "hang out" between lives, problems and conditions. It's what we'll find once we jump off our mountain of judgment.

You are without fault – one unique flower in an exquisite field of astonishing beauty and fragrance. Not one of us can replicate you – your contribution is personal, powerful, solitary and necessary."

~

"Love cannot die. Relationships may end, and in truth, through choice, death or circumstance all of them do, but the love? It exists eternally. This love is the force of creation.
This love is the initiatory spark of your existence – it is the essence of source – it is eternal."

~

"The evolution of the human is still the best show in town. As confusing and exciting and a bit worrisome as it may be for us – it is fascinating to anyone in the audience. The conversations taking place telepathically display something clearly; something important. It is time to retire the words "foreign" and "enemy" and even "alien". We are each alien in the right context; the name says nothing.
The name "telepathic empath" describes what I do. The conversations being shared in the newsletter are not channeled, but spoken to me. Telepathy with another human on earth is only slightly different. The

one reaching out must have clarity of intent. I am like a party line. I only need to pick up the receiver; there is always someone there."

~

Newsletters were now sent weekly, and the telepathic conversations taking place that year included...

~

Poseur: "It is difficult to come up with wording that is precise as this is all a dream. Certainly, in your current imagining of dimension I come from another one."

~

Angel: "The term angelic basically refers to a life form dedicated to the assistance of the human. It does not necessarily indicate wings..."

~

Chewbacca: "It is a cold climate and we have hair we do not cut covering our body. I am sorry you feel the cold so much. It is true, I am closer to "cold blooded" creatures than warm blooded and you are picking that up."

~

Pleiadians: "This is not One being, it is a group. You are familiar with us."

~

Fairies: "I am a version of life, of essence, currently exhibiting it as what you would call a "fairy". I, therefore, am on this same planet, Mother Earth, with you - yet not effected in the same way as my frequency starts out different than yours. I cannot

113

typically be seen by humans and yet I see them."

~

A Watcher, the Anunnaki, Plant People, Lyrans, Mer-folk, Ewoks, Mantids, A sentient machine, Giraffe-like beings and Star beings also joined this unusual group!

~

The blog post on Mother's Day speaks to our growing awareness; we were waking up…

~

"Mother's Day began not as an excuse to go out for brunch, but a call for a peaceful approach to solving conflict. The day was intended to honor mothering attitudes and actions – as an answer to healing the destruction of war; as a valuable solution that was not practiced.

This "watering down" of Mother's Day is yet another way we've diminished valid and effective peaceful so-lutions and replaced them with sexier and more ex-plosive and expensive ones. It takes time to negotiate peace. It is an easy and quick thing to pull a trigger (or purchase a greeting card).

The mothering instinct is not reserved for only our physical mother but a universal caretaking impulse held by us all, which is truly what the day is about. Once allowed and nourished it would change the world. That's the thing to honor today, with or without the greeting card."

~

*On May 27ᵗʰ, 2015, I sat down &
said…*

I feel someone, who is this?

You will need to release expectings and ideas of both
reasons for and methods of contact, if we are to
chat.

What do you mean by methods?

Methods are ways of producing desired effects. These must be open to alteration as my energy
is not one you've known.

Yet I hear and feel you.

You do. This is by way of introduction. I would like
to diverge from word communication to
event/idea/subject communication. This coincides
with what happens in the spaces you have labeled
"higher realms" or faster frequencies or different
densities.

Okay. I'm open.

This will require a non-judgmental allowing of an
idea, a thought – merely looking at it.

Drops of Light

In this way it is hoped that a clearer picture can be given of this other way of life. Life in 5D+. Until now you've been speaking to others. Each with valid information and told word by word. In truth you had no real picture of what was said until after the conversation completed itself.

In contrast, in densities/realms other than earth – communication is in complete thoughts. In actuality you can do that now, and do, yet the use of words interprets and gets in the way.

This is because you alter your focus from what you are communicating or receiving to what you are saying or the words you are hearing. You step away from the art of telepathy to speak and listen to words. When in fact it is all telepathy to a greater or lesser degree.

So, who are you?

I am a being from the Pleiades and we have watched eagerly your discussions, waiting to move into your field and show you what your own day to day communication will be like once you complete your shift.

Do you have a name that could be used as reference?

I am known as Helna.

H-E-L-N-A?

More like H-E-L-L-E-N-A-T.

Is the final letter silent?

It is soft, not hard.

Okay, what do we do to proceed with this new type of communicating?

You remain open and listening. I will send the idea and we'll see what gets heard by you.

(I waited and received for a bit, allowing an immersion into what I was feeling and seeing)

I would like to tell you about what I see/sense/feel and how I interpret it all.

Yes, please.

I see first swirling dresses, dancing, a rambunctious and joyful dance — a performance — reds, white, colors — clapping. This is indoors, though not on earth. Not a planet of any type but a ship. This is a celebration due to a homecoming. Those who are dancing are demonstrating overwhelming joy. Deep satisfaction in those watching at this juncture — long awaited.

Drops of Light

It feels as if you are sending these to me with a feeling of coming home. At how many beings eagerly anticipate the homecoming of those of us who have been human for so long. Those of us who will be returning home.

(Note *these images were coupled with waves of love, of joy, of immense feelings of "welcome home" ... It is a challenge to find words to describe the intensity of this gathering and its effect on me...)

You are seeing it, Sophia. If you allow without so much associative input you will see more detail; remember more detail of this home that I am sending. The challenge with the human brain is it likes to categorize. Your memories of this place have no category you are familiar with in your current life.

Yes. The dresses threw me.

The dresses are your only visual context for a mesmerizing, welcoming dance that draws you into it. You are putting in a sort of square dance type costuming. This is not a square dance. It is a deeply sacred series of movements that are practiced and then handed from dancer to dancer. I was hoping you would remember/feel the solemnity of the dance itself. It has been practiced and perfected over eons for a very specific homecoming. Yours.

You are speaking the empirical "you"?

Yes. As those humans who volunteered for this work return home, each will be welcomed in the manner significant for that specific origin. Our race holds the movement, dancelike, as both beautiful and unique. It is a gift by every measure, and requires the entire community's participation. Not only the dancers, but the musicians, choreographers, costumers, attendants and logistics personnel. It is a deep honor. We are eagerly awaiting your return. We will learn so much and we have missed you all.

Okay, I would like to try this again. I must go.

I am aware. Until then.

(Note* after this, there was an overwhelming feeling of joy and I was sort of awestruck. I wandered into the room where I work, turned on my computer and kindle and the song, "Love" by American Authors was playing.

I began to cry and to sway with the visuals and feelings I was still getting. The sense of it is so difficult to describe, it is not like the family we know here, but sort of. It is perhaps so overwhelmingly loving because it has been so very long since a reunion has actually happened.

There is a sense of being with others who "get" you completely, that is experienced at every level of being; a deep validation. The only word I have in my heart is "home"; yet even that does not do it justice. Perhaps a better word is "agape"; unconditional acceptance.

The sense I have is that this is waiting for each of us, in some method of expression. This is one family reunion you won't want to miss!"

~

"The rapid acceleration in frequency leaves a wake of energy in its path – it is here, where the rest of us hangs on, desperate to catch up so some sort of stasis can be achieved."

~

In early June…

~

"This week has gone by sooooooooooooooo slllllooowwwwwwlllllllyyyyyyyyyyyy…………… It feels like a precursor to a sudden jolt. Up until this week I could barely keep up – so change is upon us once again. The last time I felt like this was March 15th, 2015. Things shifted suddenly on that day for sure."

~

"I find myself talking and listening to off world beings on most days. My dear friend K suggested and wondered if these were fractals; fractals of me. K also suggested that what I am doing with these conversations and the sharing of them is sort of expanding consciousness in some weird and wonderful way that expands it for anyone reading…"

~

A little later that month, this conversation took place...

~

"*Is there someone specific who wants to engage?*

There is.

You are keeping me awake.

We feel a certain urgency to our information. There are many wanting an audience. It is our option to reach you now, when there is not so much static. *(This was close to midnight and I wake each day at 5 AM)*

I do not know what you mean.

You are open – we are ready – it is the good moment for a connection.

Okay. I would like an introduction. I would also like an immediate 'getting to the point". It is so very late for me now and I am not so sure how long this will last.

Yes, we feel a draining. We are not here to cause you discomfort but to supply facts; certain ones that may enlighten you further.

We are not a race that frequents earth by way of visitation or even lights in your skies. Our interest is in the stories of old that circulate and their (*they) seem to form the basis of your "history". This, we find to be a fascination into the insight of your predecessors, creators and ancestors rather than the truth it has been labeled.

How do you know our history if you've never been here?

There is a galactic truth/story if you will that Earth is a part of.

The misconceptions and falsehoods told and re-peated over your concept of time was part of the veil of secrecy man agreed to step behind.

Not being human, we have never agreed to step will-ingly into delusion. All truth is available in the Akash. This is accessible to anyone interested in dis-covery.
What we'd like to say to you is that your origin some-how incorporates a bit of all the lies/folklore/stories you've been told. Yet there is *(*are)* huge gaps and holes in knowledge.
Mankind takes the clues he finds left behind such as huge buildings and monoliths and imagines why – having no factual basis on which to stand his theo-ries.

There were giants on your Earth by your stand-ards. There were times of great advancements in structural buildings. These were not made with any tool you have today.

The years of the creation of these stone buildings go so far beyond what man has guessed as to make it unbelievable.

As man uses time in forward motion only – the truth of time confuses the issue for any of his ability to "date" artifacts and buildings.

It all has happened. Time revolves as a record and what some of the discoveries are is more man's "future" than "past".

Mankind has already decided where he is going and what will be available to him when he gets there. Mankind has succeeded in securing a stronghold of power on Earth that will/does/is containing every dream and all imaginings for past-present-future lives.

The remarkable thing is that by remaining behind the veil you've "pulled the wool" over only your own eyes. Everyone else in the cosmos has access to your story and so the ending is no surprise to us.

We are enjoying so much your pretense of not knowing that there are many who show up again and again to remind you. *(Here I felt a reference to the many channelers.)* Humans by design have limited attention spans.

I think I have to stop now.

Drops of Light

Yes, I feel your fatigue. Just know that as your story plays out for the rest of us – it makes it possible for it to be told to you before you see it for yourselves. This does not make the tellers more powerful than you – only not restricted by the curtain.

Yes. I must go."
~

And the blog posts continued...
~

"I want to tell you how extraordinary you are. How each note sent, every thought shared, all things given and whatever you show up as is the most wondrous thing. I feel you as you read these words and the gift of your reaction explodes in my heart. We give without restraint or even comprehension as we feel each other – this is love expressed.
Love is perhaps the only place we completely agree. This, because the connection starts and ends there.
You are remarkable. You've come to a place of contrast and conflict in order to embody its opposite – oneness and unification. All this in slow motion. Every feeling, deeply felt; each heartache, painfully lived through. You are not masochistic. You are determined.
There are few others in all of creation admired such as you. You are brave, strong and attempting the miraculous while blindfolded. Your intent and

determination got you here. Your love and power will see you succeed."

~

There was a conversation that month that was first shared on the newsletter, and then also on the website because of its impact. I described it to my friend this way...

"It was like, idk, like knowing what all of life is, without having a physical life, without years or opinions or pain or even the necessity of learning... It was just knowing, well, every-thing. There are not really words..."

~

"I am here now.

What do you wish to talk about?

About this notion of Ascension.

Who are you – how will you be identified?

I will be identified by my mark of birth – yes, I've been human yet not only or often.

What do you mean by "mark of birth"?

By the fact of my personhood. I have existed in the "3rd" dimension as you call it, in the denser states.

Well, I will need some other form, something unique to you.

125

Drops of Light

There is a name – yet you may not know of it – it is – I will say the letters in your tongue. S-L-O-V-E-N-T-A would be closest.

Okay. If you are not often human, who/what are you most often?

I am not in form most "often", yet it would be more accurate to say "mostly" as I Am One – occurring in many places.

Your quantum physicists are seeing the truth of this.

I have been human. It is for this reason I want to speak of "ascension". It was all the rage when I was human as well. Not for everyone, but reportedly for the sainted or holy ones.

The idea that some beings had "ascended" into "heaven" once they passed was held sacred. It was a mark and if you were one of those accomplishing ascension, well, it was the ultimate in spirituality – the apex – the goal.

We were so mistaken. Both in how we defined what we saw and what we yearned for ourselves. I see now how the yearning is all part of the journey. Yet I also see humans in your focal moment of now doing the same.

Ascension, as defined today, is something to yearn for if you are looking to escape life as it exists around you now. There is no "up" or "heaven" or place to go to. You are here now. You can transform your current life to be heaven and utilize your powers of manifestation, imagination, to *(there was a long pause)*

To what?

To maximize your manipulative abilities and have whatever is necessary for bliss. None of this is beyond you – but perhaps beyond your current imagining.

The reason I would like to speak to you of ascension is because the idea held by you *(empirical you)* about it contains polarization.

It is still all "before (ascension)" and "after (ascension)" – darkness and light – then and now – less and more. The fullness of every facet of your life is not understood.

From the place that I look – I see a mass of beings in stasis still waiting for an outside event, happening, spark or influence – to push them "forward." This is only possible if "forward" were true. It is not.

The fullness of life has to be realized from inside – like an exponentially felt **Zen moment**.

Drops of Light

I am getting a picture.

Describe it. I am sending you one.

It is light from the inside — gradual and bursting forth all at once — an internal explosion of brilliance without damage — an expansion of self that, I don't know. What I physically see is the form of a human in shadow — black — and inside the form and then beyond and the form never moves — yet the power of the light is exceptional and reaches far past the form itself.

Perhaps I'd call it a "Light-gasm".

You have captured my message/image. Ascension is not so much a climax but a maturing and a new start. A version of creation theory that is like the "big bang" on human form. Once that level of life is realized and expressed, it most naturally evolves to more life — and the cycle continues.

I see man hold a notion of climbing "up" towards ascension when there was never a "down" to move out of. Every moment of life is sacred. Held there, time is immaterial and there is no question of belief or doubt.
Life answers itself.
Everything is known.

Humans play with not knowing, not liking, not

remembering and not loving because it's a way to **re**-know, **re**-member and **re**-love. It's pretend.

If there was one thing I could get across as a bit of assistance on your current "now" it would be to stop, notice every now moment and it will share with you the secrets of life itself.

Do not imagine yourself un-ascended or with something you "must" do. Just live each moment to its extreme depths. This will give you pause enough to let your light emerge. You'll see more clearly and with greater understanding.

I did none of these things while human. It was "long ago". I too wanted a way out and tried all the "fads". I hated still, mostly myself, for reasons I could rattle off like a list of grievances – but not discern. The self-hatred comes from a stuffing of truth. It seems that this game always sounds like fun before you actually play it. Then, it gets far too real and painful.

By stifling of truth, I mean that the fullness of humanity is hidden beneath the roles they wear and take. *(Another long pause)*

Why have you stopped?

As you become weary it's like you turn the volume

down.

Well, yes, I am tired. Please explain a bit more and we'll finish up now?

I have no self-hatred when I am not human. I also have no feast of constant sensation and emotion and stimulus for creation. Here (In the non-physical) truth is known. As human, truth is what you are learning, feeling – **becoming**.

This self-hatred is a mis-identification of your actions. Somehow, your ego has gotten the message that it's done something wrong, very wrong. What is wrong is humanity's acceptance of limitations in its self-definition, not anything it is doing.

As man becomes the fullness of himself, he "ascends" – without going anywhere.

I would like to speak of this again. But I must go.

Yes. We will."

~

In July of that year, the Guardian returned. He had been absent for about 6 months. Here's what he said at that time...

~

"Right now, we GEs are in the middle of our most important mission, the one why we have been made to be GEs. **It is our life's most important one**."

~

My blog posts were less frequent that summer...

~

"The infrequency of these blog posts is a result of the thought that it's already been said. That it's **all** been said. That one more person saying it, is just, well, one more person clogging up your screen. It has come down to a single question: "To what end?""

~

""To what end?" To say that I feel you. I see you in all that I encounter, ages new to 96. A tiredness, a weariness. It is evident in your eyes, your words, your explanations. It feels like the part before the big win, the plot shift or the last yard. It feels like we are moments away from massive acceleration, choice and living the new, right now.

Perhaps Greece is a marker."

~

"The name "the Awakening" suits this time now for humanity. It is not so much a physical awakening but a spiritual and emotional resurgence of awareness; a remembering, an uncovering of truth."

~

"So many names for this time: Awakening, The Wave, The Event, The Moment of Justice, The Shift, The Party. Who to believe? When is it coming? What will happen? Where should I be? These are just a

few of the wonderings I am feeling from us all…
All is in motion now. I dislike the term "Wave"
because on the shore a wave emerges from beyond,
alters the landscape and departs.
It is more than that. Think *human* wave, the
kind routinely played out in ball fields everywhere.
Once this wave happens, everyone is still there. Some
of us start it. Others of us hold up the middle. The
last few finish it.
Remember the "wave" at the sports arena. It happens
without a plan, **yet each one knows when their
moment to stand up arrives**."
~

On August 3, 2015 I was told, by One, that the
being I had called Poseur was no longer. A recording
of that conversation is found on Soundcloud. I was
also told that some of my friends helped facilitate his
departure.
The "Call to Action", from 8/8/2014, may have
started the process. There is no way to verify that, yet
it seems plausible. At any rate, Poseur was gone from
this earth realm."
~

*The blogs continued. Eventually a series entitled
"As we Shift" was written and shared…*
~

"We are, as of late, exponentially expressing ourselves. There is no getting around or away from
whom we are. It's all okay. We're all okay.

What this looks like on the street is extremes of personality, played out before your eyes."

~

"This is, I believe, what has been happening since March of this year, and what some have called the splitting of earth. We are choosing our world. Each life is self-perceived and self-motivated, depending on our current addictions.
Whatever you believe you are, you'll see evidence of everywhere."

~

"There are none of us more "valuable", less "quirky" or "better" than any others of us. Sometimes the cast of characters reminds me of a giant game of "Whack a Mole" – we are all sitting around, equally "ascended" until one of us rises to the top – in clear view of the rest of us. This one enjoys the "specialness" of being "on top" for a few moments. Until, inevitably, they are whacked back to equality."

~

"Do you remember who you are? Perhaps with the expansion we can do away with reflections (and mirrors). Without "needing" another to mirror you – you will stand in full acceptance of your magnificence. This will occur without names or "others" to validate it for you.
You will then stand free."

~

"Maybe humans are a new kind of god – one that

needs no worship or affirmation. Maybe we just "get 'er done" at our own urging. Maybe now we have reminded ourselves enough. **Maybe the "Event" we are all planning on is self-initiated."**

~

"There is a term now used as an option when you are asked to declare your sexuality on some form or another. There is *male*. There is *female*. There is *gender fluid*[7]. I love this. We are beginning the process of losing categories.

Thus, begins Oneness…

Names, roles and categories, even those as seemingly solid as "sex", are re-defined in this new place we call home. It's now possible to be nothing specific, to remain whole and complete without a permanent attachment to any label, any "name". Wrap your head around it and begin to experience freedom. You are who you say you are. Right now."

~

"The most profound gift we have to offer is ourselves. It is something we have always with us. It is all that we came here with, and will be the only thing we take with us upon exiting. By definition then, it is rare and without equal; this is your moment to share it.

It is useful in any situation, with any population, at any locale. It is not dependent on finances, position, title or education.

If you can find no other reason to love yourself today, use this one. **There is none other than you."**

~

"This recent energetic pulse is a huge force. It will not be stopped.
It feels like this wave is meant to be ridden.
Most children and a surprising # of adults are excellent surfers.
Those that haven't yet learned to surf are crabby, sour faced and struggling to hang on.
It's sort of a glorious mess. This process, foretold and planned these many years is happening in our lifetime, right now and before our eyes.
Surf's up! Time to learn to "hang ten"."

~

"Enlightenment is not accomplished via title or specific process or group or increased vibration – it emerges from self-acceptance."

~

"The deep self-acknowledgement that accompanies sovereignty leaves no doubt as to worth. There is no room for fault or blame in absolute awareness."

~

"It sounds trite yet words have not yet been imagined for what it is we are doing. We are re-imagining ourselves. The pictures we held of need and lack are dissolving and in their places, we are inventing Agape.
I don't know your specifics but I know your blueprint. It was drawn in pure light and saturated with love.
This is the time for your emergence. **We need your**

light."

~

"Imagination is the stuff of creation. *It sees the form within the formless and the formless within the form.* It knows."

~

"The balance between self and "other" is not reached in agreement. It is realized in acceptance."

~

"Three nights ago, I was out walking and, well, something happened. It was like the earth shifted and then righted itself. A palpable movement, like I was walking on a giant ball and it rolled forward and then back. Surreal. Then, I could hear the crackles in my ears as what feels and looks to me like reality is forming before my eyes...
On my walks around the park, the lights go out as I approach... Not just one... many.
We will invent the words for this one..."

~

"As we shift, it is our humanity that rises above every disagreement and difference. We are magnificent in our uniqueness and unique in our magnificence.

~

The last month of 2015 saw us immersed in more "terror threats" & greater surveillance. Many of us were ill and/or depressed, while working more than one job to get by. Publicly, there was evidence of disclosure with "The Martian" and "The Expanse". Blog posts attempted to capture where we were...

~

"Everywhere is "evidence" of what we are not – illness and violence and loss attempt to convince us to be afraid. Be very afraid. It is only mid-week and there has been a bomb threat and lock down in 2 schools within 15 miles of my home, a shooting in San Bernardino, CA and a new "security system" installed at my workplace, a grade school. All of this in 3 days. We are now under constant surveillance and locked into our classrooms at all times."

~

"The point in mentioning any of this is to say that if I were writing this story – **and we are –** I would gradually worsen things so that hope is almost gone – just before the big (and happy) final scene. This is what makes a great story, and what you remember as you get up to leave the theater – the ending."

~

"Here's a true story.
Last week my partner had to call a cab. About the time I expected to see him, I sent a text to see what was up. He was still waiting for his ride. I was with some people and noticed, about an hour later still, that he had not arrived. I sent another text. There was no sign of the cabbie, he had gotten lost. I had a single thought upon hearing this: "Someone **needs** to pick him up, **now**."

I returned to our guests. About 20 minutes later he walked in the front door, saying:

Drops of Light

"Thank God you called someone. My guy never showed. He called me when we were just about here."
I replied, "But I didn't call anyone."
He said, dumbfounded, "But he pulled up less than 5 minutes after we texted, and asked for you, not me. I could see your name on his computer screen in the cab."

We just looked at each other. We've no real explanations as to how, but we do have evidence that *the universe has conspired to give us exactly what we intended/wished/created.*"
~

"Everything necessary to create this dream is found in you. It's been hidden beneath rules and shoulds, control and manipulation. No longer. Once we let go the stranglehold on ideas and words and dreams and possibilities – we enter unlimited.
You are a brilliant light. You are here to illuminate this golden age, which has already begun."
~

"For light is what we are. And when all is said and done, and you are asked how you did it? How you pulled off the most incredible transformation in creation? You'll say: "I let go."
For nothing is worth hanging on to, not pride or agenda or grudge or a belief or a point or a name or love or twenty bucks. There is someone always who needs what you are hanging on to – more than you

do.

The wonderful thing about our illusion is that giving it away creates more. We set it up that way. So, when this moment came, and it seemed as if all was lost or forgotten or never going to change; we'd remember to let go."

~

"2015 was preparatory and perhaps most of all it brought us to our knees for love. Not to an altar or a specific god, not to the words of a specific doctrine, but to truth – all separation is fictional.
We are One."

~

"Hugs happen a lot this time of year. For all of this I am grateful beyond words.
For our humanity is our brilliance and love is our birthright. This is who we are.
We are a generous, joyful, hugging hoard of humans in December. I predict in our shifting "5D World" that all of this and more will be our everyday – making every day a holiday. For this is who we actually are."

~

"Willingly you took this role and cheerfully you play your part, all the while wondering – When will I be saved? How will I be rescued? Who will come to heal me?

I tell you this. There is no other but you to do the saving, the rescuing and the healing. As you have

Drops of Light

played all parts – villain, victim, evil, criminal, liar and thief – you have prepared yourself to play this role. You are the one who knows, the one who heals, the one who comprehends, the one who gives.
You – who have asked, now answers.
All of this is within. It is not reserved for a "god" or a "deity". It is not held separate.

Know that there is no other; without separation all is One.
You are that One."

~

And so, 2015 came to an end. We were holding onto some questions. We had a few answers, but were expecting further clarity, and expectation for the "event" remained; a sort of remedy or savior to us all.

~

Chapter 4
These many Lights
(2016-2019)

Here,
there is a noticing of Light
beyond the realm and focus
of your everyday life.

Drops of Light

2016 began with an update from the Guardian…

~

"Now it is 2016, Followers of Light refused to stop this experiment, yet they agreed to leave Terranians alone, adding that Humanity is now "self-functioning civilization of 3rd kind.""

"In our words Terranians are now an independent Civilization with unrestricted access to space exploration. Now They can move beyond Outer Solar System. Compromise found. You know what this means - there is no more need for a'f'a (Forces of One) or AMs to directly interfere, experiment against Creation will no longer proceed further.
Confrontation avoided.

What is left to take place here is ascending to Next Stage of Development (Grand Shift, Moment of Justice, Event), and isolation (quarantine of Earth) will be lifted upon this occurrence is completed, from words of FLs (Followers of Light)."

~

Here's what mainstream media told us happened that year…

~

Flint, Michigan had a crisis, with **lead** contaminated water, when the city was switching systems.
The Zika virus outbreak began with mosquitos in Brazil and made its way to the United States.

The Syrian civil war was on its 6th year, when peace talks between Russia and the United States led to a "cessation of hostilities". An agreement was reached in mid-December to end the fighting there.

U.S. Supreme Court justice Antonin Scalia died. U.S. President **Barack Obama nominated appeals court judge Merrick Garland** to the Supreme Court.

A **7.8 magnitude earthquake happened in Ecuador**, South America.

Popstar **Prince died at the age of 57.**

NASA announced that it had examined **over 1200 planets** and that **9 of them could support life.**

A **Baltimore police officer**, the first of 6 accused, was **acquitted in the 2015 death case of Freddie Gray.**

BREXIT happened in June when the United Kingdom voted to leave the European Union.

The Pulse nightclub in Florida had a gunman open fire inside, taking the lives of approximately 50 people.

Pokémon "Go" was released in the United States as a wildly popular augmented reality game.

An act of **terror** occurred at a **Bastille Day celebration in Nice, France** when a man drove his car through the crowd, killing more than 80 people. Either Al-Qaeda or ISIS claimed responsibility that year for **terror attacks in Burkina Faso West Africa, Brussels Airport in Belgium, Istanbul airport and Berlin.**

Thousands of **DNC emails were hacked** and Russia was blamed.

The **summer Olympics** were held in **Brazil**.

Hillary Clinton became the **first female to lead a major political party in a US presidential race**.

There was a **recall of Samsung Galaxy Note 7** smartphones after some of them were either **exploding or catching fire**. The phones were banned from airplanes. **Mother Theresa** officially became a **saint**.

Hurricane Matthew grew to a Category 5 as it stormed through Haiti, the eastern Caribbean and the southwest United States.

More than **500 groups of Native American Protesters** (which included the Crow Nation and the Sioux; lifelong enemies!) **blocked access to the Dakota Access oil pipeline** in North Dakota.

Donald Trump became the 45th president of the United States, beating Hillary Clinton.

Fidel Castro died at the age of 90.

Other deaths that year included **David Bowie, Muhammad Ali, Gene Wilder, and Nancy Reagan**.

The **opioid addiction epidemic** in the United States was in the news with reports of 70+ people dying each day from overdoses.

Police violence and racial profiling were again in the news that year, with the **shooting deaths** of Alton Sterling in Baton Rouge, LA and Philando Castille in Minnesota. These deaths sparked the shooting of police officers (at a peaceful protest) in Dallas,TX, where 5 officers were killed, and in Baton Rouge, LA where 3 officers were also killed.

In baseball, the **Chicago Cubs broke a 108-year curse** by winning the World Series against the Cleveland Indians. "**Fake News**" and "**Pizzagate**" entered the conversation.

~

That year, the following "off-worlders" were ringing me up for "telepathic chats" (*names given are my own*); Merfolk, the Elders, the Anunnaki, Jellyfish beings, Sasquatch, Martians, Andromedins, Giants, Dwarves, Pleiadians, Plant-like beings, Felines, Earth Keepers, Cetaceans, Dog-like beings, Raptors and Reptilians.

~

Where was the light in all of this madness? Well, here's what others of us were thinking, saying and doing…

~

"We are the ones shifting, the ones asking, the ones wondering: if, when, why and how. We are wasting our most valuable asset. No, it's not time, its **emotion; the wind beneath our wings.** "

~

"We ask for apologies and promises, without understanding their power to distract us. **They bind us to useless emotion.** We want names and dates without realizing the names are ours and the dates self-chosen."

~

"This experiment is ending, of that there is no doubt. It can end slowly, which helps only the

145

controllers (1%) as they amass as much wealth as possible before the end (*while we continue to watch them*). It can end quickly, giving us the benefit **now** in all arenas of abundance and life (*while they quickly exit*). Demand an end now. Stretching this out until a specified "date" only harvests our hope. **It does not benefit mankind in any way.**"

~

"The Big Short" was released. Timely and powerful, the film offers an inside view of what happened when the housing market crashed 8 years ago. It explains why it crashed, and ends with a single sentence. This line tells us that the same set up is happening again, in 2015. The bankers have renamed an instrument that will glean them huge amounts of money."

~

"In 2008 no one was held accountable and the banks were bailed out. Eight million of us lost our homes here in the USA."

~

""Money Monster" (another film) was released that spring. It too exposed the manipulation on Wall Street, this time of stocks."

~

There was a lot of talk about Ascension Symptoms, and our shifting world…

~

"Each of these symptoms appears also as a sign of

what we've come to label the common cold or an ear infection or anxiety or stress or stomach flu. What happens when they show up now is that the usual meds and treatments aren't working. They seem to appear and disappear at will.

~

"Everyone is not on the same page as we head towards our new world. Some of us are not really aware we are heading anyplace new. That's right and perfect. The point here is that regardless of age or attitude, we are shifting. You can't help but notice. Our global voice has changed key."

~

"Somehow, I'm becoming the observer; the observer of my life – **while living it.**
Things are getting weird. I can hardly look at anything without seeing the bigger picture."

~

"As we move there is a oneness observed and our individual parts start to stick out... Some of us were big hits several years ago, when the crank was really stuck and needed enormous effort while it moved almost imperceptibly. Some of us showed up in between like shooting stars, illuminating things from time to time so that more of us could see what was happening. The rest of us continue to explore and elucidate and share and morph and grow and sometimes pull back a bit, keeping the momentum and flow going ever towards what we all intended and never stopped believing in."

Drops of Light

~

"You will be asked to light the way. You'll know where the switch is and when to turn it on."

~

"**This life is a living field.** It is not so much that we are altering the field with our intent. It is that we are moving to the field of our most deeply held beliefs. The Golden Age already exists. We just have to relocate."

~

"Four years ago, we were waiting for someone to "ascend us" on 12-21-12. We've changed many things since then, including ourselves. We are probably better off in all sorts of ways. Yet we are still waiting to be ascended. That's like sitting in your bedroom on Christmas morning and wondering why you didn't get any presents. You have to go to the tree!"

~

"Whomever and wherever we are, **we are this shift**. We only need decide."

~

The form and substance of my "off world" communications changed a bit that late winter...

~

"The following conversation took place yesterday. What is surprising about it is the force of the visual that accompanied it. This is a new wrinkle in this work, visions are not typically part of these connections; yesterday and today they seemed to be the whole point of the conversation. I offer this here, as confirmation of the work we are doing and the love we are realizing. It is happening, it is working, we are doing it! There is no longer any doubt.

~

The following conversation took place on March 2, 2016...

"Is there someone who wants to connect?"

There is!

Who is this? I feel exuberance and smiles and happy excitement!

We are your sisters from the Pleiades!

Hello! It is always nice to hear from you!

It is always nice to be heard! ;-) (Wink, wink)

What have you come to talk about?

About you! About your ascension or whatever it is you are calling it now! About all of the exciting progress happening on your now home world.

Sure, okay, that would be great. Go ahead then.

Drops of Light

We have been following (and closely) what is transpiring on Earth. We are very aware of the fact that you're constantly being told words like "soon" and "next week" and "any moment or day now". Those words have become empty. We will not use them.
We would however, like to offer encouragement when we see you discouraged. We know this is your current state and the state of many who call Gaia home.

Here's how it looks from here. It looks like the darkness is being forced off...

I am getting an image and it is of many people pushing off a huge dark canvas tarp that was covering them. It is a huge effort as the tarp in this vision is larger than a football stadium. The people are working as one in this visual. And every time I see it, I see children in all of their joyful exuberance. They seem to be providing the energy, not the muscles, to remove this dark tarp. I also see in the distance other tarps of darkness. They are far away. I cannot tell if they are being removed or are just there.

In this vision there is a lot of light and people with their sleeves rolled up ready to work and smiling. It is a vision with lots of energy, positive energy. The light increases in portions of the field, like segments at a time, as the tarp is pushed up.
(I was interrupted here) I'm sorry, my son began a conversation. I'm available now.

Yes! We see you have many beings with you now, who also desire your attention. We also sense a feline, who does not.

Well, no, my kitten is sleeping, but with me in the room. (My kitten was asleep on the floor nearby, lol.) What can you say regarding the vision just seen?

That we are very pleased and interested! Your method of interpretation is so very much tied to things you know of or have seen. You have seen a sports field – hence the size reference. You are human and equate the emotions to all things human.

We will say this – the picture we sent was done so to illustrate why we are so very excited for humanity right now. It is because you are working together. As One. This may not appear to be so, as you live such isolated lives – it is the internet that joins you.

What we see is the same efforts extended in many different ways – all of them towards the unveiling of truth and uncovering of hidden structures that do in fact form the base for your world. New ideas and old truths are being brought to the surface. More of your population are reading them now, hungry for them, as the limitation and starvation for truth intensifies.

This can be seen in your vision. These are no longer isolated "whistleblowers" attempting to remove what

151

amounts to a huge tarp – but you are banding together energetically and, in more and more cases, physically. *This is activated oneness. (Italics mine – Sophia)*

You cannot force disclosure – it will erupt once the demand for truth is the only thing ringing in the ears of those holding the tarps in place.

What we want you to notice is that these tarps of darkness (in your vision) were not fastened to anything at all; but seemed instead to be floating above the heads of the people.

Yes, it was weird. It was like nothing was holding them up.

There is nothing holding the darkness/control/lies/manipulation/slavery in place except the agreement of mankind. This is all illusion.

Realize too what force helped in the action – in the physical removal of the tarp.

It was the exuberance of the children. Their energy was this force, pushing the adults to let in more light by throwing back more of the tarp. It was their light.

Yes! You have received the prime component of our message today. It is the light of every portion of mankind that contributes. It may appear that only some of men and women are doing the "heavy lifting" and throwing back the tarp. This is a falsehood. It is the voice of every one of you that creates the movement into the light.

So – those of you who are light workers are probably who you see as the "rolled up sleeves" (humans) throwing back the tarp. In this picturing, it may also seem that only a few of you are strong enough to make a difference. It is a heavy tarp.

Yet realize that not only the light worker, but all of mankind will ultimately throw off the old. This is initiated by the few – and gladly picked up by those in the same area once the light shines in.

Light helps everything, and this benefit is universally felt. Notice the energetic contribution of happy children that also push forth the unveiling. It is everyone.

We who watch are so happy to see this working together happen and want you to notice its increasing not gradually, but **exponentially**. You are doing powerful work here, and as your numbers increase the load gets lighter.

Notice too those dark tarps in the distance (in your vision) shrouded in shadow. Be assured that there is movement beneath them, and as the field you are in becomes ablaze with light and free of its confining darkness, it lights the rest and their "tarp removal" is

Drops of Light

now offered assistance by the initial removers – *the light spreads. (Italics mine – Sophia)"*
~

This conversation took place on March 3, 2016.

"So, who kept waking me up last night?"

There is a group, there are many of us. We have come to communicate and would appreciate an audience with you.

Okay, you have one now. What is it you've come to say?

That the earth is being watched.

I don't follow?

The planet, known as a jewel in the galaxy, has many eyes upon her as she makes her transformation.

You woke me up to tell me that? It does not seem to be a message of urgency. As a human, I require a certain amount of un-interrupted sleep. (By way of explanation, I was a little put out. I'd been woken up 2 or three times the previous night and it was brutal getting up at 5 AM for work. I have asked before for this kind of activity to stop during the weekdays. These beings were quite insistent.)

There is more.

Please continue then.

You are a human, having life on a planet that is also having a life. You come here to evolve – this planet you rest on is also evolving.

The urgency was felt by us due to the moment you are approaching.

What moment is that? I suddenly experience an internal feeling of speed, if that makes sense, and I see/hear the word "Crash". What are you saying?

There is a ramping up that is becoming exponential on your planet. It is witnessed by us now as approaching a crescendo.

Who are you?

We are your co-occupiers of a life in a galaxy referred to as "Milky". We do not; have not before engaged the human. We hear/see/feel your beacon/call and we answer.

I am not clear. What call is being sent?

There are more than one – your own voice is one we picked up to respond to as you specifically requested "only assistance".

Drops of Light

And you can offer that?

We feel, yes, that we can. It is in this vein we reached you. There is not a concept inside of your signal/beacon that describes "sleep" or, for that matter, "off". Your signal is very strong at times, perhaps those times coincide with certain sleep patterns.

I don't know that is true, yet perhaps.
What help are you offering?

We offer a perspective, some enthusiasm and an alternative. Your race attempts something that has not been, to our knowing, consciously chosen up until this moment now. "Prior" "ascension events" happened for isolated ones or small groups of you – while the planet remained unchanged.
What you attempt with this current shift that coincides with your planets shift is a simultaneous transformation while remaining in body – a mere change of location, sort of.

This is the reason for the "all eyes" on Earth – with this event there is a new paradigm offered to all of creation.

What we want to say, and let us explain as we do, the difficulty we sense in your reception of us now. This is due to the surrounding of you with so many humans! Their energy interferes, even without engagement.

Yes, well, I'm in a coffee shop. It is quite crowded.

We know not the meaning of the words, but see the intake of substances and mutual exchanges. There are many.

There are. Can we continue anyway?

We can. We will send clear images so that you can "hear" them and this should help.

Now I see the word "collapse".

Yes.

And I see dollar bills, money, falling from a spot above. I see something slamming shut. Like a ledger. "broken" "not repairable" 'out of order" "unavailable" – these are the words I'm seeing. "Money" "cash only" "gold" "closed for eternity" "thank you for your business" "out of stock" "empty".

I see people turning away from buildings, doors to buildings that did not open. They are smiling as they turn away and shake their head "no" to other people walking also towards the same doors.

I see one man give another man a "high five" in the parking

Drops of Light

lot in front of this building. I don't know what sort of business this is. It appears formal, a dark structure, official looking but not sure what capacity. My guess would be some sort of government building or bank.

Now I see others pulling up and these men shaking their heads and the car's driver smiling and just driving away. They do not attempt to enter.

You have associated many familiar images with our sending along with words. Many words.
What we came to say is this:
What is observed right now is unprecedented. It is cataclysmic and by many will be perceived as catastrophic. Those who see it that way, (catastrophic) will not be seeing the whole picture.

This rapid influx of energy is helping what the humans are doing on their own. It is like giving them a hit of speed when they've already had a Red Bull. Does that make sense?

What is so very exciting and unusual is this human engineered shift. Right now, its speed is beyond expectation and the resulting change to the landscape is unclear.
This is an actual physical alteration to all of life on your planet. Gaia is keeping up with your movement and all of this is leading, very quickly now, to a pivotal point.

What will very likely be a cataclysmic event is more than likely going to happen for you, for her, for you all. This cannot be helped, as in order to move, the old must be left behind.

A break will necessitate a new order and a new world is what you are co-creating. This break will initiate finally the actual changes we see you make – yet the break happens first.

What will have to break is not just the planet, but the systems governing her and enslaving her people. **None of this should you consider prophecy for we are not prophets and not enmeshed in a life on your world.** *(Bold type mine – Sophia)*

Consider this a long-range view of goings on. It is offered only because without it only catastrophe and finality may be observed. This coming series of breakages are likened to the hatching of a bird or the butterfly breaking the cocoon. The current structure has to be dismantled. It is seen that a show of something forceful is what creates the final collapse. It may be that Gaia herself forces the issue with many earth changes. It may be a monetary breaking/failure that creates the chaos. Maybe something else or both will occur.

The message is that those Dark Forces controlling

the Earth is not the initiatory force; but the planet and her people. They have no more power – it has been removed. We've heard you use the words "Maybe they didn't get the memo". That may be true. These upcoming changes will be clear.

What is not clear is what mankind as a whole will do. Our coming to you now is done in an effort to say this –
Do not despair whatever comes. You and Gaia are at the helm.
(What was coming through here is that the controllers were NOT at the wheel, we've wrested control from them now, with our singular voice. I liken this to the idea that it is not initially obvious that a child has finally completed puberty. There are minor signs, sure, but until that day when the young man or young woman takes responsibility completely for their life, you are never quite sure when this process began; the release of parental control directing their life.)
And these twists, turns and dead-ends are necessary.

You are, and very quickly, writing a map for all of life.
This map takes you to the place of your wildest dreams and fondest hopes.
In every case this is true.
You are, all of you, warrior angels, and you've assured a rapid transformation.
Complete the journey with love in every case.

That is all for now.

Thank you."

~

"What we have to remember, while we listen to and read and ask about what is happening – is that **we are simultaneously making it happen.** All of this is our dream, our nightmare, our paradise, our illusion. Nothing happens without our belief, expectation and permission."

~

Later that month, another group had information about our shift…

~

" *"Is there someone who wants to connect?"*

There could be. We sense a question.

Yes. There has been a document released – I was shown this document. It supposedly is authored by the "Royals" and amongst other things, foretells of "severe space weather" approaching the earth. This was posted yesterday (3/21/16) and I'd like some comments on this, if possible, from whoever is able to offer more information.

Yes, we see that more information will be helpful. We can tell you what is seen and known from this perspective here.

Thank you. Please tell us who you are?

Drops of Light

I am a part of the **Council of Elders**. We've observed the dynamic relationship earth humans have with so many factions and races. It is a complicated, extremely active picture you paint. We, with such an expanded view, find it challenging to appreciate which specific knowledge you hold when we talk to you – so many stories!

We can only imagine how confusing and disconcerting this must be for the human.

Yes, it can be.

We will attempt clarity as we answer this question. What is seen is a force of energy which is radiating from Source itself. This will be experienced by every human and does not matter what name you give it or expectation you have for it – it will be felt and once felt, known to be an alteration of life itself. You will know this. It may be that you will even see this and subsequent reports will foretell of the end of days.

To be clear – this is not the end of days. (Italics mine, Sophia) The announcing document that alerted you to this, springs from a group heavily invested in protection of its physical assets and the control required to do so. They are not certain such control will be possible after this event and are lining up their "ducks in a row" as it were.

Things/illusions and the "gamers of creation" that helped place them there are about to unravel and quickly so.

We do not see humanity negatively impacted by this "severe space weather" event – but the opposite. Be clear however that change of massive proportions will cause upheaval to physical systems and the planets that support them. All energy has a force – this incoming force is looking like a huge ocean wave off in the distance and it grows.

You know that there is no escaping this shift.

What you don't know is what precisely is shifting. As it looks from our vantage point – this wave of love/energy/power/life essence will wash over humanity.

Those solidly rooted will bask in its effect. Those without roots will be tossed around. What is not clear is whether or not this wave is the shift, initiates the shift or neither. It was and still is meant to be a surprise.

The horizon can be deceiving. Things close look very far and things very far appear close. For this reason, we cannot give you a precise "date" or "time" for its arrival.

Drops of Light

Rest assured you and those of your "ilk" stand on solid ground and will enjoy very much what is on its way to you.

Is that all?

We feel that we've answered the question, yes.

Okay, thank you."

~

   The Pleiadians had this to tell us...

~

"What is happening that is so very exciting is portions of darkness are disappearing at a constant rate. It is as if they are being regularly and systematically zapped with light beams.

What is the source of the light? The source is absolute love. There is no other explanation.
What we wanted to say was this. Each "partial disclosure" event, however small and expected is affecting the field exponentially. It seems to be doing this against the intents of those holding the power and without the direct intention of those who are still enslaved.
As you accept yourselves your hearts expand. This expansion from your most powerful physical organ *(the heart)* creates streams of energy/light – thus the darkness is illuminated. With each new particle of

light comes a new awakening – a realization that there's been a misjudgment – and a re-alignment of focus. This only amplifies each possible beam of light and love expands.

This love, this light, this core of that which you are – is erasing the darkness and exponentially increasing the amount of love *(that is)* present.

If a gradual data release causes less shock and overall disruption, while a complete outing of truth causes more benefit – then both must occur for maximum power and appreciation of all of humanity. You are ONE. It would seem that your unity has created a scenario that allows each of you to gradually appreciate your unique contribution and perfection while accepting every facet of yourselves. It is not within the human to intentionally harm itself. It is within the human to love.

You are only at the beginning stages – what you do and how you do this will be witnessed by all of us as it unfolds."

~

And we continued to watch, wonder and wait…

~

"Four years ago, we were mostly anxious to enlighten everyone to the fact of this shift. As it approaches and rapidly, it comes with a sense of dread and uncertainty. What will it look like?"

~

Drops of Light

In mid-April of 2016, we were all noticing a sort of calm, and were given this explanation for it...

~

"This planet is no longer to be controlled by the dark ones who acted as owners. They've departed. Whether willing or at their own instigation does not matter – they are gone.

Your controllers/your owners are gone Sophia.

All of you feel this. You do not know what to say. Conversation has such a minor role in the enormous scheme that is your life today. How can you begin to introduce a change of such proportions to a race unaware?

You can't. Not really. Yet they are gone and this changes it all.
What happens from here on out is up to your race. Those left still are perhaps a bit more reckless and possibly dangerous because of fear.

You are left with the underlings. They are just as mean and are backed by no-one. It is fear and habit that keeps them moving and operating with fear tactics.
What this change will look like for you is unclear. The old systems and rules will crumble without a foundation – yet this could take a while."

~

Towards the end of April, this message came through…

~

"The introduction of your race to the many has been so long awaited. You are no longer under the confines of absolute control.

What/who is now running things is a group of humans – they are finding out now that their masters are absent.

This changes the field on which you play.

What humankind does now is determine his fate without bonds. As those elite groups serving the Draco dismantle without masters, earth humans must be ready to move and create the structure of life that is most desired.

First there must occur a visible crumbling. Then the new will rebuild.
A massive education is necessary and this is why the majority of light-workers are here.
Now your work begins and your entry into *(nothing…)*

Into what?

I am sorry. This next part is not to be told – not yet. We welcome you Humans! That is all."

~

Drops of Light

In May, Steven Greer was seeking funding to produce his film "Unacknowledged". There was a call then to contribute just $2.00 by giving up a cup of coffee. It's 2023, and that cup of coffee would at least double that!

~

"It's tempting now, with news streaming in every day, that validates what we've always known, to rest on our laurels and nod knowingly, while saying "See? I wasn't crazy/mistaken/imagining this. I told you about this years ago."

This is not a call to place your head in the sand. It's a call to remain aware of where you are directing your light. Keep looking ahead and telling the story of what you see. The power of your energy is exponential."

~

In late May there was a series of conversations with One concerning several prophetic conversations that had taken place a year earlier, in 2015, but that had never been published. They concerned the "end of the experiment". I was told that they needed to be published, and they subsequently were distributed as blog posts.
Here's a snippet...

~

"Gaia is feeling her children and right now exerts extreme force to carry them through this as gently as she is able. Yet force is necessary to impact a message and it will occur.
There will be casualties and destruction.

As you have seen on your continent with massive fires – there is destruction already. Yes, this will continue.

Know that intentions and beliefs create in a tangible way, and a goodly number of humans believe fervently in catastrophic, even apocalyptic ending events.

That being the case, there are no ways to proceed that do not mark this time in a physical and final manner.

Nothing moves without your participation. All efforts and intents, thoughts and beliefs, are creative.

You are having an effect not just on your personal life but on the ground you walk.

This effect will have a greater and clearer impact with self-awareness and acceptance. The light warriors, light workers, those reading these words, are humanities best hope for a smooth transition as the effect of a clear heart is many times greater than one caught up in and embroiled in ego, anger, fear and self-worth.

Time will show this message comes from a source interested only in truth, sovereignty and agape.

Drops of Light

The events portrayed do not have to happen in the most severe and destructive *(way)* but recall the message – as was told to you many times as you questioned it. Severe criminality requires a severe end. They are not going easily, although they know the prophecy. There are consistent attempts to side step it and outsmart the process they agreed to.

Realize they have nothing to lose, their efforts will only accelerate as these nearby "now's" approach.

Having nothing to lose creates a viciousness to the fight – either way they must leave. Many would rather take as much out for themselves before hand as they can.
This is a message from One. You are merely a messenger. Share all parts and decisions can then be made individually."
~

"A decision is being made by each human now as to how to proceed through the changes. This decision can be an informed one.

It is in the discerning and believing where intent is birthed. Conscious intent is what heralds this new earth.
It will be led by light and carried forth or through with love and clarity – honesty and deep, deep awareness.

It is suggested that the light workers bring patience to the table as your role changes from one uncovering and revealing the truth to that of validation and a calm supportive base.

You have come now to see Gaia through her physical shift while undergoing your own. All of this is upon you right now. These are not words of alarm but of announcement and joy as your beliefs and intents have created the highest and most supported outcome for all. Hold this knowing in your heart."

~

And a bit later that same month...

~

"What follows has been told to me today, and it has been confirmed by four others (*both yesterday and today*) as a true telling of what took place on Saturday, June 18th, 2016.

It was the removal of another level of control, the top most human level. The Draco's were removed in April. Two months later now, those human controllers below them have been either returned to Source, or moved elsewhere. They no longer are present in any fashion, and are not in power. Another step towards liberation has occurred.

I am sharing it here, now, because your light and power are being asked for..."

"We are a confederate, or we represent a confederate

of Light Beings whose command post includes the observance and protection of your current home planet – earth.

You have been told of more removals.

Yes, yesterday.

These will be un-mentioned in your media. Some of the sensitives felt them. Others with intel were told. Others still engaged in the work of the cleansing were there, whether or not they remember specifically. Memories are either intentionally wiped out or else forgotten as a choice of the being involved. This process has many players with many parts.

What you'll now witness is unclear. Heads of state and corporations are still present. Without their superiors now, it is uncertain what will occur.

We care for the hearts, souls and bodies of your race and planet and want to tell you to remain confident throughout this next part. With the visible authority still in place, it may seem that things are getting worse, not better. They are desperate and feel their own moment of truth is imminent. Indeed, it is. *This is so very vague.*

It is not meant to be. We wanted to say that right now your light is required - as **a force exerted in** any direction effects events.

Love has so very much more power than hate, control, and dominance. Those last three are merely disguises of fear. Your powers, and those doing light work, are therefore exponentially greater than any seemingly opposing factions."

~

There was a good deal of talk that year about how to use our power/love/light in an act of pure creation, to set things straight. There were almost daily conversations with off world beings wanting to share with or congratulate us…

~

"We've been told that this is an experiment in consciousness; to see how far we'd go to reach for the light. Those wearing the dark t-shirts have not stopped playing and we've seen the lengths they'll go to succeed.

This is a proposal to end it with a decision, a belief and intent. **Become the light.** Let go of searching, stop longing and give up needing something outside of yourself. **You are the Light.** Nothing else is needed."

~

And in late July…

~

"What follows is a verbatim account of what happened on **July 23rd, 2016**. I was told in advance of this happening. It is for this reason I then reached out for clarification. This conversation took place in two passes. The first began at 3:33 PM on the 23rd. The second I was woken up for, approximately 2:00 AM on July 24th.

"Is there someone who wants to connect who can enlighten me on what is going on right now? With One? With the Sun?"

Yes Sophia. It is I. It is One.
You have answered a call now because of the urgency of the moment.
This moment, this one you are living right now, is the same moment in which the experiment is ending.

Those in power who refuse to surrender or even to stop are being /are in the process of being physically taken out.

This plan, the one that allowed a manipulation of a race, has come to its conclusion.

The warnings did not stop this globalist agenda and they are right now being returned to Source.
It is done.
This, you will discover, is the Day of Judgment as has been foretold.
They had many chances to surrender, even to assist in the restructuring. Some took that chance. Many did not and it is those beings who've been sought out in this right now moment for an end and a return.

There is no need for regret or remorse at the end of such a being – or of any being actually. We are all at choice.

Ultimately it is the lust for power that brings on the destruction of a soul.

Things can now, with the exit of these beings, be expedited into the hands of men.

There is much work to be done.

What happened here will not be repeated. This experiment has shown the human to be a force itself; a being able to stand alone for a noble cause – for life, for each other. This is the beginning of unity, of oneness.

It has been said now, with the final act played, that above all else is One. No force exceeds One. One is power unexpected and unequaled.

The battle that ensued in these final moments did so not to crush an enemy but to return a friend. This friend was lost and had agreed at the beginning of it all to do this only if love was the answer to be given. It knew of the potential for it to be lost. Now, those beings have been found and will return anew. This is the promise for all of life.

Drops of Light

It must not be mis-told. This was not a battle of good vs evil but of power and force. What happened here was not a win. It was a return to balance. All is as it should be for a new beginning. That is all.

Let this now be told."

~

"Since 2012, throughout my conversation with The Guardian, *he said that the ending of this experiment would for sure happen in mid-August of 2016, if not before".*

~

So, what did this mean for us at this point? What actually changed? Here were some thoughts on that…

~

"It means our history will change, as with recollections of that day in Dallas, to where the story of who shot who is talked about openly. The media will be less and less suppressed; to the uninitiated, it will appear to have always been the case. The criminal actions of the controllers will become an open part of our collective history – open and (now) obvious. Without the veil we will see more clearly the host of others occupying this dream. Expect to see more out of the corner of your eyes and in our skies"

~

After this, there were comments from readers that indicated for us that change was really happening. There were quite a few, and they included reports of ships in the skies being on the news, the work of the Keshe Foundation,

and arrests of bankers, to name a few. There was a very spe-
cific validation from a health care worker...

~

"On 7/22 I cared for a man in the hospital who had
a very unique vibrational signature and spoke of
time, and the ability to be able to move through it.
On 7/23 night when I arrived at work, he was very
animated, and expressed the urgency to gather his
group for a dissolution ceremony. He revealed that
he was a founding member of the Church of Satan,
and that during their time they had amassed an unimaginable fortune/treasure. He said he was not saddened to lose it or his sect because the convergence
of time is now. That they must keep it "light", have a
picnic or supper, enjoy each other's company, then
do a ritual of release. His worry is that the treasure
would fall into the wrong hands, since some artifacts
were powerful. But nonetheless...he is ONE of the
1%, letting go because "it is time...we have run our
course" and that there is no longer the need of their
control.""

~

There was a great deal of encouragement from off-
world; this is from August of that year...

~

"What we see, as witnesses now, is a build-up of
force that compels the dark to dissipate. This force is
light. It springs or is emitted from that which is the
element within the human fiercest – **it is the force
of love.**

177

Drops of Light

It is not that the darkness is gone. Here is the part
still undone. Humanity will now be directed by a
force of light – Gaia as well. The opportunity to see
humanity's compassionate heart rule the population
is ours. …from our view, it is imminent.

We wish you honor and congratulations. We know
that the love of the human heart has been the power
right along.

We do not see dates or the passage of precise
days. We see energy and movement.

*I see what you are sending. It is a sphere, a planet, earth?
There is darkness on it. There is light sort of growing and eas-
ing out the darkness.*
*This is not light from a star but somehow from within – swirls
of light sort of growing and pushing back darkness. (Sophia)*

This light is the light sparked by humanity's love. It is
this that we see. The power grows from within. It is
this we wanted to say. …**it is your heart that is the
light.**
Be aware this happens and is now possible because
of you. **You are the light that compels the end of
this darkness.** You are the power beneath the shift
of your world, and this break-through is imminent.

We anticipate a bit of chaos. We want to say (that)
out of the chaos will come something new and it is

the power of your light that brings it forth."

~

There was an even greater degree of expectation and preparation (for the "Event") …

~

"We are ready. If your life is anything like mine now then it is expectant and as prepared as possible. I'm watching people and dreams both leaving and ending while also witnessing the new begin for others. I'm seeing banks get nervous as they invent new reasons to gain access to personal accounts. I'm watching houses sell in less than 24 hours (someone is buying up lots of land here). I see an increase in soda pop commercials and billboards as more of us now reject it; drinking water instead.

What I see mostly is humanity doing what we do best – persevering. We may be tired and we may not know precisely how this plays out, but we are not giving up. We are eternally hopeful and unrelenting in our capacity for love."

~

Some of us went on reconnaissance missions, checking out the "new earth" for the rest of us…

~

"This past weekend a friend sent this message "**Love this construct as it is now…with all you be…it'll take you there…**" At that moment I was immersed in relatives (a family reunion), it was pouring sheets of rain on us and I had just received news of a dear

179

friend's passing over. It was emotionally intense, to say the least.

My partner, Dreamhopper, chose this same weekend to, well, "hop" dreams. I wasn't sure exactly what was going on. He at first seemed just "not here", while sitting in a crowded room. Then, as I watched, his eyes would close and he'd appear to be sleeping. That is, if you weren't looking carefully. I was.

His head was straight up and sort of in motion. His eyebrows were moving up and down and his hands would gesture. It looked like he was having a conversation. I didn't want to interrupt. This only lasted a few minutes. He'd wake up, (this happened several times), look at me and say "I was someplace else, and its right here!"
After several "hops" he decided to actually go to sleep and find out what was happening. Here's what he said after he woke up:

"I went to the place we are headed. It is not far at all. It has most of the same people in it and most of the same stuff. Yet not all of the people are there, because this is by choice. It's going on right now. I have three choices. I could keep slipping back and forth, as I am now. I could wait, and go when everyone else goes. Or I could choose to not go at all and stay right here.

The pull is strong to go. It's really nice there. I have no sense of time there, or bills or requirements. Manifestation is instantaneous. If I want something it just shows up. The physics works differently. But everything looks pretty much the same there; the people, the places, all the same.

It just feels so much nicer. The energy is different, not the same pressure. And it's right here! It's not far at all! It's going on right now! It's where we are headed and it can't be long now, I can go anytime. I just need to daydream, to get in the alpha state, and I'm there!"

We talked then for a long time and concluded that, although he saw no dates, we must be extremely close if this is happening in this way for him, now and in real time. He "dream hops" (hence his nickname) often, yet this is different. This is not another time or place; it is now, and it is this place, and he remembers it vividly.
He said, **"It feels like all you have to do is let go and you are there.""**
~

In our daily lives we were feeling it and discussing it without ever precisely naming it…
~

"Humans, ages 5 to 86, are saying "My head hurts", "It just feels strange today", "I never reacted that way before", "I feel nervous", "I feel weird", "The energy

181

is just off" (*this from a cashier at a grocery store I had never met*) and "I'm just done with this part"."

~

Off world conversations chimed in...

~

"No longer will this group be allowed to continue. The human will have to see to it that some sort of justice is served. This justice will not necessarily be the typical justice as dished out by your legal system. It will be formulated by you all as new humans."

"It is love that dominates and forces this shift. This love will be evident in how you see your people treated, regardless of who they are or what they may have done."

"Now that the control is returned to humanity – we wait to see what humanity looks like as a driver of its own fortune."

"We are aware of the Event...with so many expecting one then in order to settle all accounts an Event must occur. This expectation is what drives all of creation and sets the form for your reality...Your focus of energy drives everything, especially now when so much is in disarray."

"Your people are headed for many upticks in energy. The fastest course is what you are on. We speak of an acceleration of consciousness. This acceleration arrives almost as a surprise."

"You humans continue to surpass plans for your own transformation. What interests us is these are not plans you've seen or known existed. It would seem that with very little to go on the human adapts and proceeds with an unmatched level of energy and acceleration. It may appear chaotic."

"You are on a course for ascension that there is no veering off of.""
~

   In September, One had this to say regarding the prophecy given earlier...
~

"It is I. It is One.

Hello.

Hello. There is something to be said now about the current frame of time you are focused in.

Yes. Several have asked me why the big push to release information before August of this year. There has been no discernable change or event. Would you address these concerns also please?

I would be glad to.

Drops of Light

I am only hearing the word prophecy/prophecies?

You are resisting.

Yes. I am discouraged. Please give me a moment to center myself.

As you wish.

(After stopping for a bit and going outside, I continued. All declarations were re-stated.)
Okay. Let's try again. Is there someone who wants to connect?

Yes Sophia. It is I. It is One.

Please go ahead then.

Prophecy is meant to be received and recorded. You were chosen as the recorder of the earlier prophecy. You are not the only one chosen. You were one who had a platform on which it could be read and received. It was. The point of releasing it has been completed.

So it is not truth?

It exists as possible truth and had to be recorded. In the hologram of life there are systems and events that drive it forward. Some act as springboards while others remain rooted.

The words you were given were both. They remain as well as instigate creative thought which then incites and actualizes additional possibilities.

Please be direct.
We are all so very done with this. If an awakening conscious-ness leads us to a place of nothing more than awareness of our options – what is the point of prophecy? Why make a big deal about telling us what may possibly occur in our lifetime? Certainly every sentient adult realizes disasters are possible in any given day. Is it necessary to give a date of some possible future that includes catastrophe? It came, in this case, from a source I've come to trust and was given because I trusted it.

What has been gained by the rush of anxiety over potential ca-tastrophe? I am not clear on any of this now.

Sophia, the purpose of your work is truth. It is com-munication. You are here to spread the word. There are many anxious to disseminate their words through you and to you. By now you must realize this.

I do, yes.

These prophecies are part of that truth. The possi-bilities for your world have always held the potential for global catastrophe. Indeed, there are some among you now with a wider audience predicting as

185

much.

(Note, what came with those words was an image of Keshe.)

These prophecies were not so much predictions as they were and are possibilities. At the time they were given their timing was deemed critical.

Things have changed. As a collective you've put forward an accelerated timeline towards your evolution. This puts you both in and out of harm's way. By that is meant the acceleration brings with it a speeding up of the response of all of life.
Make no mistake – humanity represents creation itself and is the reason so many outsiders are interested. You continue to shake up the plan for where this goes and how fast.

That being said, there are no constants in life save the focal point of love from which you spring.

As an expression of creation, you are uniquely fit to lead this charge to ascension.

The Earth will react as will the human. It is the human's deep desire for comfort and unity – for bringing everyone along – that changes everything.

I am feeling something…

Go ahead then, I am sending this feeling.

*It is as if we are becoming new already. Our will is creative
and right now we are creating/building this new human. He/she is focused on love and comfort and freedom of
choice for everyone.*
*There is anger and potential violence because of our strength
and it still displays polarity as it is focused on "other" –
the "other" who we've labeled as the one stopping us from freedom or love or prosperity or expression.*

*Yet I'm not sure I can express this as fiercely as I feel
her/him. These words don't convey the change happen-
ing <u>now</u>. The whole plan sort of waits and watches as this new
human evolves. It is early, yet our rapid transfer of compassion is ahead of schedule. It is looking like the ultimate transition will be seamless as so much light already exists and alters the world.*
*It is both (1) driven by obvious corruption and (2) more obvi-
ous than ever before in the contrast.*

It becomes then a new plan. The polarization stands
out blatantly. The Earth will react/respond and, as
well, offer her version of the contrast.
What is seen now is unclear yet definite. The part
lacking clarity is the timing. The part that is clear in
its definition is the part that decides. Humanity has
chosen, once again, to do things in its own unique
fashion. The Earth complies and all becomes a reflection of the energy both received and ultimately

emitted by the race.

There was always a plan. This plan exists today for the movement and ascension, simultaneously, of a planet and her people.

You will proceed as you've planned always to – driven by the accumulation of who you are. Each voice and contact and resulting response add to the way you get this done. It will get done.

Part of the current realization experienced by your readers and others is that the control is in your hands and has been always.

What has changed now is how many others are also attempting to manipulate the levers. That number is reduced and decreases every day.

Sovereignty is realized. It is not given. As soon as the human stops expecting it in every part of his or her life, he and she will be it.

All of this is part of a process. The ultimate result has no place for blame or expectation.

The end is absolute knowing - I Am.

That is all for now."

~

This also transpired that month…

~

"*These conversations took place during the last week of February, 2016. They were sparked by something I had heard. (I'd been told) that there was a possible plan for Disclosure to be stretched out and gradual, taking possibly 100 years to reach its completion. I saw no benefit to humanity in that plan.*

I was angry. I did not know if I could reach anyone involved with this, but I figured why not try? So, I did. The response, well, you will read who spoke. I have not shared this until now because I wasn't sure how helpful it would be.

We are in a different energy today and so many things are talked about, there is no reason not to add this to the mix. It becomes then, more data for us to work with. I will start with my initial statement. Most of this conversation was written in ALL CAPS, from both sides.

"*I reach out now to whomever is assuming they have the right to continue to withhold information/disclosure information regarding alternative beings and races, advanced technologies that will supply humanity with free energy, physical healing technology, food replicators and a moneyless society. These beings have been referenced by others yet I am not clear that those so referenced are the ones holding back on* **Full Disclosure**.

It is to those beings I reach out now, or a representative of them. Please come forward and introduce yourself."

189

Drops of Light

I am Ra and I speak for the collective who are in observance of human society.

Hello.

It is a delight to engage. What is it you wish to engage about?

About the holdup to Full Disclosure and reconciliation of control to humanity for the Earth's surface.

The holdup deemed necessary in order to preserve order.

Yes. It is known that it is wealth by the 1% that is being preserved and not "order". How is that in concert with the Will of One?

It is not. We are following the flow of energy that allows for the successful continuation of life on Earth. And it is seen by those doing the observing that order must be maintained - that chaos will result in destruction of too much life. That would not be productive.

This order you are maintaining keeps mankind subservient to a greater power - this power held in place by fear. I do not, humanity does not, see fear as the desire of One or as productive overall.

You speak for humanity?

Being human, I can do that. I can say now that having access to tech that affords us healing, food, free energy and sustenance on all levels will be supported by all of humanity - regardless of which "god" is worshipped or what is believed.

There is no argument with that, no.

Then what gives any race the power or right to withhold what would only promote life and expand the possibilities for the human?

By agreement these powers are held.

Agreement by who? I, a human, have made no such agreement.

By those in control of your planet.

Those whose end is here.

Those whose end is near, not here.

Which is the reason for this call to you! The end of this control is demanded. It's time for them to go. Disclosure Now.

This is your voice - a strong one yet not a majority.

Drops of Light

Only because the majority is not aware - the media is controlled and people are killed who go against the party line. It's a loop of control we cannot break without an equal hand from the likes of you - those who hold the information back from man. This is just as criminal as the acts of the controllers themselves.

This was part of the plan.

Whose plan?

The plan of One for the perpetuation of All.

Well, the one unnamed part here, the part that was not seen, is how fast humanity has woken up. We see now the jailor beyond the bars. You hold the key. Unlock the bars and give us what is rightfully ours.
It is the real criminals who are free. They need to be locked up. Disclosure and a release of all the tech mentioned will be what is needed.

We have systems in place to take care of the arrests. Disclosure is demanded. **You came now (as an answer to) my request for someone with the power to do so - will you? What will you do?**

I will take your request into the negotiations and consider it.

That is all?

That is all.

Well consider what we've been informed of then. That the per-
petuation of these crimes only creates a more negative out-
come/decision/retribution for those knowingly holding it over
the heads of 8 billion people (and NOT helping). This is
criminal. There is no reason to wait.

You have been clear. Goodbye.

Goodbye.

What follows is a second conversation on another day.

"I would like again to connect to the being I spoke with two
days ago regarding disclosure; the being representing the group
advocating its timing and its being held back. Please come for-
ward."

I am Ra.

Thank you for responding.

What is your request?

I have, since we connected, received further information. This
tells me that it is the intent of the group to delay Full Disclo-
sure for 100 years! Is this truth?

It is our current path. Yes.

Drops of Light

Explain please the reasons for this delay and period of time?

It is, we feel, necessary so that mankind has an opportunity to set in place systems. The current ones are held there by brute, if invisible, force. As these chains and threats and controllers are removed, mankind will scramble to locate and agree on appropriate rulers. Time will be necessary so that order is maintained.

Why 100 years? This seems an arbitrary and excessive number.

So that the generations of humans taking over have come to appreciate the depth and breadth of the task. This is accomplished by watching their elders gradually take the wheel and assume self-governance.

Today's potential leaders have been witnesses only to puppetry. This is not true ability to govern. Self-governance demands a deep sense of sovereignty. This sense is not held in mankind - regardless of where he rests in prosperity or rule.

It is not felt because it has not been taken or assumed. Not by man. Not by any man. It has been played at. Men kill those who take it seriously. Self-control is to be lived authentically if it is not destined to dissolve to violence and everyone for themselves. This concept is not understood by your masses.

Is it not true that there are humans on the planet now who are primed and ready for this role? That there are conscious military (men and women) in my country who are ready to protect them during the change-over? That there are forces in place and ready to be initiated that will not only ensure a smooth transition, but also massive arrests so that these criminal controllers are not strung up by the people once their crimes are public knowledge? Are not these facts being considered?

These facts are known.

Yet they have no impact on the trend that leans instead to wait 100 years?

They do not, no. These things are not spoken of here.

It sounds like a skewed conversation; one that assumes ownership and rights of control still, even in the discussion of ending it. Do you not see the folly?

Until you said it, no.

Is there no universal law that demands highest order decisions for the impact on an entire planet?

Drops of Light

There is law that dictates life must prosper - **that the continuation of the species be held as the first order of business.**

How about quality of life? I interject that this plan for a 100-year stall exists not to promote the continuation of life, but the preservation of wealth and accumulation of more in all things by a small fraction of the entire species. Not to mention the putting off of justice and karma for crimes against a species.

These things are and have always been a consideration; it is the beings themselves that dictate the scope of the talks.

Mankind the species does not represent himself in these negotiations?

He does not. It would be akin to allowing your pet a say in his food purchase.

Yet he does have a say! If he dislikes a brand or flavor, or it causes him distress, other choices are made. In this way we work together for the best solution.

This is not how it's done.

This is criminal. *In 100 years, several generations will have lived and died, still sick and poor and enslaved by this corrupt money system. We the people do speak. It is the group* *making the decision not listening to our voice.* **This is not in concert with the will of One, in my estimation.**

When one element of the whole thrives while abusing another, the purpose of life is not served. What is served is one small segment. Are you able to explain how this action serves the One of us that is creation itself?

Only this, all of life is an expression of difference it is occurring on earth now as an example to the rest.

IT'S DONE ITS PART! THE JIG IS UP! THE PRISONERS SEE THE BARS! NO FURTHER DEMONSTRATION IS NECESSARY. *Disclosure is the only decision that will begin to restore healing and promote life here. A woken-up populace requires a woken-up response.*

As this plays out, all input is considered.

By whom?

By those making the ultimate choice/holding the final say.

This notion of a few speaking for many goes against natural law. There is no doubt the many would benefit from healing technology, free energy, food replicators and a chance for a moneyless society, whether spoken out loud or not.

197

Drops of Light

This group you are a part of knows this. This needs to be considered as paramount.

You have been clear. Goodbye Sophia.

Okay then. Goodbye.

This conversation ended.
~

> *Well, that conversation inspired many of us! What stood out among those responses, was this "Disclosure Manifesto" authored by Jack S.; here's how it ended...*
~

"We the collective of planet earth, all 8 billion people, united as ONE, in ONE voice and as Co-Creators with the Will of ONE, not only request but DEMAND our release from the predation, persecution, and enslavement by the forces that have ruled this planet for thousands of years. We DEMAND the reunion with our star brothers
and sisters. They are our beloved family that we have been separated from for centuries. We further demand the release of all technologies that afford us healing, food, free energy and sustenance on all levels. This is the Will of ONE. What we demand is rightfully ours, all 8 billion of us. So be it!"
~

> *We were left wondering...*
~

"So, what's the hold up? It's us. Yet, this was part of our plan all along. We require acceptance which leads to belief which supports intention which fuels creation. The acceptance bit is where we are stuck. Or, to keep it clear, where I see we are stuck.

Acceptance of something we've yet to see is a bit of a stretch for associative beings. So, in our typical crafty and brilliant fashion, we re-define ascension while physical until all of us can see it. How is it we do this?

We use polarity and these powerful frequencies to lay out quite clearly what it is we don't want, what doesn't fit, won't resonate or will not match a comfortable range of vibration. Gradually we then find ourselves in a place surrounded by others who are resonating the same way. This becomes unity and a singular voice.
As the volume increases, creation replies in kind, and we shift. It is not that someone shifts us apart from our own actions. Essentially, we are shifting ourselves."
~

"We, in a movement of unity and love, are postponing this dance until everyone is out on the dance floor. It's more fun that way.
We are writing now what oneness looks like in a human suit. It looks like us."
~

Drops of Light

"Make no mistake – this is a planet of polarity – there are "real" forces on the "dark side". Their secret weapon? **It is our own disbelief.**

If we don't believe they are *right here* – we will do nothing to remove them. They are not interested in love, light or transformation. They want to win. Period.

Right now, those service to self-beings that remain are like junkyard dogs. They will lose and they know it and they will do anything to get that last shot in before they go. They have nothing to lose.

These light warriors who are friends of mine have seen them. They remember "dreams" or "visions" of battles. These are just as real as the location you find yourself now, reading these words. **Do not doubt your dreams; you are living one.** This is a multi-dimensional process.

Do you see what this means? Their biggest weapon is something **we are in complete control of - it is our own imagination, our own belief system.**

We are so much more powerful than we know – and they know this. Once we get, really get, that WE ARE SOURCE, its game over.

No more tricks or scary spells. **Love wins. Love**

always wins. Love is not weak and has nothing to do with "falling". Love is the force of creation."

~

"What if you knew, **before taking a test,** that you'd not only passed it, but scored 100%? What if, in this scenario, you'd actually written the test yourself and constructed the answer key specifically for you, so that you would be attracted to the correct responses in each and every case? What if you had a second, third and fourth chance to find the correct response if you somehow missed it the first time? What if you had infinite chances?

Would you still be nervous or anxious or wondering how to do it and if you did something irreconcilably wrong? Somehow, I doubt it.

There are angels. There are beings of light. They are brilliantly perfect and reading these words."

~

"There is no place to ascend to, not really. **We are beings of Light.** Period."

~

"The general subject (on my mind) is this shift...this brings up questions: "How does it feel?"
What I hear, see and feel is best described as an unravelling, discord, a revelation and emergence."

~

Drops of Light

Within days of each other that Fall, the Chicago Cubs won the World Series after 108 years, and Donald Trump won the United States presidential election. The world was laser focused; random number generators were synchronizing like crazy. Our collective energy/focus was on fire...

~

"We have not known exactly how our historical shift would play out, only because we weren't there yet. We are there now. You have brilliantly crafted a way to draw us together, to enable the manifestation of our new world.

Who would've thought? A baseball team and a reality TV star led us right to where we need to be – on the cusp of creation.

You are magnificent. I can't wait to see what you do next."

~

"Will it be like the chicken and the egg? Will future versions of us ask – which caused the other? Will they happen simultaneously? Does our worldwide debt slavery stimulate, even necessitate, our internal realization of sovereignty and result in an instant evolutionary moment?
Or...
Does a personal awareness of divinity propel a rapid-fire instant view of the chains around us and shatter them – resulting in freedom?"

~

"Which comes first, Ascension or Event?" – becomes finally answered. Both do. Infinite wisdom determines ultimately that initial blast which incorporates a moment of sovereign awareness."

~

"As we ride this current of expanding consciousness, throw your hands up!!!
Freedom is found there. Letting go is not giving in or giving up. It is allowing."

~

"We have taken the scenic route and find ourselves home.
This is a place familiar, not by sight but by feel. It peeks out from beneath the masks and whispers…
"Remember." For you are not beauty, beast, brain, brawn, rich or poor. You are the bit of brilliance beneath them all.

This name you've become will one day be added to your essence string. It will serve as a locator for you in 2016 on Earth. There are multiple locators, all of them you.

When you stand there long enough without your mask or your job or your name to cover you – what you see is the fabric of life itself. What you feel is love.

It is felt in each bird call and belly laugh. It is seen in

Drops of Light

every tree. You have to find it alone. It sometimes jumps out from a song lyric or a movie moment or a sunset. You occasionally feel it in a hug or see it in a pair of smiling eyes."

~

"Just love. It's what you came for."

~

The first few days of 2017 brought us "Robert" a human from what he called "the 5ᵗʰ dimension". Here's some of how he described his locale…

~

"We come to you from a place quieter - where the rapid changes have occurred. That place is your soon to be home.

We are healthy.

There are not corporate interests guiding what we can ingest but human ones.

We have advanced (and) very different healing technology to sustain and maintain our bodies. These are not invasive, destructive methods. All of our healing systems use waves of sound and light, as well as crystals and stones of the earth, to promote stasis.

Without the limitation of borders as you know them now, we can see and get anything from any place. The internet is more seamless and useful than you know. Holographic technology is in everything. It is not that things are all done for you without effort. It is that the effort made to get these things does not involve slave labor, money or shipping. This is more a virtual existence. We are solid, yes.

We have virtual centers for education. Our young do not leave their homes.

There is a unified global governance of which all areas take part. The health of the planet takes precedence here. There are no wars.

Drops of Light

Money is not gone. It is used as a form of exchange. What differs is how it is accumulated. Each person within the family has access to money. The family has its own hoard of money.

The systems of exchange are most likely a step toward no money at all. What is used as exchange has an agreed upon worth that varies by locale. There is a global currency and ways of exchange.

What differs most however is us. We look the same as 3D humans yet more uniformly vibrant, engaged, youthful, happy. If I had to find a word for the difference it may be autonomy. We have control over our days and our lives and thus feel better on a regular basis.

There is a sense of mutual honor here that is not relegated to you because of rank or worth but is given to everyone simply because they are alive."

~

*And right here on 3D earth, we met **Clif High** and his aggregated data forecasts. His reports were seeing our collective energy undergoing a massive shift.*

*In June of 2017, a 3-fingered mummified corpse was unearthed just outside of **Nazca, Peru**, initiating a slew of speculation as to its "alien" appearance, as well as research to establish just what it was.*

While mainstream media reported the following headlines as the things that we should be looking at ...

~

There was the investigation into possible **"Russian interference" in the 2016 US Presidential election**, led by **Robert Mueller**.

There was an **escalation of tension** between the **United States and North Korea**, as its leader, **Kim Jong Un**, announced that they were developing nuclear tipped missiles capable of reaching the US.

The **#MeToo Movement** was inspired by allegations of sexual assault against **Harvey Weinstein**, as well as **Hollywood's "Open Secret"** regarding its culture of sexual harassment and assault.

In October, the **shooting at a concert at Mandalay Bay Resort in Las Vegas** took the lives of 59 people. A month later, **a Texas church** lost 26 of its parishioners to **another shooter**.

Multiple terrorist attacks that year included vehicles running into pedestrians, and **a suicide bomber at an Ariana Grande concert in Great Britian's Manchester area**.

The **Opioid Epidemic was declared a National Emergency in the United States** in August; the CDC announced that half of the 2016 deaths due to overdose were from lab-made, illegal fentanyl.

Hurricanes Harvey, Irma and Maria caused devastation in southeast Texas, Florida and the Caribbean.

The **U.S. experienced a total solar eclipse** in late August, its first since 1918.

"Culture Wars" took place in the U.S. as the division from the 2016 presidential campaign morphed into debates about which statues should be removed due to their Confederate nature, and athletes kneeling at professional football games due to racial inequality. **Zimbabwe's Robert Mugabe was ousted**/resigned from leadership after 37 years.

Britian struggled to negotiate the terms of its "Brexit". More than 400,000 members of **the Rohingya minority group fled Myanmar** due to killings, rape and torture at the hands of the Myanmar military in an "ethnic cleansing". The Rohingya have lived there for centuries.

In June, **Mosul, Iraq was liberated from ISIS** after a three-year occupation. This was a costly win, with 40,000 civilian casualties and massive devastation of infrastructure there. **Saudi Arabia's crown Prince Mohammad bin Salman** had **11 of his cousins arrested on corruption**, in a move to consolidate power.

There were reports of **a strengthening global economy** with 3.6% growth, and a warming planet, with 2017 being the "second warmest year" on record.

Xi Jinping was named a "core leader" of the CCP, and **given a second 5-year term** as party general secretary.

U.S. President Donald Trump made good on his "America First" campaign promise by **withdrawing from the Trans-Pacific partnership and the Paris Climate agreement.** He also **recognized Jerusalem as the capital of Israel.**

Emmanuel Macron became France's youngest president.

Britain's **Prince Phillip retired** from official appearances after 70 years.

Australia became the 25th country to **legalize same-sex marriage.**

In October, a stadium sized space object, **Oumuamua**, was spotted, and we were told that it was **the first interstellar object detected passing through the Solar System**. The name comes from Hawaiian *oumuamua* - 'scout', as it was first seen by a Hawaiian Observatory.

In mid-December, the **NY Times** reported on video recordings from fighter jets based on US Naval Aircraft Carriers, of their **cockpit instrumentation, that showed "Unidentified Aerial Phenomena" (UAP's)**. They had been recorded in 2014 and 2015. The word **"TicTac"** was used to describe the grainy footage.

~

And as we strolled through our days, here's what we were seeing and saying…

~

"You see now, on social, mainstream and alternative media, the reports of those who have forgotten. They are the chicken littles of this time. The sky is not falling, we are rising up to meet it. We are entering the time of our ascension."

~

"Remember the butterfly. We have to let go of all

209

that binds us. For as surely as the cocoon ensnares the wings of the butterfly, words that separate and destroy prevent our own flight. It is upon us to love."

~

"Ascension is not for sissies.
You are a being of unimaginable power and extraordinary light, here to illuminate the world."

~

"We are tired and rightfully so. We came to free a planet and it's taken oh so much longer than we imagined it would. We want the hard part to be over. It is not, not yet."

~

"We've already done a really cool thing here, years ago, we decided on our own. We said "Thanks, but we've got this", to other groups who were ready to free us."

~

"You are no longer in the dark. You realize now the omnipotent nature of you. This is no small discovery. We are like the infant who finally forms her first word. There is such potency here! The world becomes a place to control rather than a place to be at the whim of.

Do not hide from these truths as they are revealed. Instead use them. Shout "**No More**"! Become the poster child for sovereignty. Stand in your own authority and decide.

Choose strength. Embody compassion. Walk freedom. Consciously contribute. Refuse manipulation. Walk your talk and speak only love. This is neither weak nor subservient. It is the force beneath creation itself."

~

"We are tired. There is a sense of having finished what we came to do; perhaps a feeling of completion. Or rather, maybe, a thought that says "We did all that we came for. We found each other and gathered and wrote and spoke and produced content to share and spoke and became the light that we remembered we were. It is time to go now. It is no longer up to us.

When I see the light worker/warrior community now, a picture emerges. We are brushing our hands together, having just closed the door behind us. We are standing just beyond that door, and inside the kitchen now, where all that work occurred.

The meal has been served after years of preparation. It is not a meal we came to eat; it is one we came to formulate. Yet as we look into the kitchen, we see pots, pans and numerous utensils with food still stuck to them. They need cleaning and re-purposing. There is yet work to be done.

We met online about 5 years ago, maybe more. Most of us will never meet in person. Yet there is kinship, a sense of family. We "know" each other without knowing why that is true. We are profoundly familiar; there is a sense of having done this before and of each of us having a specific role in the doing. There is deep recognition.

There is urgency felt while preparing a feast – timing is everything. Once that meal is placed on the table, we breathe a sigh of relief. It is done. There's only the enjoyment left; what remains is the devouring. It's party time, finally.

Yet we are not seeing the feasting yet, and this confuses us. It is happening much more gradually than expected."

~

"I know two people alive today that I consider Masters. You do not know them. They are not on a pulpit or an altar or a blog or Twitter. They do not know each other. They live in different parts of the world. They differ in age and sex and color and creed, yet they have one thing in common. They are highly connected. Everyone knows them. They are consistent in their search for how they can offer themselves to help you. They do not think everyone is perfect, they believe **everyone is worth their attention.** That "everyone" includes yourself."

~

"It can be hard to release things you imagined were holding this life together; things like rules and systems and even a sense of history or god. These things we imagined were the bedrock of society.

This switch will uncover the real foundation of society, and that would be us. For society is an extension of the individual. It rises and falls on what you hold to be deeply true.

Hold fast to your heart and realize in every moment you can love. It is in each small choice to accept and welcome, that mastery resides."

~

"If I had one wish for all of us, it would look like this – **a single moment of clarity.** Where what we know astounds all of our senses simultaneously and leaves behind no doubt. A universal wake up moment, where all that remains is the dream. What is true then is us – brilliant, obnoxious, glorious, vibrant, radiant, spectacular us."

~

And, like the bull a china shop… "You have come from a seemingly distant land and willingly immersed yourself in a place that has no facility to recognize your gift. But put that same bull in the ring, and all who see him appreciate his beauty, strength and magnificence.
We are sensing now our time to enter the ring."

~

"As we contemplate what this shift will ultimately look like; we live each moment portraying it."

Drops of Light

~

In looking for information/explanation about President Trump's air strike on Syria, this is what we were told by a group called "the Watchers" ...

~

"What is new, or perhaps not new, but newly realized, is the way this feels for the people of the world. It feels, on a visceral level, wrong. This is an indication of the shift, the change, the newly forming human.

It has become nearly impossible to create an event of destruction on any portion of the populace without it being felt by the whole.

This, although we see you are not experiencing it as such, is a good indication of the shift.... No longer are you able to pretend not to feel the impact of each other.

What this means in terms of timing is unclear – humanity is creating the illusion of gradual shifting, while attempting to bring the whole lot of you along.

What is now illustrated is: **what is not universally wanted.** These tactics do not work in a unified world, and this is now seen.

The planet is moving, changing, shifting towards the new. What is seen in this event is that it is not contained – almost as if **the world** was struck by these missiles. All felt the strike.

It is unknown by us what precisely will be done – it is humanity's choice. No, you have not switched time-lines and are not headed for destruction. You experience now the effect of unification.

This increases your desire for peace on all fronts. If you would like we would send a visual for you to see.

Yes, I would like that.

After a few moments, this is what I saw...
Okay, what I "see", and this has been in the corners of my perception throughout this conversation, is our planet as a bright blue and green globe. There is a bright yellow and or-ange spot – what in my mind's eye is the missile strike and Syria. The strike does not stay small – but grows, and then, from it, something... It is a covering, a shadow, it moves out and spreads, covering the globe. It is not yellow/orange but darker. I want to say blue, yet it's not a solid color. It sort of permeates everything, melts into everything without altering it, but leaving a residue. Like the planet has been tinted with a different hue.
I'm tempted to say the coloring means peace but it does not, peace would be a greener hue. This means change and the blue signifies the cool color of water; which puts out fires, maybe stops bombs. I don't' see that the bombs were put out by this tint – but that the bombs altered/colored the fabric of the illu-sion in its entirety.

Drops of Light

Nothing is seen beyond that.

A good description of how your planet is morphing, changing…

I am seeing more…

Yes, as we send other images.

These are of bombings in the past. There are numerous explosions, all over the planet (at once) and yet they remain isolated pockets.

This is given to you now for comparison, as a way to gauge what we are seeing (now).

Yes, I get it. (What I did not say to them, but "got", was the meaning of the comparison. In our past, we were able to ignore violence that did not impact us directly. We perceived it as having no effect on our daily life. This recent strike illustrates something different. We are not assuming we are separate. Violence directed to any part of the populace changes us and we feel it.)

The planet **has shifted**.

~

"In these days where daily exposure of the most heinous crimes is becoming the norm; we are finally getting down to it. For in every case, I am you. There is no sin or sacrifice I haven't committed, no repulsive or divine act undone.

If oneness is fact, then I am you right now. The lifetimes and fractals are merely remnants of a mind's shattered pictures – as it attempts to deal with infinity. I am every possibility, absent limit."

~

That year there was lots of talk about what it felt like to create a "new earth" and show up differently. A series of Love Quest journeys was started up again with these words…

~

"Our aim is deep recognition of the sacred found there. You must then follow your deepest longing. Retreat, and feel into what it is you love. It is upon you now to emerge whole and to then re-connect with the all of us held in oneness.

It is not as you think. There is nowhere to go. These incoming energies herald a moment of awakening for every single one of us. This rousing is meant to be gentle but firm and undeniable. In this remarkable time to be alive, dare to test your wings and jump. A giving of all that you have into what you love will produce for you the life that you desire."

~

Our off-world audience continued to join in…

~

"Is there someone who wants to connect now?

Drops of Light

We do Sophia, yes. Are you able now to speak with us?

I am.

Good. We desire contact. There is an event coming soon to your planet that we see erupting. It begins in small and somewhat isolated pockets of human life forms. In some cases, there is only one life form in which the energy emits from. In others, several. But not thousands and even those of you all doing the same thing are separated. It is an unusual grouping.

Connected by internet perhaps?

It appears so, yes. There is a string of data that joins you and inspires action. This data excites you.

This event we are noticing is one of great joy, great exuberance. The earth has not seen this universal feeling emitted, it is virtually the same emotion coming from each exit point and this has not been seen, **ever.**

Who are you?

We are a group, a conglomerate of beings with keen interest in the ongoing liberation of the race that is humanity.

We watch. Just now we see a change that looks unlike past alterations. What differs now is the exuberance emitted and its directed focus. There has not been such a unified emotion prior.

What is seen is this gladdening, or maybe, not so much a gladdening but a self-righteousness, self-awareness, but more than that. It is as if there is a recognition.

It is not a running away, as you would expect a slave to do once it was set free.

It is not even a rejoicing or celebration, as you may expect. No, this is something else. It is not so much awareness as acknowledgment. If I may explain with an example.

I am getting one in my head. It's been building as you transmit and search for words. I feel it, perhaps in some way embody it.

Yes. Of course, you do. It is akin to a reckoning. A being who has just begun to settle comfortably in his skin suit and is realizing just how magnificent he is in it. It has many secret powers and buttons and levers that this being is just becoming aware of. These are not separate from the being but **extensions.**

What we see happening is again unexpected. We see this human, being careful in its process as it realizes all that it is capable of. It is climbing to new heights of compassion and care rather than falling to the lowest common denominator of selfishness and gluttony.

We see the splendor of heaven being laid out before this being, and rather than grab it and run for more, the being looks back to pull its fellow man forward **so all can share in the grandeur of heaven.**

The shackles are all but removed and rather than seek vengeance, this human being worries about everyone else.

Why we reached out to you today is because we wanted to share this vision. The new human promises to be even more than was imagined, if that is possible.

I keep getting images and ideas from you guys. You are powerfully emitting, which both puts me to sleep and fills my head with images. I was not intending to write now, but I could not stop myself from doing so.

Please go ahead, describe the images.

It is as if the depth of emotion and compassion for man's fellow man is off the charts. That, when given everything, (and here it must be said that what's been given primarily is hope. There's been no actual gold or riches dropped in our laps, but a *method to possibly access them and **validation that they are real**) Man chooses always his brother and sister.*

It is in this moment where mankind's version of unity shines forth. It emanates as a ginormous field of love energy from each little pocket of beings you perceive.

*With full comprehension, this will only multiply, until **the sound of mankind becomes a clear and deafening call to the cosmos. It says we don't have to be the same – we have to care for each other as if we are.***

What is obvious to the observer is that man is not content to be freed alone. His joy and fulfillment come in the freeing others. This is unprecedented.

You are capturing our observance of you. Now there will be outliers as this spreads. Yet by the rapid and absolute joining of each other – this is only expected to be the beginning of a huge wave of compassion, a tsunami.

This is what so many of us are hoping for.

Well mankind, expect it. It happens now. Congratulations and well done. You've exceeded the expectations of us all.

Thank you. Goodbye then."

~

Drops of Light

In July and August, we were focused on a trial in Washington, D.C....

~

"In regards to the incarceration of Randy and Heather; what is clear is that this is playing out precisely as it had to, **in order to be perfectly done**. It is brilliantly orchestrated for maximum effect. The ending of the slavery mechanism is accomplished already. Send love their way, not only to them, but to all involved. Reports are saying they can feel it and it is making a difference."

~

"What is happening in Washington, DC this coming Friday, is that someone (Heather Ann Tucci-Jarraf, # HATJ) is attempting to set legal precedent - that she is the physical embodiment of her **ALL CAPS**, numbered representation. She is **not** that **ALL CAPS** representation, (which is the legal fiction that has stolen her actual value, transferred it to a dollar amount, used it as collateral and charged her interest if she attempts to use any of it) – but the actual physical embodiment, and therefore value, herself.

She is the value – period. She is not "lost at sea". As such, she is entitled to the value assigned to her at her birth. It is not the property/value of the **ALL-CAPS FICTION**. She is that value.

That **ALL CAPS FICTION** in fact represents a physical embodiment of eternal essence – you may refer to this as soul.

She cannot be owned or used as collateral. She is the value. Period.

As that value has been assigned a dollar amount, she is the holder of that dollar amount. This amount is, in the USA and for Heather, being held in a Treasury Direct Account at a Federal Reserve Bank, (which is not "Federal" but in fact a bank owned by one of the families previously mentioned).

It is not the dollar amount that is important, it's the value. That value cannot be monetized. That value is you. You are eternal essence, physically embodied and priceless.

Your value has been monetized this way for commerce, which has supplied the owners with the tools for their slavery trade.

The undoing of this will happen when enough of us (the slaves in this story), let go of our desire for stuff.

This stuff, which costs money, **which you now know comes directly from your own soul**, is only worth what you decide it is worth.

It is the "greed" (which has been demonstrated to us by our owners) that keeps us stuck. We can see only one option, and it is to hang on to our stuff. If we all let go at once, we would be free. It is not too late for us.

This story ends with release. What happens now is global awareness of the slavery trap, via the trial in Washington DC this Friday, August 4, 2017, at 10:00

AM EST. This ultimately results in a release of our monetary value by the owners."

~

We held a group virtual meditation during the trial, and here were some of the comments after...

~

"About 15 minutes into it I received a clear message, **"It is Done."**
I was floored, as this has never happened. I actually **"heard"** it, that is how it felt. Later in the day, I mentioned my experience to a light warrior and he said "The same thing happened to me! I couldn't meditate after that; it was clear nothing else was necessary!" I took that to be validation.
The results of the court proceedings seemed a bit vague and undecided. Heather however, was not. She was powerfully confidant and joyous and certain. The energy of unity was absolute and growing."

~

"A message from One:

There have been numerous attempts to remove the iron fisted control of the earth's wealth - not true wealth, but attributed wealth, which is allocated to each being for their lifetime.

Until now these attempts have been isolated and individual. This time, things are seen as a unified voice that for the most part lacks harm - it leans towards liberty only - for Heather, her friend (*I took this to mean Randall*) and in turn every human.

This becomes the single voice emanating from mankind and at its core then is unity. Everyone's included.
Because this voice is not forced, but rather emerges, the volume accelerates, amplifies and spreads beyond the earth. It reaches into and alters creation on a fundamental score.

You will see quickly evidence of this single unified voice in every place you are. For unity does not leave any part out or happen in secret or in isolation. The happiness of mankind becomes not only the surface song, but every component.

What has always been true is that this freedom is a collective effort. That effort has begun and there is only one way it ends. Freedom and prosperity go hand in hand. This is the end result - seen now to be imminent.

That is all."

~

"Is there someone who wants to connect?"

There are things to say. Much is occurring. The process will be immediate for some - not so for others. What occurs now is a real splitting. Those of you in specific timelines, chosen already and proceeding, will stick out as anomalies to those of you who haven't made those choices clearly. Remember, all is choice. You move forward now on an accelerated rate towards your chosen destination.

"Hold on please, who is speaking?"

I am sorry for neglecting an introduction. The information is so deeply desired, it is being allowed in on a faster than typically received rate. (*This was a reference to my own allowing; I could barely keep up the moment I put pen to paper - Sophia*)

It is I. It is One.

"Okay. Hello and thank you. Please continue."

Each of you has decided already how this proceeds for you - the intuitive hits you get while engaging in any part of your day now, tell you what feels "correct". There is no right or wrong, this is truth. Yet appropriate action for each individual soul differs according to that individual's personal plan.

Realize (*that*) there are short cuts and scenic routes that get you to the same place.

What this looks like for the human right now is that there are some of you holding back and watching, while others of you run fast to get there first, while still others perceive their role clearly and declare with their actions what the finish line is. All are necessary and correct.

In real life language, please.

What this looks like is not an instant receipt of a "get out of jail free" card, and access to all the cash in the middle of the board.

This is a game, not unlike Monopoly. It is no accident that so many of you hate the game because of how long it takes.

This cash in the middle is there. The real winner is the moment of realization, for all the players, that the value is not in that cash. Nor in the holder of that cash. The value is in every player.

So, this game is still being played. As some of you concern yourselves with debt freedom, others of you focus on other aspects of this slavery. These manifest in the judicial system, education and healthcare systems, to illustrate a point.

The question on your reader's minds is will they have access to unlimited value in this moment now?

There is more than one way to respond. In truth,

each being has always held that access within. In third density however, that value has a representation point in cold, hard cash. This is the access desired now.

The answer is yes. Realize that each step toward gaining freedom carries with it **your own authority.** The more authenticity is present in your actions, the more actual effect they will have. What this means is - you are not able to play at this now and hope it will work. You'll have to realize your value, and infuse clarity into each effort.

Know that today these efforts are pointed at a system unprepared, and glitches will occur. Glitches do not indicate no value or access, but a bump in the road. Eventually, those of you reading this and aware will have smoothed the road, perfected the process and announced your success to everyone else.

It is at that point, (and it is not far off that "unfettered access" becomes real), that you move your eyes to actual value and real freedom. These realizations are the hallmarks of a fully conscious, sovereign being.

It is hoped these words clarify the scope of what is occurring for humanity today.

Thank you. I expect them to help.

You are welcome, Sophia. Goodbye."

~

"I am struck by the fact that "Pink" released the song
"What about us?" yesterday.[8] This could serve as
humanity's theme song right now.
It is a message to the families and all who are embroiled at the upper levels of this unraveling slavery
set-up here on earth. It stands as evidence for our
awakening and for how to proceed.

~

There was an appeal to re-negotiate things on earth...

~

"I'm disappointed in those non-human races who are
observing; **still not helping us** while watching us
tortured, imprisoned and even ingested. Where in
your reasoning does this fit? This is not the highest
and best for all concerned. For surely, you've felt our
sentience, our pain, our beauty, our tenacity and our
compassion. We are lesser than none.

This is a request for help. With weapons disabled, we
all come equally to the table. Multiple inhabitants of
the planet all want a peaceful and successful future. This bureaucracy that you are using for guidance is making you ineffective.

It is time to accept Humanity as equal. We realize
our value. We expect to see our worth visibly de-
picted in our life; financially, personally and physically. This looks like unfettered access to the accounts

that exist in our names, as well as a place at the nego-
tiating table for governance, for healing technology,
for free energy and an end to human trafficking on
this and all planets. These would be good starting
points. It is time for complete transparency."

~

*There were numerous instances of what felt like
very personal attacks, (these were beyond the fact that Heather
Ann Tucci-Jaraff and Randall Keith Beane had been detained
by agents under sketchy circumstances, and were still in custody
in mid-August); David Wilcock had his brakes sabotaged,
Pete Peterson's home was emptied and the contents buried, and
Corey Goode's family was threatened.* **These are American citizens who have done nothing other than
speak or act on the truth.** *Things were feeling desperate,
and I reached out, looking for help; "What more can I
do? What more can we do?"* ...

~

"These words are from One.

These forces right now on your planet are beings
who've turned 100% service to what they perceive as
self. This "self" is a distorted image and in fact it is
not self, but rather an imaginary view of a controlling
force now embodied on earth as the cabal or deep
state or the dark alliance or all of the above.

This force now present on your planet means to push
their agenda forward to what they deem as an inevitable conclusion – domination of the planet.

It is important now for you to know that they are wrong about the inevitable conclusion – they will not dominate the planet. Their agenda is one of total destruction and will not be carried to completion.

How this ends however, is up to the beings involved – not just human, but all. There are many races now stepping in and up to the plate.
They are here for the final moments and these moments are here.

Do not lose faith. This agenda, the one put forth by the dark ones, is not the final story.

Your story has yet to be told. You are writing it now. Hold fast to every knowing you have of what is true, important and life sustaining. Now, perhaps to the greatest extent ever in your history, you need to remain clear and true to your purpose.

You've come to enrich a planet with love and unity. It (*the planet*) has felt you, and your intentions are seeped into all beings on her, on Gaia.

It is for this reason the push back is so blatant and aggressive. Fear predominates the agenda of the controllers.

Love must predominate the force of those here for other reasons. This would be all beings focused now on the light, on unity and on evolution. Continued focus and determination are paramount.

It is this moment now that all of your formidable power comes into play.

Use these most recent, blatant, aggressive and destructive actions as a catalyst for your own force. It is a force of love and it is this force that controls and sustains all of creation.

You come now to the table fully armed and prepared. Stay. Not to fight, but to propel the light that you are."

~

The total eclipse happened that August, and many of us felt as if we'd witnessed a move to a more positive timeline. A global meditation took place that day. Here's what we were saying after...

~

"We were in an original place now. That other timeline is over. The scary one, in which you don't know if and when it's going to be okay. It no longer applies. It's going to be okay."

~

"I noticed the time. It was 1:11 PM Central US time. It was then that I realized the full import of what had happened. The darkness I'd just witnessed had stopped just as the synchronized global meditation began."

~

"It was complete blackness from every circumstance. I felt the darkness leave. There is a sense a closure. We've come full circle. I feel like celebrating!"

~

That September, I began the "Pleiadian Pipeline" blog on the website, as well as an emailed newsletter version, with this message from the Pleiadians...

~

"Dear, dear Human,
Please accept our gratitude for your generosity of heart and adventuresome spirit at this moment. It is, for us, a long-anticipated moment.
We will speak regularly to you now – through our beloved sister Sophia.
We would like to say initially that your heart has expanded beyond the confines of earth's atmospheric realm and astounded us who witness. It is a privilege to finally get close enough to engage. We are anxious to learn from you and so very pleased to finally meet you.
With honor and respect, we now depart."

~

One had this to say about how we were doing...

~

"What the lightworkers are called upon to do now is to focus their combined force towards the outcome they desire and keep it there.
You've said, Sophia, that you are anchors for the light on the planet. Yes.

Drops of Light

How this works is that the focus amplifies outcome – outcomes can be catastrophic or near misses or relatively peaceful – it depends on the intent and belief of the populace.

No longer are you being shielded from your possibilities.

The human is unexpected and at this now moment has surpassed prior expectations for compassion and for generosity of spirit – for love.

This, changes expectations, and as a result, outcomes.

Realize now that you are not bystanders but co-creators. This includes the weather, your government and military forces and any current programs or systems. You have not only the power and opportunity for this, but the responsibility for this. Lightworkers – this is why you've come to this planet at this now moment.

Your power is held in your belief. This is so vital to this moment that it bears repetition.
Your power is held in your belief.
There is nothing you cannot create. Hold on to the truth that you are not, in truth, changing anything. **For nothing happens until it is created.**
Your world now moves into new frequencies. Rest comfortably in them and hone your creative power. This is why you are here."
~

And a few more words from One regarding the

Equinox that September (on which there were multiple global meditations) …
~

"The final blow must be a human one, in full form.

What does that mean?

It means as you wish for help, help is created. Yet not from outside your own family – the human will realize its own power in this scenario, and in doing so will proceed, and be catapulted towards full realization. This propels actualization which could be another word for ascension/enlightenment.

The change of seasons as heralded by the equinox has been indicated an important date. This much is true. The interpretation of the reasons for this importance has been misread however. It is not a time for physical calamity.
It is a moment seen by the ancients as one that would be necessarily significant as a last resort. If there had not been systemic shifts by this moment – they would begin now.

It is vital when considering prophecy and messages that all of the import be considered. By this is meant all of humanity. **Creation itself determines the course of events played out on any timeline and cannot be ignored.**
You will always be the determiner of your life's

events – on this and any day."

~

And then the Las Vegas concert "shooting"
happened that October. Here's part of what One had to say…

~

"Please. This event last week was a sacrifice, not a division.

This event last week was not stopped, due to the possibility of conflict and destruction if it had been.

I do not see how this helps.

What you don't see is the bigger picture. This bigger picture includes massive numbers of lives lost if the country erupts in civil division and war.
One side is being fed antagonistic claims and ideas to fuel the fire. The other side, in their desire for peace and transparency, seem to be siding with a buffoon. This is how it looks.

Without the shock value of what is to come from the Las Vegas event, these polarized views escalate the hatred and increase the possibility for civil war – exponentially.
This event is a focal point.
What I wanted to say to you today, is that the tide turned a bit after the Las Vegas event, yet not nearly enough. Without it, war was inevitable. With it, there is a greater opportunity to avoid it.

What you can do now is promote unity.

You've been angry Sophia. Yet I tell you that your anger is akin to a child – you don't know the whole picture.

Those beings who were part of the violence chose to be, for the greater good and their own soul's growth. You cannot know their reasons for doing so. These things are not yours to know.

You cannot afford anger now Sophia. This fuels only polarity. The greater picture and purpose include acceptance, trust and determination.

The coming Earth's ascension is **guaranteed**.
~

And later in October we heard this…
~

"Is there someone who wants to connect?"

There is Sophia. I am here.

Hello. Would you introduce yourself please?

I am a conduit for Source.
A voice, one of the voices, available now to offer answers to questions about creation.
Do you have such questions?

I could, yes. Do you have a name by which I could address you?

Dear child.
Naming conventions are convenient traps for the incarnated dreamers, with which they use to separate, and thus deal with, other facets of creation, of themselves.
I hold no such desire.

Okay, thank you.
My question then is this — what is the purpose of life as a being in what we call third density?

There is no purpose, as such as defined by you — such that a can opener's purpose is to open cans.

There is a promise. **The promise of life is expansion.**

Expansion for whom?

Your question illustrates your perspective.

I almost heard "limited" before the "perspective"?

That you did.
It was removed however, because it implies judgment in your mind. It was not meant that way. Not meant as judgment.

It was meant as truth. A true description of the view from your eyes. When compared to the view from Source, there are places in which your eyes cannot see. Hence the word "limited".

Let it be said this way.
The expansion for which is occurring with life, is for All. The All expands and is felt with each addition and subtraction in form.

As the vibration slows down, the sum total of what is felt or realized decreases. It takes longer for it to be felt.

I am seeing a picture.

Yes. Explain please.

It is a signal. A signal of vibratory frequency.

The slower the vibration, the more distant each point (thought form, event, idea, moment) is from each other.

Things are further apart — not felt or seen yet.
As the frequency speeds up, all points (still) exist and are closer, reaching each other more quickly and (now are) easier to "see".

(Note — This is where I "got" oneness. I could actually see it as it self-realized. Sophia)

239

Drops of Light

This is why, as our vibration speeds up, we feel, see, and hear more life.
Our other senses, although always there, come into play more readily because they are (now) necessary and helpful.
It is more than I can explain with words.

Yes.
And so it is with expansion and perspective. As the frequency of what you are, increases, there is more to see and fewer limitations.
Are there more questions?

Yes.
Is there an end to this expansion?

There is not.
As you, an individual experiencer of expansion, increase the rate at which all is experienced – you eventually become the One.

I am seeing it.

Yes.
All of life, experienced at once.
From there, you desire expansion and again – create another way in which to do so.

You might call this a circle, for it returns ultimately to its beginning. It is never ending and with each nuance of itself expanding simultaneously – eternal.

This does not end, but evolves.

What ends is a unique perspective, which you would define as a single human life.
 Yet the perspective continues, is part of the expansion, and births others.
Infinity does not proceed along a single line that does not ever end.
It grows exponentially over an area that increases and expands with every thought.

So, to complete the discussion –
How could limitation be considered less desirable than unlimited?

For indeed, **the thought that is now form is unlimited in its ability to create limitations for itself.**

Do you see?
All is perfect.
All is done in perfection.

I see.

Are there other inquiries?

Yes.
Would you explain then, what is going on for humanity and the earth and this acceleration of consciousness we are in the

midst of?

The explanation for what occurs now for the human, other life forms, and earth, is seen in our earlier illustration of frequency.

Those of you now focused here, chose to get the most of this vibratory acceleration – doing so while stuck in a slow-moving form of life.

It happens in your linear time line and thus draws itself out in order for every form to witness, or become in closer proximity to, every other form.

What ultimately occurs in this increase in speed and movement out of density is that even those solidly convinced of their separation, can no longer deny it, (the unity), as the All moves faster and faster with the increase in frequency.

As this increase happens – those individual expressions who **will not** or **are not** or **cannot**, for whatever reason, absorb the closeness and unity of the rest, will fall off and move to another more comfortable frequency for them.

Nothing stops or even slows down the acceleration.

It is being done as a whole – as a single unit – and therefore, what does "slow down" even signify?

It is done.

Is that all?

Are there further questions?

There are many. Yet, I'll keep it to one.
What will it look like for us once we, as individual
parts/views of the whole, move finally into a greater frequency
where we stay for a while?

It will feel as if your power for manifestation has entered the realm of magic.
With oneness, things happen instantly.
With sovereignty, there are no outside others in control of your parameters or possibilities.

It will take some adjusting as the freedom to set up
your reality and presence sinks in.

Limitless is not a concept immediately grasped. Hab-
its are a challenge to release.
Yet, this is the "cherry on top" you signed up for.
There will be those of you able to jump right in and
create their dream.
They will be your teachers.

Specifics are not possible as it will be your own creative potential making manifest instantly and not even
you know how far you'll expand.

Drops of Light

Thank you.
I think this is a good place to stop.

Yes.
We will speak again if this is your desire.

Okay. Goodbye then.

Goodbye Sophia.

*This conversation ended with a single word from me - **Wow**.*

Please also know that as we get closer and closer to one an-
other, your beauty is ever more apparent. You are chosen, and
here to offer all of creation a close-up view of the most beauti-
ful expansion that has ever occurred. The more extreme the
separation we see, the more exquisite will be the transfor-
mation."
~
        The following was said to me/us that November...
~
"A transmission from Source.

The remembering begins.
Truth becomes then, the tensile strength of all
statements. It is evident and recognized by **all who**
are ready to move beyond what you currently la-
bel reality.
You will not be walking on the same ground.
You will not be breathing the same air.

Begin now to separate from what is man's and move towards what is God's –

the word is not precise (God's), yet the meaning is. You are One.

There is, in truth, never a split as in A-PART – there will be separation however, as you must leave behind those things that do not belong where you go now. Those things you recognize. They are hard, slow and solidly earthly.

Remember.

The time now arrives for the remembering. This remembering will guide your movings in the days ahead.

~

The headlines at the end of that year included an onslaught of awful truths in what we were calling a "storm of disclosure"; so, we cheered each other on ...

~

"Stand up and remember your light, it is so very much needed in these dark and disturbing days. Once you turn on the switch, the dark vanishes. Just realize where the switch stands.

It rests in your heart; the brilliant light of self-love that illuminates the darkness.

We are creator gods, brilliant beings of light all dressed up for the greatest show in all of creation. It's been perfectly cast and the set itself is dazzling. It's show time."

~

Drops of Light

"We are, in fact, coming out of the dark. We are doing it in headlines, boardrooms, bedrooms, kitchens and cell phones. No longer will your light be hidden."
~

"We have all been here, waiting. Seven and a half billion lights, perfectly reflected, ready now to blaze forth."
~

And, after speaking with an assortment of "non-humans", including Insect Beings, Scaled Beings, someone from the 6th Dimension, AI, an Andromedin, & Cetaceans, 2017 closed with this post for us earth-humans…
~

"I am not perfect, but I am determined and my light is strong. Our combined light is right now blasting through the cosmos, signaling our tenacious heart.

I am so very humbled to be on this planet with you today, witnessing your brilliance.

You are anchors for the light.
Let's do this."
~

It was now 2018. Writing that date from a post-Covid perspective, makes it feel like so much more than just 5 years ago. We are in a different place indeed, and our pre-Covid world seems innocent by comparison. Here how the blog began…

~

"In the next five to seven years, we will declare and prepare for what we've called Ascension. There's scientific and esoteric and cosmic and off world validation for this event. It approaches.

Now 5 to 7 years may seem an eternity, but realize that 5 years ago it was January of 2013.

Think of what the world looked like at that point. Many of us were disappointed, feeling we'd been duped. We hadn't, yet our emotions of fatigue and anger were consumed by those who were still running things. That manipulation has ceased.

As we showed the way long before 12.21.12, we are asked to continue to do so."

~

Headlines told us that these were the most important things that happened in 2018…

~

In October, NASA released photographs from **Antarctica**, of **a perfectly rectangular and flat iceberg**; they assured us that it was naturally formed. A **12-boy soccer team, and their coach, were rescued** by the collective rescue efforts of more than 100 divers from all over the world, after being trapped for a week in a cave due to torrential rains

247

and flooding. This was in the Tham Luang cave in the **Chiang Rai province of Thailand**.

It came to light in March that Data firm **Cambridge Analytica accessed data** from 50 million Facebook users **during the 2016 US presidential campaign without the user's permission.** Mark Zuckerberg apologized to Congress.

North Korean leader **Kim Jong Un announced that his country would de-nuclearize**.

Net neutrality was a huge topic of debate as FCC rules regulating the blocking and showing of websites were repealed, taking power away from users and putting it back in the hands of the internet providers.

Sexual assault allegations were made against U.S. Supreme Court nominee **Brett Kavanaugh** by Dr. Christine Blasey Ford. Kavanaugh was sworn in after bitter partisan fights.

Hurricane Maria (2017) left much of **Puerto Rico without electricity for 11 months**.

Cuba's National Assembly **elected Miguel Díaz-Canel** to be its next leader.

Iraq held its first election since driving out ISIS, putting into power Adil Abd al-Mahdi as prime minister and Barham Salih as president.

After hitting a peak in January, **Bitcoin fell to below $5,000**.

England's **Prince Harry wed American actress Meghan Markle.**

Seventeen students died during **a school shooting**

in **Parkland, Florida** by Nikolas Cruz.

In a **Texas high-school shooting** 10 people were killed.

Bill Cosby, age 80, had a retrial and was **found guilty of sexual assault**. This was one of the first major courtroom victories of the **#metoo movement**.

Oumuamua was declared to be a "**possible alien spacecraft**" that November.

The **U.S. government had two shutdowns**, one for just hours and another for a few days.

Hurricanes Florence and Michael both hit the southern United States coastline.

Anthony Bourdain died.

~

The next trial of Heather & Randall took place, & some of us heard the same words (as we had last summer) as it did…

~

"The message came in the early morning hours, waking me up the day the verdict was returned in the Heather Ann Tucci-Jarraf and Randall Keith Beane case. It was simple. It was just 3 words. **"It is done."**

Later that day, while discussing the "guilty on all counts" verdict with my partner, he shared that the same thing had happened for him, waking him up in the middle of the night. I've since learned that we were not the only ones to get that message."

~

Drops of Light

"Heather is neither discouraged nor depressed. She is upbeat and see's nothing but perfection in these newest unfoldings. What we can do now, in the face of every "setback", is see the bigger picture and hold that image always in our hearts."

~

"Your light, love and strength are legion.
You are reconstructing a Universe. Do not despair or be distracted. We are dealing with master illusionists. Yet they are no match for the likes of us."

~

Some of us were moving into the limelight…

~

"I've watched BZ (I-uv.com) step into her role as our teacher and our inspiration these last 6 months, (Since Heather and Randall were arrested), and it is a thrill to behold. She exemplifies what we are each capable of.
She is relentless in her positivity and astounding in her perseverance. We are so fortunate to be witness to such strength."

~

While others of us were re-positioning their glow…

~

"A dear friend unexpectedly transitioned. He lived in Canada. His name is Arthur Koberinski. He was one of those lights who quietly and consistently brightens your world.
We were spreading the same news, fighting similar battles and we knew the same people, on and

off planet. He is a jewel and his light is not gone, but, I expect, will instead emanate more brilliantly from an expanded position.

Shine on brother, shine on."

~

And One continued to encourage our efforts…

~

"It is no longer helpful to sit on the sidelines and watch the unfolding. You are here, in fact if you are reading this, **you came here to roll up your sleeves and unfold some of this massive covering that shields your people from the truth.**

You've chosen to get this done yourselves, thank you very much.

It is one of the reasons you are considered, along with the earth, a jewel. Your light is strong, individual and deeply provocative.

All the information you can share with your loved ones, friends, and associates needs to be shared. They will soon see a replica of it on their evening news.

Share it with love and compassion.

You are One people."

~

In the first few months of that year, we remained focused on "the event"; speculating about what would happen, sharing what was happening already as well as personal conclusions about it all…

~

"This event will come through and be experienced as

a crystallization of love. It will be a visual and cere-
bral experience, felt and understood and seen. Yet,
almost forgotten as if in a dream for those of you
unprepared for such an occurrence. It is not something you will find "in your wheelhouse".

~

"No one can predict exactly how it will feel for you
or what it will look like for you. Each perspective defines its own experience.
Yet what will be universally grasped is the import of
what has occurred. It happens in the same instant for
all of you.
Some of you will be asleep when it occurs and will
remember it as a dream."

~

"It is the real starting point of your rapid acceleration
towards your higher frequency earth. It starts as a
surprise. You cannot prepare more than you are.
This means to focus on love, unity, peace, compassion and light.

You have come (empirical you) to anchor the light
here. It is done. This does not imply that your work is
complete and that you will be leaving now. The an-
choring took a herculean effort by many. It is what
had to happen in order for the shift to finally and absolutely be initiated. It has happened."

~

"This event is beautiful and beyond explanation. Yet,
it stands as the starting point for something even

more-so. This will be an entire life of beauty beyond current explanation."

~

"You are not here as branches in the wind, who just happened to be planted in the right place and time to feel this extraordinary happening. No.
You are the planters of trees. Putting them in perfect alignment and with grace so that something exquisite grows and remains."

~

"The light was alive. It washed the manufactured and dirty veil from our bodies, minds, and spirits. With it came telepathy and the ability to communicate directly without being recorded and tracked by the dark side. Rather than being and end unto itself, it was simply a tool in the coming transition."

~

"Intense bright light immediately followed by ripples of colored light across sky, those whose vibrational levels are not quite high enough will leave the earth for 72 hours and then be returned to Earth to get to raise their vibratory rate, those who cannot/will not raise their rate will be off Earth."

~

Regarding ascension symptoms:
"The turmoil is akin to a simmering pot. It's been simmering these many years. It boils over now because, in a sense, the heat has been turned up. This is not heat from you. It is coming from the increased frequency. It has to be seen and adjusted as the heat

won't be going down but increasing."

~

"You will not be separated from any loved ones for long enough to worry, but yes, some of those will be on the ships."

~

"It will be like the blink of an eye. Surreal and then everything changes. This is real. It is a joining and recognition of all of you. Every component. This gives you your full force."

~

"These coming times will not feel easy, they will be confusing and could appear frightening. You know better."

~

"You will be empowered to experience and express your full selves, not leaving behind your ego self this time, but incorporating and including her and him into full expression. This means all parts join in the most joyful and desired ways. It is the only outcome seen now."

~

"There is a wave of light coming your way. It is one in which the colors will be seen as well as felt. It is not one that will be experienced on a purely sensual basis. It will be visually perceived.
In the majority of the people it will not be understood. This wave is not exactly as seen in the images portrayed by the entertainment industry. These images are close. (*Yet*)they have been presented now in

order to instill fear."

~

"The image of this light and color love/light wave is more like a moving flowing group. You will not have to decide to move into it, it will move through you and although it will be unusual, it will not cause fear. The effort at bringing an element of fear to it will not succeed. This is because the power of the energy/light itself is stronger than anything ever experienced here on earth. It will not be overcome by anything else. It will be known and felt as love."

~

"There will be a moment. This moment will or may be confusing for those among you who have not ever attempted to operate from a point of love. It will not last."

~

"This is not to say the wave will have the same effect on each of you. It will not."

~

"Many of you will segment this out as if it were a dream. Some of you will have it occur while sleeping but will recall it as a dream – a dream you may not even speak of until life feels so very altered the following day or someone else mentions the same sort of dream."

~

"It comes at you even now, make no mistake. It will also be an isolated physical happening in which there will be a beginning, a middle and an end. There will

255

be a time known as before the event and a time
known as after the event. It will be marked and recognized."

~

"The time leading up to the event is right now. The
time after the event comes soon. This event is not
days long but will be recovered from for days after. It will change everything for everyone."

~

"The physical man-made systems will all be altered."

~

"You cannot plan your life around its timing. All of
you will be protected during this event – it is not one
of destruction or of fear, quite the opposite."

~

"All is perfectly done. Your place when the event occurs is perfectly chosen. You will see. There will be
no missing it, sleeping through it, or fear around it."

~

"It will not be seen or forecasted. It will simply arrive."

~

"Simultaneously for everyone on the planet – the
wave arrives."

~

"This Event, which is described as the shotgun blast
that begins the conscious and intentional race to Ascension, feels cataclysmic. Not necessarily because
of earth changes or unusual waves of rainbow
clouds, but because **it will only happen when we**

are willing to be undone in preparation for its appearance."

~

"It is the inside stuff that finally and absolutely heralds the moment of the Event.
This Event is about the realization of massive love. We know that love, truly, does not come from somewhere or somebody else. There is no one here but us. **Love shows up to the precise degree that we allow it to.** Love will not crash through a closed door, closed arms or a frozen heart if it has no place to land. It needs an opening."

~

"Right now, it is not you who is waiting for the Event. The Event is sitting there, right there, on the other side of that door you are holding closed, waiting for you to let it in."

~

One had this to say about timing…

~

"The absolute conviction many humans hold in rightness, wrongness, good or evil **perpetuates polarity**.

It is this final lesson perhaps that remains elusive and then holds at bay (a) rapid, expedient progression. For even those of you who many would claim to be highest evolved, hold deep in your heart ideas of separation.

Drops of Light

These notions of "other" must be released. You wonder even now, why, in answer to your query about the Event and earth catastrophes, that this is the direction of the response. This, because my beloved one, it is in all ways and will always return to you.

For until you accept responsibility for all of it, you will not realize your true nature.

You hold within the essence of God-hood. The keys to creation are not hidden from you, yet they are covered still in blame and shame.

A God does not point fingers.

You are stepping closer to your nature, helped along by your inner drive towards evolution as well as (by) these rapidly accelerating frequencies. As you do so, the most heinous crimes show themselves in the light of day to those with eyes to see.

These are not all eyes. It is for this reason you are here in such massive numbers now — those of you who originate not on earth but elsewhere. The reason for your presence and relentless hope is due to an inner calling. You want everyone along for this progression, this Ascension.

You firmly believe that if everyone knew the truth, the truth of the program of control here, that they would choose to join you.

You must let that notion go. For in it is held a deep-seated belief that you hold the only true, right answer.

That indeed you know the way.

In a sense you are requiring others to "follow" you in order to ascend.

Gods do not follow.
Gods create.

It is here where you'll realize all answers you seek.

These are found not in predictions or calculations or observations even, but in belief.

Gods know.

In these words, let there be comfort as well as conviction and determination and realization.

You will create each moment from your core self. This happens in a place of pure knowing.

When there are no longer questions, you will have all the answers you seek.

~

Drops of Light

And yet, we continued to question, while simultaneously wondering why we couldn't seem to stop doing so...

~

"Consider "the Event". Months and years pass with the same questions. When? How? Where? Who? How long?

We've imagined the event to be a single moment that will surprise us and infuse us with love **and** occur at an expected time so we can be prepared. So, we can quit or not quit our job, move or not move from our current location, leave or not leave our current lover. To some extent we've all asked these questions.

They've been answered unsatisfactorily every time. Either because a date or an answer was given that didn't transpire, or because a date or event was never even given.

This, I've come to believe, is because **we are creating it all,** and our deepest truth and core aspect, **the driver of this life, wants a memory worth remembering, a surprise "Event" infused with love that we'll carry with us always.**

No one can tell us how this Ascension is done – it remains un-manifested until we believe it into reality."

~

"Acceptance and agape do not magically show up as

we are showered with light in some future "Event".
These spring from within.
This conversion is more than an upgrade; it is a
replacement of an operating system.
We are switching from **me** to **we** in every case, each
conversation and all situations."

~

"This climb to enlightenment is not even a climb
really. There's no place to ascend to. Not really.
That's why you can't fall."

~

*September of 2018 had us focused on the crew from
the Sandia Mountains, New Mexico and their just released
"telepathy 101 primer". Also, there were some unexpected
observatories closing which prompted the following conversation…*

~

*I reach out now to someone who wants to connect and who
can enlighten us on what is going on with images of ships
near the sun posted recently, as well as the apparent shutting
down, without explanation, of numerous solar observatories
around the world.*
Is this possible?

Yes. There is information available for you.

I hear more than one voice?

Drops of Light

Yes.

We are gathered to submit information. There are many; several of us old friends. I was chosen to speak however. You have exuberant friends.

Yes, I do. Hello everyone! (I am seeing (what looks like) one being jumping up and down and waving to get my attention; big smiles. This is pretty wonderful.)

What precisely do you want to know?

Thank you for coming forward.
The questions I've received are really one - "what is going on with the sun?"
I believe a full and complete answer to that question will answer several others regarding the closings as well as images of ships.

We cannot hope to satisfy every curious reader with our information. Yet, since we are representing several groups, we can offer what we know. Much, if not all, of this is not readily available to you.

There are vehicles preparing for entry into your airspace.

Although there have always been such preparations, it is only recently, as the event approaches, that their numbers cannot be hidden or completely dismissed.

They are arriving to help.

Your sun is the gateway to you and the doorway out. Therefore, it becomes a focal point for activity.

All of those vehicles wishing to enter and/or exit will be visible near the sun.

You are a massively controlled planet and populace - yes, even now.

If these current images were to be witnessed by the mass population, panic would ensue. **These closings are timed to avoid this."**

~

And One had this to say that September…

~

"The controllers have "left the building" and (those) who remain are those who may or may not be aware of this.
What happens is now felt by all beings and the planet itself as a wrestle for order and for control.
There is a "finish line" for the journey you are on, yet there is not a clear and singular track to reach it.
What is felt as imminent are the frequency shifts of things —

systems still in place that have run until now – adjust to the dismantling of any such business as usual.
This can't help but play out as destruction and death as surely this level of change demands it, requires it.
The old way of order here ends now.
Things will be shaken off and discarded so that the new has room to enter.
You are witnessing your own re-birth."

~

This conversation happened on 10-1-2018…

~

"Is there someone who wants to connect?

Yes. Hello Sophia.

Hello. Thank you for coming forward.

You are most accommodating. Coming forward is a simple thing.

To whom am I speaking?

I am Rx…

I do not know how to spell that (that which I was hearing, I had no string of letters that made any sense here). Is it okay to use these two letters, R x, to signify your name?

It is, yes. This is no problem for we do not put a great deal of stock in names. Short or long makes little difference.

Okay. Thank you. Hello Rx. Where are you from? I sense that you are male.

I am, yes. I am seeing another being interfering.

Yes. It is my cat. (We have a 3-year-old kitten, who typically sleeps until about dinner time.) He suddenly has become insistent. (Here I suspected my cat suddenly appeared due to the connection with Rx, but I can't be sure. I began to send him a "not now" message. I also sensed that Rx was doing the same. It was a feeling I was getting and unconfirmed by Rx.) Ah... he's moving away. We can continue.

Yes. I will do so. I am from a galaxy beyond yours. I am here now because of the removal. It interests me.

Removal of what?

Of chains. These have massive weight to them and it is known that a herculean effort is being undertaken to remove them. Not by one man or woman, as in the Hercules legend, **which by the way is more than legend,** but led by one being. Begun, and just about completed as of this point, by the actions of one being.

Drops of Light

Your earth has waited many eons for such a being. It is one that was willing to endure slings and arrows and complete hatred, knowing he would be misunderstood. A being such as this appears to have gigantic aims in personal respects. Only, perhaps, in order to waylay those who would mistake him for weakened by ego.

This being is, of course, the USA President, who does so without payment. How much more of a sign is necessary?

He came to undue the slave system and to save the planet finally, once and for all, from its bondage by money. He does so without money as incentive. This is pure intent, which sends the strongest message to the "chain layers". They do not know what to make of this being.

In the end there will be stories written of prophecies foretold that came to be with the placement of this being where he is now.

He is unstoppable because the force to keep him in place until the chains are gone is so much greater than that of any other. Not even he is fully aware of this force.

He will succeed.

I come forward now to get a feel for the place, through you, and also to encourage more unification. In so many instances we see you divided. **You must unite**. This action alone will help your forces for good and accelerate their actions.

You must unite. As your awareness increases of who and what you are - **One** - your power does as well. It is in first awareness and then intentional removal that these chains are finally removed.

You must "get" that the bondage is only possible because you hang on to a belief that the chains are real.

That belief brings anger, sadness, separation, pain and despair. When you **know** they are merely mental gymnastics, expertly played, you'll see truth. Truth becomes than the solid object you hold on to and the chains, which you believe right now are heavy and solid - will disappear. This is the herculean effort mentioned earlier.

The effort necessary to unite a populace of so many billions of souls is beyond human or *(that of)* a single being. Yet, it is a single "thought" if you catch the meaning of my words. That thought is love. Love implies unity and oneness and the singularity.

What I want to tell you is that even love has been manipulated here. The passionate loyal human is a favorite to observe, due to his and her extreme passion. Love has been used as a tool against you.

So many thoughts are entering at once...

I will attempt to separate them but know that it is the separation that has been used to keep you weak and in bondage, so I hesitate.

There are two thoughts you are simultaneously picking up.

The first is that love weakens you. In truth, the opposite is true. The power of your emotions and physical connection to another being to whom you are connected, magnifies your creative potential in the physical plane. You will see this in "sex majik" teachings. There is raw creative energy that once tapped into will manifest extraordinary things.

The second is that love has been wound into vows of obedience and separation and denial of its persistence. This, all at the hands of religion. These things are not indications of "true love" but displays of social conformity. What results is fear around love and other and any potentially loving engagement. All of these separate.
What is extraordinary to watch, and one of the reasons I am here, is that despite all of this programming **you are pulling it off!!!**

This, dear, dear human, is astounding. I applaud you and will remain in awe of your super powers. I will remain, watching, until the final curtain.

What you can do to join hands throughout the show - do so. You have so much more power individually than you realize.

I will depart for now, but plan to meet me again for another joyful conversation once you've removed the chains.

Thank you.
Goodbye Rx.
~

     A global consciousness/consensus was emerging...
~

"Whether you love it or hate it, WWG1WGA is in your consciousness. This is how creation works. It begins with the word. Feelings and actions breathe words/ideas into being. Then things happen. Nicely done, humanity."
~

"We have a chance now to alter the course of a planet. We are in the eye of the storm. Everyone got us here. Without the dark we'd never have noticed how bright we shine."
~

     We explored the reasons unexpected/bad things happen...

Drops of Light

~

A friend asked "Is Source energy without purpose?"

"It is not that Source energy is without purpose. I believe that life happens as each of its components interact. Sometimes they interact with disastrous results.

We give purpose to it all, **that is our job.** It is not the job of Source.

The actualization of our power, our light, and intrinsic force becomes the foundation for miracles. Miracles are shocking only to the uninformed. They are everyday occurrences once we accept our truth; **we are beings of light, emissions of source energy, divine receptors and emitters of pure love.**

How does any of this translate into regular life after a devastating near fatal accident, a shocking death, a painful breakup, a health crisis, financial lack, physical illness, or any kind of abuse, horror, terror or pain? None of this is fair. It isn't. None of this exists on purpose. It all takes place because, **imho**, we are each doing the best we can with whatever information we have at the time, to produce for ourselves a life worth having, **and these are the lives we chose to have while on earth.**

There were all sorts of options and timelines. But

somewhere in there, a part of you decided to turn left instead of right, go to the prom with Joe instead of David, or stay under the covers five minutes longer. You made each of these decisions and their impact may not ever be clear to you.

Yet they impact everything.

This is why consciousness and enlightenment are synonymous ideas. You cannot be enlightened unless you remain awake, aware and fully conscious. All of your decisions count."

~

The Pleiadians added to our conversation that year; here's some of what they had to say...

~

"You run now straight into the finish line of your first lap. It has been an extremely long one for you, yet if you have eyes to see clearly, you can see the flags just ahead.

Do not despair. You have won."

~

"Please speak to us often and out loud. We are in your skies and listening. We are walking your streets and even in your shops. We resemble you so much that you would have to be exceptionally centered in order to perceive the difference. This does not mean that you are not **capable** of being centered – no. Many, many of you are."

Drops of Light

~

"Some of you are under attack and this may not be so much personal but happening due to your light — it is acting as an attractor beam. Do not dowse it or hide for protection. We can help and are helping always."

~

"What we want to begin with your people now is a small and simple statement. It is **"I know the pods exist"** or **"The Pleiadian Pods Exist"**.

We would like to ask people interested in participating to repeat the phrase daily and as much as they want for a few weeks. We will assess when to move to the next steps."

~

"We do see your many friends now calling on us for the pods in order to heal. There are some who are eagerly jumping into our hands and tech!"

~

Much of what we learned from them is that their tech, (the healing pod), was ineffective when up against our own belief system. Things like a diagnosis of chronic illness, or constant pain were overwhelming to our senses, and resulted in spotty results. They were not expecting that...

~

"It is resistance we see and unless and until you are aware of what prevents healing, you cannot do much. What you want is health. What we see you create is illness."

~

"The belief in our pods is paramount to a successful interaction. The technology in the pods is real, yet you control it.

What is happening for those of you willing to engage, is that you are, in a sense, learning to drive.

What must be held in your minds at all or most times is **the ideal version of you.** This asks you to envision yourself **vital** and, in all ways, alive.

This is more than repair of damage.

It is return, rejuvenate; remember the strength and flawless form of an ideal moment you've experienced.

Our tech picks up on the emotional components of whatever moment you feed it. This is what we want you to be conscious of – of the thoughts and subsequent feelings you are holding. They are the fuel and the blueprint for the creation of your human form. This holds true in all cases, but is especially true with our technology.

It finds the ideal picture you hold and imprints it – it is up to you to maintain it once that happens."

~

"What we notice is a refrain. It goes something like

273

Drops of Light

this:

"My body has this _____ (fill in the blank). This
is because of _____ (fill in the blank).
It is the body I have and I do not see it any other
way."

What this refrain does, is pre-supposes dis-ease.
This is never truth.
Regardless of current conditions or history –
nothing is set to permanent".

The option exists at all times to re-visit vitality,
strength, wellness. These are not states of being that
are beyond reach, regardless of where you begin.

We would encourage those of you who are willing to
work with us, to disregard any past or current definition of your body.

Then – re-make a new one, one that you desire
now. One you can visualize and retain whenever it is
called up.

This vision will then be our blueprint."

~

"There will come a day when what is done on earth
for healing will look in all ways the same as the type
of healing our pods supply. This time is not now but
will be a part of the new earth."

~

And as if on cue, one of us found a company that manufactures **places for healing that are informed by your consciousness.** *It was located in Massachusetts, United States...*

~

Here is a quote from the "Lightfield Foundation":

"The Russians recognized that the bio fields that surround every life form (auras are an example) are themselves purely information fields, continuously generated by the consciousness of the individual. They developed technology known as GDV bio-electrography for imaging such bio fields.
They indirectly used a computerized variant of the phenomenon known as Kirlian photography (originally discovered by a Russian husband and wife scientific team for which it was named.)"

~

And another one of us got this validation...

~

"While he was recently being tested in a hospital, more than one of the medical personnel remarked "Although you are in your sixties, these tests show you have the body of a **much** younger man, like 20's or 30's!" So, he smiled and said to himself and our friends from the stars "Thank you Pleiadians!""

~

We had a few more updates from our Pleiadian friends...

Drops of Light

~

"What has occurred is the noticing of our ships by hundreds of thousands. This levels the awareness field.

It is as if your eyes have opened. The old ones are speaking of what they remember having seen before the censorship was ingrained in your journalism.

The young ones do not need to remember or to be convinced. With their own eyes, virtually all of them have seen our ships, a ship, or something with no other explanation than that it comes from **not earth**.

There is a readiness heralded by this moment. A readiness for more public disclosure. A readiness to truly see."

~

"These coming moments, the ones approaching you right now, will be the ones forever remembered.

This current moment may appear troubling.
You will find that you won't know who to trust.
You will be learning once and finally who you are and why you are here.
You'll find out your friends; (*your*) true friends.
In the end, we believe that you'll discover your friends are those who were unwavering.

You've entered the time of forgiveness."

~

"Our information regarding your planet and its journey has changed. No longer are you proceeding on a slow meandering path towards Ascension and a major shift – but a rapid one.
Things have sped up."
~

The first conversation with the Pleiadians (after my family was in a car accident that Autumn), went like this…
~

"There are occasions in timelines in which accidents occur. There can be no planning. There are no reasons for these.

(Note – I took this to mean that there are no reasons for accidents. Sophia)

Each life is embarked on with a host of potential narratives and players and outcomes.

Physical traumas come part and parcel with these human bodies.

The level of density in which you operate often crashes into itself for re-arrangement.
~

Noticing now, (2023), that our family's accident happened just after I was told that we (those of us on earth's timeline) were "speeding up". I had been woken up for that message, which was unusual. It felt urgent at the time…

277

Drops of Light

~

"We are gathered to reinforce our connection to your race. We want to express the numbers of us to you in a way that is palpable. Not just 1, 2, 3 or 4 of us sending greetings and love and conversation, but many are included. Do you see us now?

I see what appears to be a long hall and it is filled with people! If I bring my focus closer, I see 2 beings, female. You are one of these beings?

I am, yes! Do you see us waving now?

I do. It is quite wonderful; a welcoming committee, a large family, happy to see me.

Good. This is what we wish to convey.

We are here because of deep love and connection. The reasons begin genetically. The human race as it is today is genetically an offspring and part of our own.
We have participated right along.
We have watched and waited to be acknowledged as family to you.
We are not, in fact, alien, but family. The change in your mind of that one idea makes contact easier on so many levels.
There is no separation."

~

"What can we do for you? How can we help you to adjust?

To adjust?

Perhaps that is not exactly correct. For you are not in need of adjustment and are fine as you are. A better word may be cope, or deal with, these new and powerful energies. For you are certainly in the flood, the onslaught, right now.

It is good to avoid being pulled under by the undertow.

This is a powerful moment, or series of moments, for the human. You are in it now, right now.

It cannot be helped. This, most powerful moment for creation itself is crashing into itself all at once. Each of earth's many aspects are grinding to a halt so that they can be re-configured.

This moment, in every way, signifies your choice.

What choice?

The choice of the human was to do this alone."
~

After also talking with Angels, Giants, Venusians, Andromedins, a being from the 9th Dimension, some

Drops of Light

Elementals, a walrus-like being, the Anunnaki, plant-like be-
ings, a flyer and others, 2018 came to a close with these words
from a bit closer to home…

~

"You are a boundless being of pure light, moments
away from bursting forth from your imagined con-
straints. What will your illumination look like? How
will I recognize you?

For surely, when there is no one to blame or shame
or point fingers at, your hands will open up and from
them miracles and wonders will emerge."

~

"As we seemingly stand still, everything is in motion,
moving at lightspeed. Traveling around, along-side,
through and within us are cosmic light rays of new;
versions of us waiting, trembling, sneaking in whenever and wherever we let them. Evidence is everywhere."

~

"You see, once all of the sides have been exposed
and explored and hated and loved and believed and
denied and stood on, what's left is seeing things
from *every* side. Joni Mitchell said it quite well. She
narrowed it down to "both sides now", yet truly,
once you notice there is more than one side as a valid
option, then the next obvious thing is to notice that
there are no sides at all. There is only One.

We are as divided as we'll ever be. There is no place

left to go, except together.

We must notice our humanity."
~

"Welcome 2019 with an open and willing heart.

Leave those pointing fingers behind and wrap them around someone's hand instead.

Next year, follow only one lead. Your heart will guide you always towards love. Whatever trends, explodes, shouts or tweets around you, remember this: The goal of division has been realized. This was not your goal, but an experimentation in manipulation of energy and emotion. This time now is for another purpose and a different goal. Pick one that serves you, that helps your fellow human, that promotes love, that allows expansion, that facilitates growth, that bolsters prosperity, that provides healing and that feels like joy.

You get to. It's your turn.

You are the one you've been waiting for.
You have anchored the light.
It is done."
~

Drops of Light

And this was our focus as we began the year 2019...

~

"2019 is the year of manifestation.

What will you create?

Dream big, dear one. Whenever you can. Do not plan as much as experience each coming moment. Utilize your imagination. See Paradise. Visualize Freedom. Feel Joy. Think on Peace. Actualize Laughter.

With the holiday season so recently finished, a reflection of what was reported may help us. Reports of relatives "telling it like it is" (both positive and negative) were mixed with "it was a quiet holiday, we mostly talked" and "we didn't go anywhere this year, just stayed in and caught up, played games, it was nice".

These stories of time spent with honesty and reflection were heard so often that I came to expect them. 2018 ended quietly and together.

I'm struck by the lack of eyeball-to-eyeball contact in social media, and how, with this trend of filming every conversation we have and then posting it, we seem to be yearning for it, seeking it, paying for it even. There are no pretenses or fancy studios with wardrobe or make-up. We want to see each other, feel each other, know each other.

We **need** to.

This is all part of our awakening as One.

Regardless of how far removed from ourselves technology seeks to take us, we yearn for home. Home is truth.

Home is where we reside. We reside in that place when we connect. We connect heart to heart, one to one, person to person, you to me."

~

James Gilliland coined for us a new term early that year: "Truckma". This, as opposed to "Karma". If "Karma" is a gentle version of driving straight into what you once left behind, then "Truckma" feels, instead, like being hit by a mack-truck…

~

"Truckma comes full speed, downhill, on a cliff. There is no escape. There are no explanations. There will be a mess when it is over, and there will be casualties. 2018 was filled with Truckma for me.

Right up until it began, (December 2017) there were feelings of "I've got this", "I know there is personal work to be done but basically, I am not in too bad a shape." Who was I kidding?

Then: Truckma. It manifested as serious, sudden & terrifying illness for me and multiple family members, painful relationship breakups and breakdowns, near fatal automobile accidents, to name just a few; each of which are still being deciphered in real time. I'd like to say that with hindsight their reasons and lessons are clear, but I cannot. I don't think that was the point.

What Truckma does is it leaves you humble. It levels the playing field, erases the irrelevant, raises more questions than it answers and **it questions the purpose of everything you do**."

~

My higher self & I had this conversation…

~

"What you must do, my child, is comfort your deepest wound.

"How?"

It is healed only with love. It cannot be erased, yet it can be super-imposed with feelings of actual love. This feeling of actual love comes to you from only one Source, and that is self.

You have to **release expectations.**

Keep talking to others, in any way that you can.

There was nothing for a moment
"Are you still with me?"

I am. One day you will realize that I have never left you."

~

Our Pleiadian friends started out the year with this message...

~

"I feel that there are many of you here, more than one, more than three.

We are seven. We have come to introduce to you now, some of our sub-categories of contact. You see, some humans hear us in this manner and telepathically. Others are in direct communication and although the ideas are shared telepathically in those cases, there is also a visual component.

Some of you have clear recall.

Others have dreams and still others see us in this physical realm. For those of you able to see us, it was an arrangement made prior to now.

Our messengers are many.

Our messages, you will discover, are suited to the audience and the transmitter of them.

Your readers want to know if they'll have contact. Contact in this current life place. The answer is an individual one, yet we are pleased to tell you that, &

especially right now in your collective awareness &
cycle — what you find yourselves drawn to, and interested in, is absolutely telling you more about who you
are than what is in store for you.

There is no focus without consequence.

There is no focus irrelevant.

Those of you now finding your way to these words
do so because we are connected and have experienced worlds together.

Our memories co-mingle.

You are not alone, and visits from us will most assur-
edly happen in this current life-cycle.

In order to prepare, you will have to de-sensitize
yourselves. We do not follow an earth-written protocol, and it can be off-putting and feel strange to you
to be around us, while at the same time feel very
much like home.

Ideas of love and acceptance will have to take precedence in your heart. These, over thoughts of **alien**
and **fear**.

You will not recognize us precisely, but magnetically
the pull will be there.

You'll have to trust that pull. It will not be because we are doing something to you to cause you to accept us. These are tricks perpetrated by your own kind.

You won't forget meeting us.

When we show up physically for you, it will be because you are ready to accept us.

We look as you look and there will be no physical recoiling.

These are things you have heard, most likely.

What you may not know is how quickly you'll accept our arrivals and interactions as commonplace. It will coincide with our initial arrival.

In other words, we will not land and leave; but stay and interject ourselves into your world."
~
A reader, Djon, predicted in January that the Guardian would return in a few months. He did! In March, the Guardian greeted us this way...
~
"Hello Dear Friend Sophia!
IT'S BEEN A LONG TIME! Hey? :)
I have returned!

My apologize for not being with You or Anyone
287

during passed time. **How was Time of Revelation?** It hits pretty hard, but overall, everything is nice and great as I see and that is awesome for Everyone! :)

How was Your time, Sophia? What important I missed while I wasn't here? Tell everything, I will be happy to hear anything! ;)"
~

He stayed with us until December of 2019. The last information he left us with can be found on his blog page on the web site. It was what he said were unknown truths about our human history. It was available in Russian, and that was his source for it. He said at the time that he wasn't sure how long he'd be around. We have not heard from him since (It is September of 2023).
~

And here are the things that mainstream media told us we should be focused on in 2019…
~

"Empire" actor **Jussee Smollett's claim** of a "hate crime.

The mosque **mass-shooting in Christchurch, New Zealand**, where fifty people died.

The kidnapping of Jayme Closs, and her parent's murders.

The **embellishment of some student's college applications** to elite institutions, paid for by their wealthy parents.

The **grounding of the Boing 737 Max**, after two airplane crashes and over 300 deaths.

The **fire at the Notre Dame cathedral in Paris**, and the destruction of its 850-year-old spire.

The **first-ever photo of a black hole**, which was put together using the Event Horizon Telescope.

Robert Mueller's 400-page "Russian Interference in the 2016 Election" report. Not enough evidence of criminal conspiracy was found in all those pages.

Archie was born to Prince Harry and Meghan Markle.

Theresa May resigned as Prime Minister of Great Britain. **Boris Johnson took over.**

There were **student-led protests** about government policy in **Hong Kong** that lasted for 6-months.

The **US Women's National Soccer Team won its fourth world cup.**

The **Amazon Rainforest** had more than 70,000 **wildfires**.

A **20-day manhunt in Canada for 2 teenage boys** who were murder suspects. It ended when they were found dead by self-inflicted gunshot wounds.

Jeffrey Epstein died by "suicide" while awaiting trial in a NYC prison.

Two US mass shootings within 24 hours, in Texas and Ohio, took the lives of 31 people.

16-year-old climate activist **Greta Thunberg** spoke at the UN "Climate Action Summit".

Bombings in Sri Lankan churches and hotels left more than 200 people dead.

The **first "all female" spacewalk** took place outside the International Space Station.

Drops of Light

Australia's Cardinal George Pell, was **convicted of sexually abusing two choirboys** while he was archbishop of Melbourne.
Lung illness due to vaping, not smoking, was found to possibly be linked to dozens of deaths in the US.
A volcano erupted on White Island in New Zealand, with sixteen fatalities as a result.
President Donald Trump was impeached over the testimony of an unidentified "whistleblower", who said he had "abused his office for personal gain". This was not quite "mainstream", but it happened, and with it, came a great deal of disclosure. It was a newly released film by Chad Calek - "Two Face: The Grey". It was a sequel to "Sir No-Face".

~

Blog posts & messages reflected our learning & our subsequent progression...

~

"The freedom of a race comes from more than removing shackles.

I sense more here...

You do. Many are here.

Our unified presence is due to the threshold crossed by mankind in this now moment.

I sense the presence of One.

I am here Sophia. You have sensed correctly.
It is I. It is One.
This message comes, however, differently than those
in our past conversations.
This is due to the current moment.

For oneness is upon your doorstep and it is a sight to
see - there are many voices.
This unification that happens does so as the separation collapses.
The separation collapses ("dissolves" is actually a better word), as each voice is recognized as necessary
parts of the whole.

Love does that.

It recognizes "other" as a bit of its (own) makeup,
that at the moment it is being observed and considered is providing a platform for emotion.

Emotion, once recognized as the learning tool that it
is, needs a platform on which to be expressed.
Once expressed, it can then be witnessed and experienced.

Experiencers do so from many vantage points - they
could be right on the plat-form and feeling the emotion as they are having it - thus demonstrating it for
all others.

Drops of Light

These others may be witnessing it first-hand so that they get the full force of its expression incorporated into a moment in their life.

Or...

They could be hearing about it after it took place, via social media communications. What these differing possibilities provide for you, dear humans, are moments in which you can and do choose the depth and intensity of this life lesson, this love lesson.

All action is a gift. All reaction is always a choice. All response is a decision. It is through making decisions, **responding with full depth of character and emotion and then following through with further action that agrees with that decision**, that true growth happens.

You have, oh so gradually, and some would say **not very** gracefully, reached here today to a pivotal stimulus for rapid growth.

Examine your life, your observance of emotions played out on various platforms before you.

Choose absolutely. No longer are you looking at the carrot on the stick. It is not out of reach. Yet in order to do so you'll have to use the right tool. You are equipped for this.

Love allows for a response that does not flatter or conform, but instead assures there is genuine compassion and...

I'm not hearing anything.

This, my dear, dear human, would be because **the response of absolute pure love has words that define it that remain unused in your vocabulary.**

(Wow!)

You will have to allow them to appear and the only way to do that is to let your mind go blank for a moment.

Will you do that? Now?

Yes.

Fortitude, generosity, self-effacing, courageous, gentle, fierce, nonplussed.

I feel as if I need to stop you there. These are many words with a great many definitions*.

* *Compassion* - sympathetic pity and concern for the sufferings or misfortunes of others
Fortitude - courage in pain or adversity
Generosity - the quality of being kind and generous

Drops of Light

Self-effacing - not claiming attention for oneself; retiring and modest
Courageous - not deterred by danger or pain; brave
Gentle - moderate in action, effect, or degree; not harsh or severe
Fierce - showing a heartfelt and powerful intensity
Nonplussed - (of a person) not disconcerted; unperturbed.

Yes. This is what together forms **the composite structure of a pure love response**.

~

"Love is massive, everywhere, and beyond definition. Like the air, you only need to breathe it in and **allow its release.**

Relationships, by definition, exist between two separate unique individuals. The only way they work is when each of the partners establish boundaries and rules for their crossing. If the rules aren't followed, the boundaries fail, and the relationship eventually follows suit.

What I'm attempting to say here, is that it is not the love that needs the boundaries in order to exist – **it is the relationship**. The love exists regardless."

~

"The ego is a powerful paintbrush.

It holds onto each drop of color, knowing any

minute the perfect placement will emerge. It waits, unpainted potential.

You notice, and hurriedly rush to coat it with, well, with you. Yet, right now those colors look wrong. No, not wrong yet out of place. Like the mustard yellows and olive greens of your grandmother's kitchen.

These are yesterday's hues… complaining, blaming, self-pity, self-absorption, righteousness, judgment, hoarding and hating. They no longer work.

Today requires a new pallet; more luminous and a bit less dense. Shades of understanding, patience, response, action, collaboration, humility, generosity and compassion create the look you seek.

These new colors need a skilled artist; yet this is why **you** hold the brush."
~

"These are not regular days. These are the ends of days. **You are not following a path – you are forging one.**"
~

"Each day it seems someone else is "called out publicly"; an old tape/recording found of something said, something done, something or someone harmed, ridiculed, insulted or infringed upon."
~

Some reptilians shared their insights…
295

Drops of Light

~

"I'm sorry, who are you?

We come to you now in an effort to assist. We are those whom you've labeled on a negative scale, along with the ones on your planet called lizards.

You are reptilian?

Our appearance is similar to that of your reptiles. We are attempting to transmit an image...

I see reds and golds...I also see tails.

Yes. You are picking it up then. This is helpful. May we continue now?

Go ahead then.

Our information has to do with subterfuge, with stealth, with intentional mis-direction. It has been and is being used now by not only the controllers but by "lackeys". Those with no power who are only interested in gaining a few minutes of fame. Many of these types are present in your population.

They are generally "asleep" and have only a limited sense of the "big picture" of life. Their version typically includes delusions of grandeur. It is **not**, as you may be imagining...

I am getting all of your ideas as a body of knowledge now, rapidly and too fast for me to transcribe...If you'd slow down a bit it would be more accurate a transcription. I have to get this on paper.

Yes. We see that. We will temper our transmission for you then.

Thank you.

It is not, as many are imagining, specific extremists who are members of a religious sect who are willing to carry these acts of terror out.

The population is getting to the point where there is nothing to lose. They are inundated with apocalyptic scenarios and are broke, sick and lonely.
This has been a gradual degradation. The self-glorification now available with instant social media, coupled with large numbers living isolated lives of loneliness and routine are creating a population of younger beings who are all too eager for attention - at any cost.

The easy availability of violent media has made death a hobby with little impact - turn the game off and the players all disappear, only to be re-animated then at any time.

Drops of Light

You are not then, under attack by any specific entity - but by the same group who has played this end game many times. They have brilliant methods of deception and distraction.

The easiest part of a successful operation is in the story told. If it comes from the right source, an authoritative one, it will be believed. What the population has been schooled in is that how someone dresses, where they work, how much money they have or what color their skin is, are valid indicators of their integrity and honesty. All of this was intentional.

So, rule **# 1** is have **a believable and authoritative source** for all explanations and answers.

Rule **#2** is **the element of surprise**. Once a target has been used, it is all important to abandon that location and use another. Any other. This will increase the level of fear overall.

Rule **#3** will be to **vary the specifics**. Meaning age of victims, time of day, country, type of weapons used, how they are used.

Rule **#4**. Remove all doubt as to guilt of suspects by **planting evidence** at their home. This could be done with or without their knowledge.

Rule **#5. Use perpetrators willing to go out in a blaze of glory.**

Rule **#6.** Have **plenty of "coincidental" circumstances** in place days or weeks prior to the event - job loss, unusual travel, drug use, comments by "a friend". In truth, these perpetrators are most often brain-washed, drugged, triggered loners. There will be few, if any, "friends" available to offcr valid appraisals of their mental state.

Rule **#7.** Use a host of accomplices to create an effective film of the event - meant to be played and played and played. These are known as **"crisis actors"**.

Rule **#8.** Create **massive media coverage** in places where it is not found typically. Be comprehensive in scope. You are creating fear at all costs.

It becomes critical then that those of you versed in the falsity going on **do not succumb to fear yourself**. The balance will eventually shift from fear to trust, but only with constant effort.

These are expert tactics and they will always be there waiting to shock you. **Do not be fooled**. This game isn't yet over. And even once **love prevails**, it will be some time and generations before mistrust, fear and power tactics are <u>not</u> common occurrences.

Drops of Light

It took many generations to make this absolutely mind-controlled state. The efforts were deliberate and innocuous initially. This blatant manipulation is only obvious because you've woken up. Many are waking up each day.

The numbers of sheep are diminishing, yet desperation is an obvious part of this end game - as was planned at its outset.

The reason we speak to you is because you offer hope and love - more exponentially powerful emotions than fear, if quieter.

Our race is one that played the game of deception in many arenas. There are among you now, many warriors with memories of lifetimes in conflict. Some of those exist on both "sides".

In truth, it is one continuing saga, played out together and its ultimate conclusion already stands as the only possibility.

Where it pops up on the journey is determined by the intents and beliefs of the ones taking this trip.

That would be you. It is for this reason we wanted to say to you now -

Hope and belief should rise to the top of your exhalations! Absorb the fear and watch as it dissipates. **What will remain is an enlightened populace, capable of dominance yet not likely to use it.** Instead, they'll witness the creation of a new era, one they pulled out of the darkest time known to all of creation.

It is this we are all watching for - the human version of realized essence. It promises to be capable of all expressions, resulting in something never before seen.

Note – This is being written in 2023; those 8 "rules" look, very obviously, to be the Pandemic's "rulebook" for 2020."

~

       The Pleiadians added their observations…

~

"As we witness your current planet in what appears to be escalating chaos, we simultaneously watch **a most extraordinary circumstance**. It is a reaction of some sort to the escalation of energy that looks like fear. The reaction is more of a response, we suspect, and it is showing up naturally.

That is, it seems to be a by-product. Something automatically occurring in the lightworkers/volunteers who've shown up for this moment now on earth. It is showing up in equal volume to the fear (*meaning the fear/chaos that is present on the planet right now*), and **it is**

power. It is steadfast love. It is pure light.

This is not something that any of you are trying to do or even attempting to carry out (*meaning consciously and on purpose*).

It seems to be an effect that is triggered by the escalation into chaos that occurs now on earth.

Please hear what we are saying as we feel it will encourage you and even validate your purpose.

It is as if there is something that had to happen.

A recognition perhaps of a moment or circumstance or specific level of demonstrable fear. (*And*) that this level, once reached, has had the effect of **turning up your light's force.**

And without any conscious effort **you are working as a team to carry Gaia through her transition."**

~

And this blog post was shared that April…

~

"I died this morning.
It was right before I woke up.
I woke up from the dream then; the dream where I died.

In that moment, the dying moment, not the waking

up moment, I knew everything.
I felt myself die. It was as real as real is.
It was visceral.

I actually died this morning.

I knew that I was dying, and, in that eternal moment, I knew that it was not me that was dying at all.

*It was **the idea of me** that died.*

The idea of me is what had been alive this whole time. Alive in the dream. The dream where I died. The idea of me included everyone I know right now, everyone I love right now and everyone who I was, in that dying moment, leaving right now.

Yet, I wasn't leaving at all. I was right there.
I was watching myself leave, feeling myself die and simultaneously seeing the truth about death. **Death ends only an idea.**

This idea, that ends with death, is an idea held by me alone. Me. Alone.

This idea of a solitary death was my first revelation.

Not that I was alone when I died, because I wasn't. I was with everyone that my life is about.

Drops of Light

This life, the one I am living right now.

In that eternal death moment, I realized a profound truth.

I saw what it was all about, and there is no easy way to say this.

It was all about me.

I died alone because I lived alone.

Alone is not quite accurate because the word "alone" invokes a comparison to something, as in "not in the company of others".

I died alone *while in the company of others*; that would be more precise.

The others didn't die. My idea of them *as my puppet masters* did.

Equate a death moment to watching a puppet, a puppet with strings. During all of its life, it imagines those strings. They are operated by the most important people, events, illnesses, circumstances and abilities in that puppet's "life".

The puppet dies when the strings are cut.

Now dead, the puppet, who is no longer attached to anyone or anything at all, stands up. It moves freely on its own. It leaves.

Yet it is not dead and not gone. The *idea of itself as a puppet (which was how it had lived its entire life) is the only part that "died".*

In death, the puppet sees its strings for what they are. The puppet is not really a puppet at all. It held an idea of itself as a puppet only. In death, it walks away. It leaves that idea behind.

In that moment, the puppet has a revelation. It realizes it was never about anyone or anything else, never about how they moved it or where they pushed it or pulled it or inspired it or devalued it or loved it or hated it or "wronged" it or helped it or stopped it from going. *It was always moving on its own.*

Always.
All alone.
The puppet only imagined the puppet masters.

In death, the puppet leaves behind the idea of itself as a puppet. **The puppet**, the one holding this idea of itself as a puppet, **is still going strong**.

The level of importance that the puppet gave to the puppet masters is irrelevant upon its death.

Drops of Light

None of that matters.

It was always the puppet in control.

Always about the puppet.

The second revelation was more than likely the reason I woke up.

This was a dream. A dream where I died.

I actually died this morning.

That moment, that dying moment, held everything and everyone and every time and no time at all. That dying moment held eternity.

Death is not real. I watched my death, felt my death and witnessed all of me continue as it happened.

It was simple, miraculous, astounding, quick and forever.

This all of me that continued, watched an idea disappear; the idea of me.

This idea disappeared in an instant. This is the instant that we call "death".

This moment encompassed the whole.

Immediate comprehension of the meaning and purpose of life itself, resulted.

Yet it felt as if *I had merely turned a page.*

There was no pain, no fear, no pearly gates or white light. It was a moment of recognition, of awareness, of truth.

It was shocking in its simplicity, its purity, its fullness.

It was an eternal nanosecond.

Death holds forever in its grip and is not at all as advertised.

This idea of waking up, which happens after death, is truth.

I died last night and then I woke up. Nothing is the same.

You are, in every sense, me. You are not mirrors, reflecting me, *you are me.* I only imagine that you show me who I am. In truth, I am showing myself. I am only using you to do it.

When I died last night, I knew deeply and internally

Drops of Light

that it was actually *and only* me all along. Then I woke up. I woke up this morning.

From one dream, the one where I died, to this dream, the one where this idea of me (*as Sophia*) is now telling you about it in this blog post.

I died last night and today I feel absolutely and specifically alive. More so than I ever have.

Do not be afraid of death nor seek it.

You are so much more than you realize."
~
"Here are words you may not hear today. Perhaps not ever. Yet they are yours. Unwrap the feeling that encases them and feel now the radiance of your soul. For you are exquisite and no one has told you this. Hear me now. For all those times of pretend smiles and fearful shattering's… I've seen you. I've felt you. I've held you.
My wings, unseen, encase your heart.
Dear one, nothing can subtract from your worth. Bruised, beaten, disregarded and dismissed – you shine. There is nothing insignificant about you. **Nothing compares to your light**.
You are loved without limit, adored beyond restraint; a cherished bit of radiance all squished into a human. You, yes you, are perfect. Take that in. Now breathe. It's going to be all right.

You've got this."

~

"There are other things you may need to hear. Perhaps these are not obvious things, yet they are true things.

You exist beyond your skin. That part of you, the essence that was gently ushered in to this body of yours, encases you completely with love.
Astounded by the grace and fortitude you walk in each day; it blazes forth with pride and oozes compassion.

You are cherished beyond what you know is possible. Feel that. Hold it close.

Dear, dear human, you are doing the best you can, *and your best is enough*. In every moment and with every effort, you fulfill your mission here.

What is that mission, you wonder?

It is to explore life itself. It is to respond with passion to every nuance you are presented with, to the best of your ability, with all of your current wisdom and as much consideration as you believe is necessary. It is to live, full out. It is to offer this one precious life of yours, maximum expression and deep curiosity. It is authentic exploration of all that you are.

Drops of Light

For you are so much more than you know. And it is your discovery of yourself that supports life itself; bolstering each of us, embracing all of us, expanding the whole of us – Oneness.

So, **thank you, radiant one, for joining our journey and for lighting the way.** Your efforts have been noticed and you are so very much appreciated for all of them, past, present and future.

Without you, there can be no us.

And we, are the ones we've been waiting for."

~

In May, the Pleiadians gave us a protocol to use when seeking their assistance. ***"I enlist the assistance of the Pleiadian Pods."*** *This was eventually translated into multiple languages, and pinned to the top of their blog page on the website. It's still there. With these words came a reminder of how powerful our intent is.*

The following message from Poseur, received a few years prior, seems to fit these discussions about healing our physical selves…

~

"This is a physical world, and to accomplish an alteration of the physical means a departure from thinking of it as final and complete. Rather, regard the pain, the body, all with skepticism and ask – "who are you and what right do you have to occur this way in my creation?"

Refuse to observe a way that does not serve your intent. Only observe the possibility of wholeness and completeness that serves your desire.

This is your creation, all of it is. Everything you take in and regurgitate is creative. Consciousness is all the time. What do you want?"
~

In July, the entire Sovereignty series, a total of 20 conversations with One from 2013-2014, was finally converted into audio files and shared on Soundcloud as well as on the website. This was felt to be some of the most important work accomplished to date.
~

In August, my partner and I got caught up in what we were told was an "inter-galactic feud". We were deceived by a group claiming to be the Pleiadians whom I had been speaking with for years. Here's some of what happened...
~

"It is I. It is One. How may I assist you, Sophia?

Thank you for coming forward.
We've had two instances where someone from outside this dream, beyond this dimension/assumption has come in and altered things.
(The first one concerns my partner and isn't relevant to this conversation)
Then, I was woken at 2 in the morning and told that it was

Drops of Light

the P's and they wanted to set up a situation with some local P's and myself and my mate to hold and house and share their healing pods with the world. Meetings were arranged and never materialized. Obviously, these are lies and we feel manipulated and unsure how to regain any sense of control here.
Who is doing this?
For what purpose?
How can we stop this and prevent any other intrusions like this?
These are my questions today. Thank you for considering them. We are quite upset.

Sophia. Certainly, you are aware that there are beings beyond your realm and existing in assumptions with other boundaries – boundaries that encompass your current earth's working level and moving beyond it. In these assumptions, the rules differ, as do methods. There are no access points for you currently into these. You have not achieved a vision that reaches there.
It is, as you imagine, like looking into the sky without your night vision goggles, and then with them.
Entire worlds exist that you have not been able to see or to interact with.

Yes, okay, but in this circumstance, they've not only seen, but interfered with us.

Yes. This has occurred for you because you both come from elsewhere.

That is not satisfactory and does not answer anything.
They are not in this dream, not recognizable to our higher
selves.
How is this possible? Why is this happening? Who are they?

This is not a singular force. More than one instance and source have interfered.

(Here, the situation with my partner, which had occurred a few weeks ago, was explained. The explanation satisfied all of us, and included the following words:
"This is due in a great extent to the level of unity achieved by the being and by your partner, who, at the time was beyond the 3D realm and easily seen/reached.")

For the question around the clear deception regarding the Pods, there is a different answer and one that may disturb you.

These, the ones who spoke to you as the "P's" and offered physical manifestation, were and are **not** the P's. You've been deceived.

This is not strictly off world technology or beings. This is a force interested in undermining the efforts of the Pleiadians.

It is an effort to put doubt in the minds of the earthlings as to the beneficial nature of the P's.

Yes, you were contacted. And yes, they "sounded" as exuberant as your friends the "P's" typically do. The 2AM time frame is a hint at this deception and the fact that you noticed gives credence to your power of

discernment Sophia – don't lose sight of that.
Once the deception was made and you believed it
was the P's, no further effort on their part to deceive
you was needed.

The plan was to have you disregard your faith in the
P's and their words and more importantly, their **tech**.

Remember here something crucial, you **do** create
your own reality. Once you believe or disbelieve
something, it is made manifest for you.

Just recently your voice gained a larger audience. Had
you advertised your fiasco, disappointment and subsequent disillusion with the P's and Pods, then a
whole lot of forward momentum and **sovereign
thought** would have been halted as well.
What their aim was/is to discredit the P's, not you
personally. There are old feuds that do not involve
you.
Your words could discredit their efforts. This is what
the goal was.

It does not mean your work is targeted by anyone in
control on your planet. **You got caught in an inter-
galactic feud.**

How did they come in past my declarations then?
I declare "Complete truth regarding your origin and identity
"and I did that every time. Yet I see now that I asked for them

and defined them specifically from the beginning. I asked to speak to the P's directly, the "ones who woke me".

Yes. And it is in your own definition, your own words, they slipped in. The Poseur taught you how powerful words are. Now use them. Use them every time and **be clear of intent.**
You remain the most powerful beings here, if unaware.
Do not despair. In both instances your power remains strong and you would say defined more clearly because of what occurred. It is not beyond the dream, but you are bringing in factions not usually dealt with — by your higher selves.

In order to regain control, you only need to extend your vision and intentions to reach areas as yet unseen and not known. This can be done with belief and intent.
You are getting stronger. In order for this trend to continue there will be greater expanses of influence within your lives.

You've chosen expansion while living human lives, all occurring in synchronization with global awakening and human expansion of awareness. This may confuse the issue at times, yet it should not alter your perception.

Think always beyond your 3D perception when

something doesn't add up.

You are no longer targeted for take-down. You are continuously progressing and reaching new and unknown heights of influence and awareness and action.

Re-assert your trust in your power and your higher self. It is not diminished. In all cases it remains on a journey and is gaining experience. Experience for even more encompassing adventures.

I believe your questions are answered then.
Reach out if there are others.

Thank you."
~

    We talked a lot about creation and how to consciously control it, every single time...
~

"Conscious creation takes effort now because we've been put to sleep by a system of control. This was **their intent. It is time to utilize the force of ours**. Our intent, by our sheer numbers, will change everything.

The system was designed to overload our minds with ideas that weaken our resolve and lull us into conformity; making us submissive slaves.
Freedom is a natural outcome of creative self-

control.

We've come so far since we found each other here 8 years ago. By sharing stories, we help to increase our collective power, expand our expectations and solidify our beliefs. This will add the fantastic to our list of outcomes, and allow for the force of our light and the power of our love to run the show. We've got this."

~

"One had a message in October that included these words…"

~

"Things are about to pop.
These are delicate new beginnings.
You are about to see evidence of crimes exposed.
The levels of awareness and enlightenment have reached critical mass.

As One, you will see beneath the deception that constitutes your social structure."

~

And we continued our journey…

~

"Each of us came for this moment. It is upon us right now. It is not something that ends with any single thing. It is something that leads to **more**."

~

"There are so many things to forgive.
As our social media feeds light up with validation of

Drops of Light

what we have suspected for many years, we become out-raged, horrified and so, so saddened.

Our worst suspicions are now trending.
We are told they are but tips of deeply hidden ice-bergs.

This may feel like a sinking Titanic, *yet it will not go un-der.*

It is being held afloat by angels. It is being propelled aloft with powerful emanations from light beings. It is lit up with the seeds of the stars, here to carry it through.

We see the iceberg this time. It is not a surprise for us; not crashing into us in the dead of night.
We've been broadcasting its location for decades.

Some of us, those early trail blazers, have already gone on. They left a trail of warning lights for us, lighting our way.

There will be calls for executions. These will seem, at first, to be the only solution.

Yet, *and remember this part*, the energy we con-clude this era with, now becomes the soil for our next season of growth.
Our new world will not be built on blood-soaked

streets.

Fellow light carriers and star seeds, *you are here to show the way."*

~

"Time is not a linear construct. From any point it moves in all directions. It is more like a sphere. As we vibrate more quickly, we access more possibilities.

Time is not linear, nor does it follow any specific form of measurement. **All moments are now."**

~

"Here's a bit of a telepathic conversation that happened about 2 years ago *(2017)* with a non-earth life form. It feels relevant to what we face on the planet right now; part and parcel to our Ascension.

"You are learning of the origin of life itself as your life forms expand consciousness. The intelligence of all of it, comes from all of it.

It is not that One Supreme Being commands the air, minerals, water, gases, etc., to behave in a certain fashion in order for life to be promoted. The instructions come from all parts of the whole themselves. The Supreme Being is then One.

All is unified by purpose and goal. The initiation, development and experience of growth, collaborates to create life. It appears (in) as many ways as there are possibilities, and these are infinite.

As the expansion for you continues, you will be asked by everything around you to be considerate, and demonstrate compassion. It is in this act alone that a unified existence thrives and expands."

I believe that compassion is the final stage of this Ascension."
~

The Pleiadians were asked a lot of questions in the last quarter of that year about the healing pods and how they work. Here's just one of the responses they gave us…
~

"What would seem most helpful is letting go – a letting go of the pictures painted for you, we notice, by words.

These words come from your current medical establishment. Words are not innocuous or harmless or merely informative and explanatory. Words such as cancer and tumor and chronic and genetic are loaded with energy. This is the barrier we see.

This is not to chastise or implicate you in wrong action. It is to shine light on your inner vocabulary, which speaks to you nonverbally as a response to your outer vocabulary.

Rather than thinking and speaking definitively, with diagnosis and conditions, it will assist you to speak and think of symptoms. Then, once their healing has been created, either through intent or desire – **let even those words go**.

As you see your body, mind and spirit as a whole and unified in voice, this gets easier and easier."

~

In November, "Tales from the Front" was started on the blog; a place to relate/share the changes we were all noticing...

~

"I woke this morning, opened my eyes and before them was what I'll call a vortex, a spiral. It was swirling very quickly, bright light and shadow, which defined/outlined the spinning lines of movement. I looked around a bit. It was everywhere my eyes looked. I closed my eyes.

The vortex was still there. White light and shadows whirling quite quickly. I realized then that this was real (as opposed to being a "trick of the eyes"). I sort of adjusted my shoulders, sat up, leaned back and smiled. This was going to be fun!

There was **no fear**.

With open eyes, I looked around a bit to see if it was a stationary thing or my perception/view of reality. The vortex moved with my gaze and was everywhere that I looked. It was not stable or in one place in the room.

I just watched. I had the thought "I wonder where we are going?" I did not experience a sense of movement but of transformation; *transformation of our reality*.

To describe a bit of what I was seeing: it was not a tunnel and I did not feel as if I was seeing beyond its beginning. I felt as if I was watching our reality shift/change.

As I watched, the distinct lines of the swirling vortex grew fainter and it eventually became a white light. It was still moving/swirling but pure white now; there were no shadow lines to be seen.

As I watched, this mass of white light also faded into the surrounding color of the wall or whatever was "behind" where I was looking. It grew fainter and fainter as the movement became less of a swirling vortex and more of a circular/spinning vibration.

Eventually this became the color of the wall but with a localized circular/spinning vibration beneath it. Gradually this converted into only a vibration (no longer circular or localized) and when it did, it seemed as if the entire wall and room was actually vibrating.

This vibration slowed down and eventually, everywhere I looked appeared to be stable once more.

The whole thing took less than 10 minutes and perhaps only 5 minutes. I am not sure. Time was irrelevant to it."

~

"What we believe and thus think about and then imagine becomes our life. It is not that love or freedom or health or any sort of shift happens beyond our own frequency. It is that our frequency, (*our energy*) creates a state in which love or freedom or prosperity or vitality or anything else, exists as a possibility and then… it is.

The overwhelming nature of corporate controlled mass media is, therefore, the most powerful weapon/tool available. We now carry this manipulation tool around with us, in our devices. Think about that."

~

"This change that you see all around you, is merely a physical mirror for an inside alteration. Within and beyond are merely perspectives. We place them both in perfect balance so that our life is realized and remembered full. Remembered by us. The ones doing the placing and the living.

We've divided ourselves completely so that we can one day come back together. It will happen

Drops of Light

when there is no other thing to do; when there are no other choices to choose. When the only thing we can see, that holds us together, is our humanity. When we are together huddled at the bottom of this mess, needing each other to climb up and out, with and on and around. It'll be the same answer for all of us then. Nothing to argue about. "Take my hand. Let's do this."

You are creators - what you create, you become. Every single time.

You are exquisite. A being of unimaginable brilliance residing in skin and bones, with bruises and beatings and heartaches and headaches and unimaginable pain.

You've been lied to and there is a reason that you are still standing. It is because you knew that when the world was collapsing, **you'd be needed**."
~

"I had the chance to see the film "Frozen II" yesterday. The song "Show Yourself" includes the line *"You are the one you've been waiting for"*.
It is thrilling to see how we, as One, have now created a commercial and mainstream version of our journey."
~

"2019 slams its doors for one last time. We wonder what else has ended. We peek at what is gestating.

Division has escalated. In our most intimate defini-
tions of ourselves, our sexual identity, there are new
labels and additional lines drawn. Some say "This is
ridiculous!" "This is so confusing!" "This is bad!"
"This is a (*fill in the blank*) plot!" or "It's about time."

Instead, we might celebrate the possibilities this introduces. Options never before available are now out
loud. These previously labeled and hidden possibilities today lie out in the open, exposed for a new generation to choose from.

Welcome to multi-dimensionality - where you now
confront every unusual possibility and potential
choice. Soon you will embody them. For you and I
have done them all. If not here and now, at some
other where, during some other when.

From each perspective we are right. Snowflakes,
Maga hats, yellow vests, Boomers, Millennials, Jewish,
Christian and Muslim each carry truth and hold ac-
cess to things we can all learn from.

Step away far enough and you'll see both the ending
and beginning. It's a circle. **Acceptance is birthed in
embodiment."**

~

*Before we leave 2019, let's hear a few "off-world" con-
versations. I spoke with Elders, Bigfoot, the 8th dimension, a
Hindu god, One, an ancient race, aquatic beings, bat-like*

Drops of Light

beings, a Lyran, doctors, scientists, someone from Orion, and others. Here are a few words that stand out...

~

An Elder: "A call was put out for help for the earth. To increase the light quotient to a sufficient enough level that the humans would evolve and end the reign of the controllers who prevented that with their slavery program.

You've answered the call and succeeded. The light quotient increased and the race is throwing off the controlling faction and evolving.

This evolution takes "time" to manifest in physical form on your earth.

What both complicates and speeds up the process is the one thing humans hold a very large amount of; **emotion**. Feelings become your battery and your downfall, your gasoline and your brakes.

What I want to share with you now is the inevitability of what is coming. It is the blossoming of a race held down, *now unchained*, by all things external."

~

One: "You have entered now a point of no return. It is as if you have chosen...*you have*. You **will** continue, for indeed you've decided to. You are here to assist, and you will. This cannot be stopped.

You are caught between two worlds right now. The pull of the old creates turbulence.

The calming and healing will be sustained.

Opposing forces cause this. It is responding to them (*the opposing forces*) and will continue to do so. Some (*people*) will be calmed and that will facilitate a predominant energy. This will help, **but it will not halt the friction.**

Some things have to be ridden through. In a physical way, you can use this (*meaning this rocky plane ride*) as a metaphor. **It is like this for the planet.**

I don't understand.

There is anger. Much has happened and been covered up, flat-out denied.

What will you do?

You harbor so much anger. You hold so much love. These beings are in your life right now and here for your unraveling, for you do deal with.

What will you do?
What is wrong? (*What is right?*)

Drops of Light

You will have to determine the best way to handle this.

It will not be handled easily or smoothly but you will get to the other end.

You've entered now the final phase of your Ascension. It is the **morphosis** stage - you are about to transform."

~

Emissaries of light: *How is your light essence different from the one I hold?*

"Oh Sophia, we thought we were clear at the outset - we are not different from you specifically - we are different as a whole from the light beings who originate in this galaxy.

This galaxy is not your origin.

We cannot make a general comparison with you.

Have you compared your light then to those who are from here?

Why, yes. We differ to a great extent from these beings.

The light they bear is concentrated. It is as if it has been held in stasis.

Indeed, it will be a wonder when it is "re-constituted" as it were, and all of its parts emerge in full form.
It will be wondrous indeed. It will be a surprise to us all, the humans included!

Yes.

Is there anything else you would ask of us?

Just one thing. As you are "scientists", have you ever seen light like this before, in your travels?

We have. Once.
It was held within a race of very, very dark beings who were stifled.
Their emergence was indeed magnificent and unprecedented.

The human has allowed its light to partially emerge and the end/the opening will not be as brutal for it.
Some are holding space to ease the transition.

Many who do so are children. Most who do so do not know they are doing so.

Is there anything else Sophia?

Not right now, no. Thank you for coming forward.

You're welcome!

Drops of Light

Be well, Sophia. You have the best seat in the house for this process."

~

Chapter 5
Noticing the Light within
(2020)

You begin to accept the Light within
as valid and true.
Yet, there is a cost to this acceptance,
as you identify it as a separator
between you
and what you perceive as
"not light".

Drops of Light

We strolled into that pivotal year...

~

In January I received information about a website: "Glamis Calling" which is a sort of portal for something called the WGC, or "World Governing Council". The site is still active in 2023. Researching it introduced a whole new level of "controllers", as well as specific instructions for Mankind's Awakening. To say that it is fascinating is an understatement. There are blog posts starting in 2016, there is a mention of "Q", and so much detail that by itself would be another very weighty book. Here's a quote from something that was posted there, in February of 2020:

"We, who are more accustomed to working in the dark, must tread lightly into a more public arena, but we understand we must enter that arena as part of our commitment to ethical stewardship."

2020 began in earnest...

~

"I am breathless with the force of this year...
Eyes opened cannot un-see.

What are these visions?

They are populated with personalities... Epstein, Weinstein, Trump, Bernie, Schiff, Thunberg, Biden, Hillary, Andrew, Putin, and places... Richmond, Iran, France, Puerto Rico, and things...yellow vests, Space

Force Uniforms, tic tac UFOs, and conditions…
coronavirus, autism spectrum disorder.
Wearing or holding each of these is a human.
A human. Like you and I. Each of us going through
this mass awakening. Together."

~

*Here's a partial recounting of what the mainstream
media directed our focus towards for that year. Although for
most of us, **2020 was a year that would never be
forgotten…***

~

The **coronavirus** travelled out of **Wuhan**, China and
made its way everywhere else; the WHO called it a
global pandemic that March and the world stopped.
Lockdowns, social distancing, 6 feet apart, 2 weeks to
"flatten the curve", masks, curbside delivery, zoom
meetings, temperature checks, closed businesses,
closed religious services, cancelled family gatherings,
"fact checkers" on social media, and an increase in
poverty, mental illness and suicides followed.

President Trump was impeached and acquitted.
The Olympics were postponed.
The death of **George Floyd** by a police officer
incited violent, fiery protests in multiple US cities
that summer.
Cardboard cutouts of fans were the only "people"
present when **US Major League Baseball** started
again in July.
Hurricane Laura devastated the Louisiana Gulf

Coast and was one of 12 named storms in a record-breaking year.

US Supreme Court Justice **Ruth Bader Ginsberg died; Amy Coney Barrett replaced her.**

Joe Biden was declared the winner of the US Presidential race that November. President Trump refused to concede.

Covid-19 vaccines arrived that December.

Qasem Soleimani - one of Iran's most senior military figures - was **killed in a US drone strike.** Days later, **Iran launched missiles** at bases in Iraq housing the US military, but no-one was hurt in the strikes.

A passenger plane was "unintentionally" shot down by Islamic Revolutionary Guard Corps. All 176 people aboard the Ukraine International Airlines flight were killed. Tensions escalated between the US & Iran all year.

Harry and Meghan announce their decision to "step back" as senior members of the British Royal Family.

Destructive bushfires destroyed millions of hectares of land, thousands of homes and an untold number of wildlife habitats and wildlife **in Australia**.

Oil prices fell dramatically.

The **"Abraham Accords"** was signed in August between Israel and the United Arab Emirates (UAE) providing hope for eventual peace in the Middle East as some other countries gradually joined.

Southwestern United States suffered a **prolonged drought. Western US** faced record breaking **wildfires**.

Belarus erupted with protests for free & fair elections after Alexander Lukashenko, a man known as "Europe's last dictator", claimed he had won 80 percent of the vote in the country's presidential election, thereby entitling him to a sixth term in office.

~

In the winter/spring, One asked me to write a series of books, 7 in total, about what was happening on the planet. I agreed. The first book in the "Words of One" series was published that June. The last was released about a year and ½ later. This meant that for most of that time, just about all of my telepathic conversations were with One.

Here are some other things we were talking about….

~

"If you had any questions about whether or not you were born in the right "time" or life, doubt no more. You've come for this and it happens now; *we need everyone's voice.* Can you feel the acceleration?"

~

"The hierarchy (*as I see it now*) here is pretty much laid out in this quote from Wikipedia:

"All forms of life were believed to have been created by Ra. In some accounts, humans were created from Ra's tears and sweat, hence the

335

Drops of Light

Egyptians call themselves *the "Cattle of Ra"."*

~

This is how the hierarchy appears to be organized, bottom up:

Humanity (the cattle) -->
Illuminati -->
Priest Class (Upper Chambers) -->
Queen of Illuminati (may be on same level as Upper Chambers, just different role) -->
Queen of England -->
(This next position is now vacant, but was filled until 2016) -->
RA

These are personal conclusions, drawn from personal conversations and my own research.

I am troubled with the following idea. It is the message being told, as some sort of explanation, that we are still under the control of a hierarchy in order to allow for a gentle and gradual letting go of the controls; *to avoid violence and destruction as we figure out how to lead ourselves.* It is too late for that.

Violence and destruction shout from every continent.

Instead, it appears that the real reason for this delay, is to allow those who sit at the wealthy and powerful end of the hierarchy to get whatever they want, and just as much as they can before it's over. Because they know it is over. But we do too."

"What troubles me is the moral conscience of the folks sitting up there at the top of the hierarchy. *I see no evidence of one.* What I also don't see is anyone taking responsibility to hold one. It would seem that the morally correct thing to do and asap, is to stop the abuse and torture and robbery of humanity at the hands of this "hidden hand". To see that it stops now, not at some future moment decided by someone not feeling either the abuse or torture or the robbery.

And it is in this question that our humanity is most revealed. It is the question of morality. **It is the hallmark of our species that we desire freedom and vitality and prosperity and love *for all of us.*** Not just a few of us. We *do have* a moral conscience."

~

"What feels like the end of days, is also the beginning of them. We are opening the package of our new earth. There is a lot of packaging that must be removed and it looks sort of a mess right now."

~

"We are being asked to become investigators into our core beliefs. It is these beliefs that will hold steady as this current reality devolves into a chaotic blend of media parrots and real heroes and true catastrophe. This is how a civilization becomes new. It must first be undone. Then it is re-imagined."

~

In those early, innocent, pandemic-saturated days, there was confusion and a fair amount of fear; our world had changed seemingly overnight. We were all trying to figure out what this new intruder was, and who we were as we dealt with it…

~

"We must build up more than our immune systems. We must strengthen our resolve with authenticity, and pad all of our interactions with compassion. Covid19 does not care what religion you believe in, who you love, how much land you own, what your title is, or what your education is."

~

"At the end of the day, we will all see each other. We've been hiding behind righteousness and anger and fear and despair and pretense, trying not to face each other.

The world needs you now. It does not need your opinions or your shame or your reasons for either. It needs your strength. It needs your light. It needs your help."

~

"More than once I've been assured that "a cure exists" *(for COVID-19).* Actually, from three different sources, none of them human. I have not been told precisely what that cure is. So, is it a vaccine? I doubt it, as there are many of us who wouldn't want one/trust one. Is it something else, non-medicinal? I do not have that information. I've come to understand that this story is more complex than we know. It must play out in a scenario that allows "highest and best for all concerned" to evolve *as we collectively intend it.*

That means there are reasons, not obvious, for the outbreak at all. As well as reasons, not obvious, for the things we are being told by government and health officials. *This is not* the fulfillment of the Georgia Guidestones to:

"Maintain humanity under 500,000,000 in perpetual balance with nature."

This virus will die off and there will be plenty of us still here when it does.

Yet this *is* biblical. There are now rivers running red and locust swarms, as well as a global pandemic. Yes, there are reasons in nature that exist to explain it all, yet realize what this means.

We've been told this would happen. Someone *had to be here* to tell us, and they actually wrote it down. We survive this, as have those who came before us. The virus was intended/created by those who would

Drops of Light

not become sick from it. *It is a bio-weapon."*
~

In late March, a new sort of series is begun on Me-
dium — "Corona-Daze". 17 installments chronicled the Pan-
demic in real time. Here's how the first entry began...
~

"In order of appearance, here are *2020's uninvited*
guests:

Fire. Australia is burning up.
Insects. Locusts are swarming Africa. F***ing locusts.
Plague. Wuhan can't breathe... An alarming virus has
surfaced, filling lungs and killing quickly. Initial explanation: Open air market + chemical warfare lab
within miles of
each other?   What??? This sounds like a #bio-
weapon. It is only January. This is looking to be a set-
up of biblical proportions.

Death of a loved one. Unexpected, and devastating all
of us who loved him. A huge loss.

Obsessed now with the path of this Wuhan Virus,
that is walking, driving, flying and sailing out of Wuhan without restraint.

Watching Chinese reporting. The rate of infection is
not statistically probable. Questions.

Stories emerging from some Chinese... saying not

thousands, but actually millions of people in Wuhan are dead. Shocking numbers. Reports of crematoriums operating 24/7. Satellite images seem to confirm this.

Beginning to feel fear… Reinforce my decision **never to get on a cruise ship.**

Who would do this? The crying begins in earnest… The World Health Organization won't call it a Pandemic. Yet.

Videos of Chinese citizens falling down dead in the streets. This is unreal.

Constant Twitter obsession… #Coronavirus. It is barely February. More videos of the Chinese people being boarded up in their houses. Wuhan looks to be imprisoned by its own government.

Having trouble sleeping. Phone is on 24/7, pinned on Twitter. Major purchases of vitamins, mushrooms, immune system supplements, canned food, liquor, cleaning supplies and toilet paper. It is still February, but later now.

Road trip, within our state, to visit family. Washed hands. A lot. Stayed in all weekend. Stopped checking Twitter for two days. It was wonderful. Return home and the Twitter obsession continues. #Coronavirus.

Drops of Light

#Covid19. New names and voices emerge. Can't sleep at all. Obsessively taking vitamin C and Chaga mushroom.

It is early March. China has shut down WeChat, so there are no more alarming videos. We must guess about the truth in Wuhan... And pray.
The focus changes now, to other emerging case levels in Europe. Italy, Iran, Spain...

We quit out-of-the-house activities that require social contact with groups. Family visit, here this time. We'd just found out there was a case of #Coronavirus confirmed just 2.5 miles away. Washed our hands. A lot. We did go out to dinner though. That would be the last time we were able to in the foreseeable future.

Found out there is a website that shows numbers of cases worldwide.
On March 9th there were 550 cases in the USA.

I am still staring at my phone. Watching Italy erupt and dissolve before our eyes...

Social distancing begins to be a thing here now in Illinois.

A family birthday dinner *was held over skype* between 3 households. This virus has instantly gotten very real. We laughed and joked and kept it light. After 1.5 hours, we all signed off. It was weird. There were no hugs. We agree to keep closer in touch now.

On March 15th there were 3499 cases in the USA.

My family finds out, that someone who attended a concert in which one of us performed last month, has tested positive for COVID19. We start looking at the calendar to see if the danger has passed. It seems unlikely that there could be infection at this point. We are tentatively relieved and wash down a few extra Vitamin C tablets.

My partner and I work from home and are still able to. The house is spotless and germ free.

One of our children works in the food industry and is right now on unemployment. Three others are able to work from home, at least for now, at some level. One of them manages a gym, and he sees the writing on the wall, yet scrambles to restructure and hopefully save the gym as a necessary community resource. Another one provides a vital community service as a manager and technician, so is still employed out of the house. But he has 2 co-workers who are ill, having returned from a conference in Las Vegas, Nevada before that city shut down. So, there are doubts and worries for him there.

A family wedding shower, scheduled for the end of March, is cancelled. It is unknown if the wedding, scheduled for May, will happen at all.

It is quiet outside. Our home is near an elementary school. Typically, there are families and children running back and forth to the playground there. This street is barren now.

The shock is morphing into reality as Illinois shuts down.

At this point, we had begun removing cash from our savings account as the interest rate approaches 0% and we are unsure whether or not the banks will fail. On 3.17.2020, the ATM at our local credit union was out of cash. It was late morning. We were not given any information as to why.

Later that night, it was functioning again. We continue making withdrawals, not huge ones, but regularly. Just in case.

Multiple videos of Hollywood types, looking pretty rough around the edges, surface this week, with bizarre references and questionable performances. Words like "fried fish" (Fe Fe) enter the lexicon. There are a great many images and references to roses.

Multiple government officials go missing or "self-quarantine".

On March 22nd there were 35,211 cases in the USA. That's about 10X the number of cases from a week earlier. It is doubling about every 2 days now, here in the USA. Knowing this is due to testing finally being available *doesn't stave off the alarm it raises for us.*

It is our anniversary. We have a nice meal delivered to celebrate. The driver leaves it on the front step, not even knocking on the door to tell us. He did text us when he did this, but we missed his text. It is like 28 degrees out and he leaves it almost 30 minutes before we expected it, so by the time we notice it, *it is dead cold.* Happy Anniversary in a new world. We are all adjusting to this new unsocial way of being human.

I begin reaching out to a few friends each day, checking in, saying hello, seeing if they need anything. Quarantine becomes the norm. Any sort of human contact is appreciated.

On March 24th, 2020 1/3 of the planet, or 2.5 billion humans were in some form of lock-down."

Drops of Light

~

The final installment (of the "Corona-Daze" series) was published in October 2020, and sounded a good deal different…
~

"This writer is done having her opinion skewed by newly emerging and conflicting data. She's gone from terrified to denial to anger to personal authority.

This virus is not separate from our awakening. It is enmeshed deep within it; its inroads weaving in and out of our individual awareness and confrontations with global conversation and self-talk. Through all of that, and as we approach the close of 2020, we come face to face with ourselves. It is, as it was always intended to be, a full circle journey and one that is inescapable. For you. For me. For us."
~

  The Pleiadians were still in contact, though less frequently. They said that they were in mass production, building the healing pods, but…

"I am so very conflicted about talking to you now. The world desperately needs the tech you have. Yet, it's not available.

We are saddened by your disappointment in our ability to help. We are discouraged as well. The world as it stands, is in such a divisive state. Half of the population refuses to accept an earth-born remedy that has been proven to work. How do you suspect they'd accept a tech from beyond earth?

There are still forces holding power, who are able to shut down what it is they desire to shut down. We will not put the operation at risk. We will arrive Sophia. When there is an open arena for acceptance we will arrive."

~

As the initial shock of the Pandemic wore off, we began to pull ourselves together, and utilize the possibilities now before us...

~

"We hold a singular focus, the likes of which has never been held or witnessed here on Gaia.

Go anywhere on earth today and utter the word *coronavirus* and you will be immediately understood. **Every single continent, nation-state, and citizen. This is unprecedented.** This has never been possible. Until now. A single word/subject that is globally held in our minds at the same time. The unification of our species is held in this pandemic."

~

Some of us shared fascinating, enlightening information...

~

Here's Clif High: "Here's some interesting things about this virus. It has four signatures in its envelope. It has the coronavirus, which is the virus that effects ... any mammal with an advancing vagus nervous system, okay. It effects pigs, humans...**It doesn't affect lizards."**

Drops of Light

"There was the smoking gun, the nail in the coffin. If we had any doubts about this *coronavirus* as a #bio-weapon, or about its origin, they were erased with those words. It was a sobering moment to be sure.

Whether you believe in the fact that it was lizards or not doesn't change what is happening right now. You believe in the fact of the *coronavirus*. That is sufficient. This is the awful truth that unifies our efforts and guides a single purpose. We will survive this as One. We are united with intent.

Our human nature brings to the surface things like heroism and compassion and bravery and reckless offerings of help when the going gets rough. **These attributes are not present in the reptilian race, and so are never factored in to their efforts. They simply don't have them.**

Motivation is exposed right now. We are a practical and loving and joyful people. Each of us human; all of us One. We are now exposing the truth of our human nature.

The most effective use of this moment is to love constantly. Share your light."

~

"This is only the beginning everyone. It will not be easy, yet you are armed with the only thing necessary. It is the stuff of giants, warriors, poets, healers and angels. It is a desire to serve. Humanity needs you now."

~

"Your power is as yet untapped.

This power you hold has not diminished. Your power hides beneath years of control, programming, illness, confusion, debt of every kind, discouragement and fear. All of this can end now. It can end because you deem it so. Imagine. Believe. Intend.

You have been told that you cannot command such power; the power of creation. You have been ridiculed, ignored as trivial even. It is time to throw away your tin foil hat and stand tall.

Show your brilliance, for *every time you light the way, the darkness is eradicated.*

The aliens are not coming to save us. We are here to save ourselves."

~

Our global meditations continued in earnest that year...

~

"Humanity, this was not a drill.
The truth of this will get sorted out. It will be told,

eventually. All of the voices will be heard. All of the secrets revealed. All of the guilty, identified.

What matters now is how you will respond. This is a crisis of sovereignty.

Your participation is required. The race is planning an event and you are invited. You are all at home. Join us.

Please show up. Think of nice things. Think of freedom and outside and hugs and laughter and parties and beauty and music and dancing and singing and us. We are extraordinary beings, bursting with passion, creativity, compassion and love. It is love that unites us still. It is love that will save us."

~

"We've begun our Ascension Song.
What we hear now are gasping breaths of desperation. These frantic sounds come from members of the non-meditating faction, those illusory controllers. Imagine, if you will, that you've held onto a thing, a sentient thing, a living, sentient thing such as a pet or a plant, (*or a planet*), for so long that you forgot it had a mind of its own. Over the course of its life, you've had to enact more elaborate and brilliant schemes to convince it where it should stay or grow or not go; what it should do and who's rules it should abide by.

Most times, you ignored it. You fed it just enough to keep it moving and supplying you with entertainment. You allowed it some light/freedom, but mostly kept it in the dark. You owned it, you reasoned, and could do whatever you wanted to with it.

Then one day, it stepped out of the dark. It did not wait for you there. It did not need the meager allowance of light you provided; **it was illuminated all on its own.**"
~

Because of our burgeoning unity, our active participation in earth's liberation was necessary. This was in early April…
~

"Two things are simultaneously happening.

The first is that the Dark Side is ramping up its efforts here on earth because of our volume.

Note the obvious plays being made to inoculate the "herd" and restrict movement. Humanity, now as One, is portraying fear due to this virus.

The second is that the Dark Side NOT on earth, has heard that unified fear response *as a very loud cry of weakness* and considers it an opportunity to once more enter and take over to ensure the enslavement continues.

Drops of Light

They will not. This is mandated, confirmed, and absolute. If you are a light warrior, you may have been recently called back into service.

Many have. I am being told this by those of you here on planet, that it feels the same way it did a few years ago, when the Dark Side was eradicated in the first place. Waking up, with no memories, exhausted and sometimes bruised."

~

A global freedom declaration was held in mid-April...

~

"It is time everyone. There are a few women whom are stating that very thing. Declarations of Sovereignty and Consent and Intent need to be made. Here are some suggested videos: BZ Riger. Laura Eisenhower. Magenta Pixie.

It is the female, collaborative, cooperative energetic that will take us all home. I am thrilled for these voices emerging right now to lead us there."

~

One said this...

~

"You will see people tell the truth. They will do so because of who they are. This will help to quell hysteria. **It will be then you'll know, without a doubt, that you've reached the final pages in this final chapter of the shift.**"

~

And then, this happened…

~

"The first was CNN's Chris Cuomo, who made a sudden announcement that he hates his job. The second comes from the UK, where a popular host went "off script" about the narrative on 5G.

Both are highly public Main Stream Media news personnel who are suddenly truth telling."

~

While we continued to adjust…

~

"Grief bursts forth randomly, awkwardly, and without boundaries. The world grieves now, do you see it? Step back, you will. There are stages and we've named them to imply a sense of order; some sort of control.

1. Denial and isolation; 2. Anger; 3. Bargaining; 4. Depression; 5. Acceptance.

It's not a linear process.

The thing is, none of us have ever grieved a loss of this magnitude. Prior training or education will not assist here. This moment is beyond the scope of what any of us expected.

The loss of a world, a way of life, a future… This is

Drops of Light

not an exaggeration. No emotion is over the top. Feel them all and appreciate the rest of us as we express ours out loud and on camera and at your dining room table. We are all doing the best we can. Be generous. This was the mother of all curve balls.

Leaders will emerge. So will healers, peacemakers, entertainers, producers, workers, inventors, builders, artists, musicians, chefs, innovators, angels. You'll see. We have to grieve now. Not forever, but for now.

You must be true to your essence with each and every breath. It is the only way to move on.

For this end will not destroy you, that is not what ends are for. Ends are here to pave the way for beginnings. Sometimes it's hard to see what's starting, the ending is just so damn consuming and heartbreaking. This is one of those times.

Yet the beginning exists. And, as in all things, the depth and breadth of the ending is in equal proportion to the depth and breadth of what is yet to come. Be assured. Be comforted. Be absolute in your knowing that what is to come is brilliant beyond your imaging and suitable for one such as you."

~

"Dust off your wings. For you will have to fly.

You've been ignoring them, hiding them. Beneath shrugged shoulders and heavy burdens and tattered dreams.

Their colors forgotten; their strength minimized; their purpose misunderstood. You've been imagining yourself needing new ones.

Well my warrior, the stores are all closed, there is nothing to purchase. You'll have to make-do with your original equipment.

And oh, what wings they are!
Do you see?

Breathtaking. Forged in titanium. Wrapped in luminescence. Brilliant beacons. Coronas. Now called forth. To unite. To multiply. To spread.

One.

The only response is the one you know intimately. It is your solitary choice. It is what remains when all else has failed you. The ultimate answer. Your singular solution. The promise birthed when you were. Your core. Your absolute knowing. Your essence. Your being.

You do not need armor. You need conviction. You require nothing but belief. Extend your faith to the one you know deeply.

This is a call for truth. Nothing withstands truth. Nothing destroys it. It can be dismissed but not erased. Your truth. You. Us. One. All that is.

This is not hopeless and you have not been forgotten. You've been waiting. All this time you've imagined the goddess or the god or the dude in the space ship who will be coming to save you. I tell you she is underneath your breath; he is urging you forward in whispers. It has always been you.

You.

It has always been you.

The bravest among you have already met the enemy. You've faced them and stood your ground. You've called their bluff, called them out, stopped them cold. **The bravest among you know the secret.**

The secret is found here... Acceptance. Self-referral. Authority. Unconditional love. Compassion. Badd-Assery. All of these are yours. Somewhere you recognize this. It is your deepest knowing, your base emotion, your energetic blueprint and, as human, your most cherished and unspoken wish.

Do you know what you look like out of body? **A**

huge beacon of light is your true form. Absolute energy. The ultimate powerful being of brilliance.

Once you locate the source of your light, you will discover that it was hidden beneath your darkness.

That's why you haven't been able to see it, until now.

Do not be afraid of the dark. Embrace it. Dust off your wings, and pick up all those parts hiding there. You'll need every one of them now.

This next part is not beyond you. It was made for one such as you.

No, do not be afraid of your dark or your light. They are your wings.

It's time to fly."

~

"Let's talk a bit about light. Your light. My light. Our light.

The Light.

Most supporting descriptive words are overwhelmingly positive for light. It is a word, like love, that is used both as a noun and a verb, even an adjective.

You can turn on the light. Your face can "light up"

when you see a loved one. You can light a candle to illuminate the darkness. There is light in your eyes. When carrying a loved child, they will feel "light" as opposed to "heavy". You can "see the light" when you finally "get" a concept that was shrouded in darkness for you.

We've spoken a bit about recognizing your brilliance. Let's assume for this moment that you have. You've accepted yourself, and know your true form. You've realized or at the very least, you suspect, your purpose for being here.

You are here to establish, hold and anchor the light.

You've found your switch and can turn it on. You are ready and willing. You might even go so far as to say that *you are eager* to fulfill your purpose.

Finally. Your time has arrived. You sense it. Smell it. *Know it.*

You can see the ink-black darkness that oozes into social consciousness now. It has left its shelter and any moment now will reach those you love, those you work with, those you are related to, those you talk to on social media or those you live with each day.

You notice the drops of this ink-black darkness

creeping gradually nearby. It looks to be everywhere. You wonder, "Do they see it?" "How could they miss it?"

Here's the thing.

It's not your job to wonder when or to orchestrate how the ink-black darkness here will be noticed by those who are sleeping. It will. It will not overtake them or drown them before they see it.

You are the light.

When you are needed, you will be called.

You want to draw them to your light. Be gentle, and like the morning breeze, consistent and welcoming. Allow them to blink a few times and get used to your brilliance. Wait for them to seek you out. They will.

This moment is one for the history books, the adjustment will take a while. As you consistently wrap your light with love and open arms and gentle, warm movements, you will attract legions to it. That's a promise."

~

The following conversation with One was translated into several languages, at reader's requests, as it was originally only in a video recording. It took place in May. It included a predicted time-frame, which did not happen. Here's the English

Drops of Light

version…
~

"There are things to say. These things concern the place to which you are heading. These are possibilities and probabilities and potential truths. They have not been carved in stone. Not yet.

This, because the heart of man has not done so at this moment in your time line. Here, linear time is the referenced moment.

For there are nuances and absolutes in the construct known as time. It is these qualifiers that account for differences in prophecy and precise eventual outcome.

Time is a visual process, relative to both distance and preparedness or you might say, ability to see.

There **is** such a quality as time, yet it exists within a singular reality, created and experienced in one place. As such, it contains powerful energy and can be, if used intentionally with conviction, a sort of engine of creative potential.

Once activated, things happen, all at a singular significant moment in "time".

It is for this reason I come to you now. You approach

such a moment. It is significant in your current time-line. There are numerological coordinate points, in time, that create an absolute perfect moment for an event, or series of them, to transpire.

This is highly probable and it approaches now.

You will be completely surprised by this event. It is not in your specific consciousness.

The mind of man is not what creates this event, it is, rather, a precise convergence of evolutionary forces that have come together. They "meet" so to speak, and in their meeting, this event is sparked.

There are a series of occurrences that have and are occurring, that have a high probability, the highest probability, for this outcome now. These were not clear until now.

They have begun a process that will not be stopped. You have mentioned the comparison to a snowball, rolling downhill. It is an appropriate comparison to what happens on Earth now. It is for this reason that I reach you now.

I'd like to tell you about the snowball.

This is your future and is does not just effect you, but all of mankind.

Drops of Light

You approach your singularity. It arrives to you bundled among packaging that distorts it for you.

It may appear to originate from a source that has intents that are harmful to the human. It does not. It is, rather, an eventuality that has been initiated by man's desire to reach beyond this physical nightmare of confrontation that approaches.

It is supported and encouraged by a celestial convergence and the will of the creative force for Ascension.

What approaches is a moment. It is a zero-field moment in which is held the ultimate atmosphere of potentiality.

It will be experienced as a decision point.

It will be felt viscerally.

It will be understood at your base frequency and it will appear chaotic in real time.

This moment that approaches will be a whittling down of your potentials to a single point of clarity. It will bring into your field, in precise clarity, your truth.

No one escapes this.

For some, it will be glossed over and too much for their current life form to comprehend, utilize or appreciate.

For some, it will initiate their departure.

For many, it will be a moment of bliss, of absolute pure knowing of everything that ever was, is, and could be.

It cannot be precisely visualized for you. This is because each ascending, leading moment contributes to it, and they have not yet occurred.

Such is the power of potentiality and the ultimate force of time.

This moment is a moment of singular focus of pure creative potential. You get there rapidly, absolutely, and without doubt.

What can be said for you is this. In ways of preparation what you can do is retain your focus on joy.

Imagine you are adjusting an eyepiece that somehow is both a microscope and a telescope. There is a "sweet-spot" that allows for absolute clarity. That "sweet-spot" is most easily maintained within a state and movement towards love. It feels like happiness. It strengthens and holds within unconditional

Drops of Light

acceptance.

There is a relative experience of "time" spent there, connected to that frequency. Your experience will reflect your state of allowing this joy to take hold.

Your visceral hold of pure potential, of absolute love, will feel solid and eternal, or fleeting and dream-like by your intention, by your attention.

The experience of the singularity approaches for all of you. It has been foretold.

It is in your line of sight, and each of you adjusts your personal eyepiece now.

When will this occur?
Why do I keep seeing this face as it sees a blast of brilliant light?

The timing is not to be told. It will not be long now, not be a year.

The image before you, illustrates the component of light to this moment, as well as your 3D experience of it. Light is truth, energy and the point of creative potential.

It is that point you are seeing.

Do all that you can to steady your focus on joy.

The power for you is found there.

That is all.

~

In June much of our focus was pinned on our burning cities (#GeorgeFloyd) and violent protests. We stood with eyes wide open, attempting to find the truth and an appropriate direction to follow…

~

"We are in the midst of spectacular global upheaval. A system of governance that was politely invisible, today stands naked in front of humanity. It's not a pretty sight. Most of these governing "bodies" are ancient, immovable, dried out, un-bendable and hideous to behold. They were never meant to see the light of day. These are what's been holding society up these many generations. It was bound to collapse, and we are just the humans to see that it does.

You are lucky enough to participate in the awakening. This is not a spectator sport. You didn't show up to observe. You are here to engage.

There will be a moment when oneness is realized. That moment approaches. Everyone is right. Be generous with those whom see things from another angle. They have just as much light as you do. They are just shining it from a different perspective."

Drops of Light

~

"Physical Ascension in a Holistic Universe implies systemic change. It is really happening and we are witnessing it now and now and now and now in all of our parts. It is glorious and it is terrible. It will be even more of both and soon.

This is because we, humanity, are both – terrible and glorious. We've been hiding from ourselves."

~

Here's a few words from One...

~

"Tolerance, patience, and keen interest in each other's stories will only enrich your own, not deny the truth of your own. For alterations in point of view do not weaken your own point of view, but instead outline it; framing it into your own self-portrait."

~

There were debates and divisions on all fronts. There were masks, and what wearing one signified and accomplished...

~

"I'm writing now to ask us to consider what just may be true. That we've been attacked as a race and it is time to stop pointing fingers at each other and instead consider what is really going on here. We are being played, again, and this mask discussion is mere diversion. It is meant to separate us.

We are here for this moment and it is about to be unmasked.

Once the absolute truth is revealed, you'll remember what is true. It will resonate as nothing about this Pandemic has. Trust."

~

By July, real grief was happening for all of us...

~

"We experience now the grieving of our way of life, our world.

Words said past week, by folks both old and young, included "We've been robbed" "It has to be someone's fault" "I'm more stressed now than when I lost my child, and that was loss of life" "I can't sleep" "It doesn't really matter what I do" "I will never own a home" "I will never have kids, I wouldn't wish this on anybody" "People my age (this was someone aged 20-something) feel like they have to do something, so they march, because at this point if they lose their life because of it, at least then it (their life) will have meant something" "I have no future. I have no plans" "Should I leave the country?" "Should I stay and fight?" "I wear a mask because I care about society. Even if it doesn't work, at least I tried." "I don't think these masks do anything, yet I have to wear one so I can work" "When I see someone without a mask, that tells me all I need to know"

Drops of Light

That's just some of it. These are real people. These were accompanied with real tears.

So here is the point of this post. It is to say - let's just stop pointing fingers. Let's instead join hands and intertwine them.

This is not the sort of ending where somebody with all the right answers wins. **The winners are all of us hue-mans. Not some of us. All of us.** You'll know what it was we won, and who it was that we were actually fighting, soon enough. The sooner we unite in this fight, the less collateral damage we'll have to clean up when it's over.

It is up to us. Whatever idea you hold that separates you from anyone else, it is time to let it go.

With everything you can muster, love. Love it all.

Our children are in so much pain. Gaia will not allow this to go on much longer. We've begun our last lap. It is happening. We are One. Do nothing but love."

~

The conversations in 2020 were primarily with One, yet a few others showed up occasionally. We heard from Arcturians, Pleiadians, RA, Lemur-like beings, Giants, Progenitors as well as individuals named Em, Tee and Crison. These last two shared their Ascension story...

~

"It was the same; a similar trajectory was experienced here. This is one told of by the Ancients, it is not one we've seen, nor they, for that matter. It has been passed from elder to elder for a very long chain of elders.

We are very thrilled to witness an ascension process like the earth's in our lifetimes. It was hoped for, yet not a sure thing until recently.

Can you tell us the stories you've been told by your people? By those who heard it from their elders?

We can!

It is a jubilant tale of much heroism and fantastic moments.

Here is the way it was relayed to us.

Now bear in mind, we are a joyful race now. Some would say jubilant and peaceful.

This was not always the way here.

It has become so, once freedom and sovereignty became assumptions and self-governed.

What we've been told is that all races and beings and this planet itself was ruled by a sort of darkness.

Drops of Light

Their motivation was to rule over for the benefit exclusive to them. This is the same governing agenda on your earth now.

As the plan for domination and control took many generations to enact, so our plan for self-governance did also.

We took the reins gradually and strategically until one terrible day, the ruse was up and all was exposed.

A confusing moment happened then, as subjects/beings were not sure whose side to join and which answer was the one that would set them free. Many did not even know of their imprisonment. It had been dark for a long time.

Then a light happened.

Not just any light, but a light from seemingly the heavens.

It was everywhere at once and many, many beings felt its purity and in a singular moment transformed. Their sovereign inner guidance took over and, for an eternal instant, there was clarity.

Those that could not adopt the clarity were filled with fear in that moment.

It was an eternal moment that was soon forgotten, yet changed everything.

A sort of division took place, and the words "the world split" have been repeated again and again to tell us what happened.

Yet the words don't describe a physical split – not one that divided the land or the people on that land.

All beings chose, in that moment, what filled them, and it is what filled them and became their light *that then divided them.*

Those filled now predominantly with fear, lived a world where fear was evident everywhere and each day.

Those filled with love, lived a world where love was shown in all they experienced.

It was two worlds, yes, but one planet and in the splitting became two.

Neither could reach the other once the light descended and defined their inner calling. Neither could see the other.

There were some who chose both. Not because there was no definitive choice in them. No. But instead

371

because their light was needed as a beacon still in place for those living out their lives in fear. This too was their choice.

We, those who come to you now, are generations beyond that moment. Our days and lives are governed by joy, and ruled by compassion and love.

We have no stories from beyond that day, and do not know of numbers or of how it played out for those who remained.

There are stories of mass exits, yet they are unconfirmed.

We watch now your world. There are technologies here, and it is not intrusive but used as a teaching for us. You are seen at a distance. Masses of light, and it overcomes the darkness.

We are able to get closer and at times, and due to synchronicity, we do. It is then when numbers and timing become more evident. Now is one of those times. We see so much light and bursts of it in the midst of attacks of ill-conceived plans.

You are at a pivotal time. It appears to us from here that your light bursts are massively increasing the speed of your ascension. It is an unpredictable process, at best, but we wanted to cheer you on."

~

We were becoming aware of the tools utilized in our enslavement, and the invisible power they wielded over our lives...

~

"The "Social Dilemma" is a fascinating documentary, outlining the way technology mirrors truth. It concludes that we construct our own reality, and that reality is informed today by our news-feeds. Each of these news-feeds is tailor made for us individually, using a blueprint drawn by how many seconds we spend looking at this item or that video.

It is designed to keep us engaged. Period. It has no conscience or purpose other than continuous engagement. It is not interested in whose side of the story we are viewing or any such notion of "balance". It does not care about the truth. Its only purpose is engagement.

We are watching, feeling, living in and responding to a unique world; it is a world of our own making and unlike any other world – singularly comprehended by no one but ourselves."

~

Personal news feeds all contained one story that November; the US Presidential election...

~

"Many of us fell asleep on Election night, with one candidate clearly leading; Donald J Trump. The next morning, we woke up to what felt like an illusion, as many thousands of "just found" ballots, almost 100% of them for Joe Biden, *which is a mathematical impossibility*, were added to tallies. We watched as history was attempted to be re-written. It was awesome.

For you are witnessing the Fall of Evil and it will be blatant and it will be ugly."

~

As our personal lives continued…

~

"If you haven't known anyone who has gotten ill with this CCP virus, you do now. Her name is Jan. I have known a total of 5 people, two of whom did not survive. They were also mid-stride and vibrant when the CCP virus took them; adults in their 40's.

There is a 20-something young man and an 80-something young woman who have both survived and are no longer ill.

They beat the CCP virus. Finally, there is this most recent news and it is playing out in our family right now. She has just been put back on a ventilator, after a brief time off. Please pray for Jan. Send her your light.

Our very human, visceral emotions are pulsing through our brilliant light bodies, while our brain attempts to put words together to express something worthwhile. Something of comfort, something to heal a loved one, someplace where our fellow light bearers can rest for a moment.

Or, we would like to rest for a moment ourselves. To lay down our swords or fold up our wings and watch a sunset, hold a puppy, hug someone. It is all very comprehensive and confusing. It is all part of where we walk now.

For this is our Ascension everyone.

There may be a blast of light somewhere ahead, yet right now, it is all happening wherever you find yourself.

Stand up and wherever you are, love fiercely whomever you hold in your sights; you chose to complete this part together. Whatever side they are playing, **they need your light**. They need your love. They need your truth.

Remember."

~

"When we started, about a decade ago, it was "*We are the ones we've been waiting for*". A few years ago, it changed to "*We are the Ones. We have anchored the light. It is done*". We have since unified and become a conscious single voice – the singularity approaches. So today it changes once more to "**We are One. This is** *our planet. We are freeing her now."*

Take up your armor and turn on your light. We'll do this together. You are necessary. You are brilliant. You are powerful. You are love. Remember."

~

"Everyone here right now is a Master. We are walking among Angels and Warriors. That's it. No exceptions.

The privilege held in this year, and this moment for the race, is found in each other. There is no other who chose your spot here, your place in line, for earth 2020. It's yours. You chose it. You've made it. You're here. Your purpose? To illustrate love in human form.

What is witnessed here and now is the awesome drive of our human spirit, the determination to complete this life with purpose, and with love.

It looks different than expected. It does not disappoint however. It sustains and holds and allows. It averts our eyes from judgment and directs them towards gentility. It holds us together, even when masks and social distancing conspire to keep us apart.

We cannot be held apart. The single most perfect element of a human being is his or her heart. From there, love finds a way and carries the rest through. The rest of the humans. Us.

It is humbling to be here with you at all. It is an honor to witness this transformation; to share the journey with so many gorgeous beings of brilliant light."

~

"There is a cloud of our light and as it builds, it pushes the dark away, taking its place. The dark does not resonate with our light, and this, this cloud of light, is what heralds our new earth."

~

"In the past month there have been monoliths appearing all over the world. Their source or purpose is unknown. A global memory for the monolith comes from the Stanley Kubrick film in 1968: 2001 – A Space Odyssey. This iconic image for the dawn of man, from the beginning of the film, is familiar to the entire world."

~

"There are reports of a machine on the moon that is pointed at earth and used to harvest souls for some sort of cruel recycling program. It is said that it has been put there, purposely, in order to get the most repeated use of our energy as we reincarnate again and again within its grip, without memory or any ability to escape."

~

Accompanying those stories were explanations reporting that the monoliths were to be used as truth transmitters once we were free. Also, that we'd see them "light up" once the "false reality" moon machine was switched off.

Drops of Light

There were several powerful, global meditations on 12-21-2020…

~

"There was such force and immediacy in yesterday's mass meditation that I opened my eyes as it was felt.

I entered into a meditative state, and "looked" around for everyone. In a matter of a few minutes, I felt a gathering. It was of such magnitude and volume that I was taken aback, and a bit mesmerized. There were so many of us! The earth was emblazoned with light.

Then I experienced something new. A surge of light moved through my body from the heavens and through me, and into the earth. I moved as it flowed through, in a sort of wave. It was consuming and brilliant. With it, there was a sense of completion. I knew we had done it. Our light is no longer just a visitor here. **We have anchored the light.** Astounding.

Once that happened, it was over. I was done and sat there for a moment, amazed at the definitive nature of what had just happened. Just then, my partner opened the door to the room where I was meditating. He been doing so as well, but in another room. His eyes were open wide and he said "Did you feel it?" I said "Yes! We did it! We anchored the light!" He said "I could see it! I saw the whole planet and all of the energy was there! It was huge!" We both had tears in our eyes.

It was after that event that this conversation (*with One*) took place" …

"The light is not only here, it has taken root, taken hold, and thus begun to quickly spread planet-wide.

Your light emerges everywhere now. Visualize the root system of your lilies in the field. They are connected, entangled and spread everywhere; regardless of efforts to keep them contained. The reference is a quite literal one, and meant to be physical. Light, specifically your light, and today, has embedded itself with Gaia.

You've become One, in a literal moment of singularity.

Many, many star seeds, light workers, light walkers, light warriors, angels and wanderers have arrived for this moment. It was an amplified, synchronized effort from all dimensions.

What is seen next will leave you breathless in its force, clarity and brevity.

The light has won."

~

Drops of Light

And so, 2020 came to an end.

Chapter 6
Listening to the Light
(2021-2022)

Digging deeper now,
you recognize a consistency to the voice within;
the Light that you are.
It agrees with these other voices –
the Light above and beyond you –
or what is perceived to be.
You now hear it as
One Voice ~
many verses/songs/perspectives.

Drops of Light

2021 begins. January 6th of that year will forever be recalled as the date of the "Capitol Riot" in Washington, DC. I watched the coverage live that day from our home, and witnessed people being let inside the barriers to the capitol by uniformed police. The fact that it was being called a "riot" was a surprise when I heard "the news" reports on it later.

Here's what the media told us was important that year…

~

Riots by "violent insurrectionists" stormed the **US Capitol** on January 6, 2021, during the time when Congress was meeting to confirm Joe Biden's electoral victory.

President Trump was impeached for a 2nd time as a result, for "incitement of insurrection", with just one week left in his term. He was acquitted in February. This, for the first time in US history was not a "peaceful transition of power". Similar disruptions in the countries of India and Brazil, as well as coups in Myanmar, Chad, Mali, Guinea and Sudan illustrate global unrest and alterations of power.

Joe Biden was inaugurated as President and **Kamala Harris** became the first woman as well as the first person of African American descent to be a Vice-President of the US.

GameStop stock went from $5 to $350 in 6 months-time, and short sellers lost over 25 billion in the "short-squeeze" initiated by followers of a subreddit trading thread. Investment app. "Robinhood" halted trading of the stock as this was happening, on January 28th, initiating a lawsuit.

The cargo ship **"Ever Given"** got stuck in the **Suez Canal** in March, blocking more than 400 cargo ships for 6 days. This caused up to 60-day shipping delays and increased consumer awareness of the fragility of our global supply chains.

NFT's, non-fungible tokens, grew in significance that year, as a novel way to authenticate digital art as well as real world items. In March, Christie's sold the first NFT artwork for 69 million dollars.

Covid-19 vaccines were released in May.

Private space travel, with Jeff Bezos, Elon Musk and Richard Branson competing for headlines and customers in this new "astro-tourism" market.

Gymnast Simone Biles withdrew from the Team USA final during the Tokyo **Olympics** in July, citing **mental health concerns.**

The United States clumsily & hastily withdrew from Afghanistan in August, after a 20-year war-effort, leaving behind equipment, as well as people. Afghan forces were still falling to the Taliban at the time. 175 people lost their lives during the withdrawal, including 13 US soldiers, in a bombing by ISIS-K. By years end, the Taliban were in power there.

The **"Facebook Files"**, in the Wall Street Journal, exposed censorship, hate speech and numerous systemic issues, all contributing real harm to vulnerable groups worldwide.

This was thanks to a whistleblower who worked for the company, Frances Haugen, who later testified to Congress.

A migration crisis: By October, the number of people entering the US illegally hit 1.7 million over the prior year. This was the highest number since 1960. The European Union saw a 70 percent rise, compared to 2020, in the number of people entering illegally.

Ethiopia was embroiled in a bitter **civil war**.

Extreme weather included record drought in the American southwest. Record flooding devastated Belgium and western Germany. Wildfires tore through Greece. Monsoons ravaged India and Nepal.

The Pandora Papers: 12 million documents illustrating how the wealthy and powerful use off-shore accounts to evade taxes and hide money were released by an International Consortium of Investigative Journalists.

In December, **Russia built-up their military near the Ukraine border**, prompting Joe Biden to issue a warning to Vladimir Putin against invading the Ukraine.

~

There were no shared conversations with the Pleiadians that year, as the intent was to wait until I had seen/touched a medical pod before doing so. As that didn't happen, there was no helpful reason to post...

~

I was talking to One almost daily. Three volumes in the "Words of One" series were published between February and August of 2021...

~

This year is challenging to pen, and as it is re-visited now, I gradually remember how it felt. At different moments it felt shocking, and sad, and emotionally devastating. There were times when I didn't think my heart would withstand the pain. It felt as if everything was breaking, my body, my family, my faith. A constant flow of inspiration from One was interrupted regularly with illness, argument, separation, physical hardship, pain and loss. The only thing left to do was to refuse to succumb to fear. So that is what I did, and that decision is what held me together...

~

One had this to say in early January...

~

"You have learned well, dear human.
Now is the great un-learning.
That is what this new year represents.

You will experience cognitive dissonance. You will not be as confused as some, those who are not reading messages such as these, with warnings and truths. But make no mistake, there will be confusion for you as well.

Rest assured the old world ended with the Solstice of 2020 – yet, as was said earlier, the structures remain. Therefore, its ending is not apparent to anyone not participating in the ceremonies of light.

Many did participate, but not all. Enough of you carried and held the light. Your New Earth enters the birth canal.

It is Painful and Messy and can feel interminably long in there. This is called "Labor" with good reason.

Keep your eyes on the prize. Visualize, visualize, visualize.

Your New Earth comes at your beckoning, and all of you are on board with that.

The "Un-learning" will take a while. You are in for some shocks. These will both please and horrify you.

Remember that change is happening and these shocks and horrors are what you are leaving behind.

Seeing them is necessary. Seeing everything is necessary in order to prepare for the birth. Everything is swept away. This is a new start.

This year will feel a bit like a roller coaster, with sharp turns, fast declines and the highest highs.

Through it all, remember that you've created this ride yourselves, for the benefit of all of creation. It is not to be missed."

"The force of the people, the physical force of the numbers (*of people*) who were present in Washington DC for the "counting" this week was a powerful force. Hundreds of thousands of you were there. It was a calling, a statement of such energy and force that if anything it has cemented and solidified the voice of truth and love and integrity and freedom – rather than be a "violent over-throw". Everyone played their part. Even the media.

Now know that there are still steps to be taken. There are things to be made public.

The show continues.

It will be vital that you lead the way with your love, your light, your truth. Where you are heading is a place of Unity, where Oneness is felt in real time."

"The full expression of Man is a long-anticipated moment for all of creation.

You are in the first phases of actualizing your true nature – which is love.

Drops of Light

Nothing can get in the way of this, and nothing, in all of creation, can prepare you for the glory of what you are about to witness."

~

The year continued to be chronicled…

~

'The veil is about to be lifted my friends. You have waited such a long time for this moment and we are here.

It is your love and light and tenacity that got us here.

It is you. You are ready. Know that whatever you see or hear will be best explained by how you feel about it, rather than what anyone in the media attempts to tell you to think about it. Go within for answers now and trust what you find there.

Know that the light holds throughout every step of the way, and it is the depth of blackness that offers us this spectacular contrast. Your light, my light, our light stands brilliantly against such darkness."

~

"Here's a few things that have happened, announcing this frequency shift and pointing out the dissolving veil. They are offered as examples.

While conversing with my partner yesterday his eyes closed for a nanosecond and I saw someone else show up. For those of you unaware, he's a deep trance channel. I was surprised, there was no warning and after a few moments he said "What were we saying?" I responded, "Where did you go?" "I didn't go anywhere. It was like someone walked through me!" His eyes were wide open. "That was weird."

A few minutes and sentences later, it happened again. "The veil must be really thin right now" he told me. I agreed and we laughed.

We've been told more than once that we are in a crowd, shoulder to shoulder with beings in various frequencies that we don't perceive. Yesterday, my partner felt them for the first time. *The veil is thinning.*"
~
"You are here now, that is all that needs to be known. Generations of ancestors have combined their essence in order for you to step forward today.

They are with you now, surrounding you with love, enrobing you in a cloak of comfort.

This is not a small thing; it is the only thing.

Right here, right now, you have arrived for this very moment.

For you are the combination of every wish for love, every longing for freedom, every desire for happiness; each of these making up the layers of you.

Drops of Light

For you are infinite as much as you are solid.

Realize the scope of your knowing; it reaches beyond the confines of your physical self.

It is there where your ancestors, guides and angels are waiting.

As real as your heart feels love's longing, and as inspiration arrives without being sought.

They are with you now.

For the torn places of your heart are held together by the luminescent strands of connection to every unseen realm.

You are not alone.

You were never alone.

You are the totality of pure love, the summary of each life lived before yours now, a unique combination of pure light – existing now as you.

Your full range of expertise has been anticipated and factored in to our collective uprising.

We wake with wide open eyes to the beauty that we are, and we stand, enrobed in each other's brilliance.

This is our moment."

~

"So, we are getting tired of being told to "Buckle Up" and/or "Hang on to your hats". It's real. Yet here's a thought that may help. **We were never told just how long a ride it was.**

There's a reason for that, and we uncover it now. It depends on the speed with which we are equipped to travel. It depends on the vehicle we occupy. It depends on the terrain. It depends on who is driving and what speed limits are in place. In all of these varying conditions, we remain buckled up. In all of these varying states, we remain focused on the destination.

It's the only way to guarantee we'll ever arrive.

For we did not come here to give up before the finish line."

~

"What I see with all the rhetoric/publicity around the virus, masks, jab, political players, etc., is a monster-mash-up called FEAR. It looks to be the dying gasps or desperate grabs of some **make-believe creature**.

Its whole point is to **make-you-believe** that it is both real and important. As well as to make you afraid.

What you are here to do (*with this current onslaught of*

Drops of Light

fear) is to let it go. You are actually here to usher it out of here.

You can do that by holding onto just one thing. Your light. Hold onto your light, and let the rest of it go.

Hold the light.
Hold the light.
Hold the light.

A special location is not required.

A special job is not required.

Special equipment is not required.

A large bank account is not required.

All that is necessary – is you.

The release of Heather Ann Tucci-Jaraff is a pivotal moment. We can support and amplify this moment with love. We can illuminate it with our light.

We came here for this time and this doing. It is happening now. Turn on your light, and hold it steady.

Keep it on until our arrival is assured.

Let go of fear.

Hold on to the light.

Refuse the fear.

Say yes to the light.

It is there where you'll find your deepest truth.

It is there where love's essence rests."

~

"These are the end times.

They must take place before the beginning times.

These are the beginning times. Like a child taking its
first steps, we can expect to be a little unsteady, and
prepare to fall a few times. Those falls haven't
stopped us from walking, and they won't stop us
from completing this process either. This is why we
came. We are birthing a new world.

We are the ones we've been waiting for. (2011)
We are the Ones. We have anchored the light. It is
done. (2016)
We are One. This is our planet. We are freeing her
now. (2021)"

~

Mid-year sounded like this…

~

"We have arrived at a point, which I believe is **the**

point. The moment of **surrender**.

Here's what it looks like:

It looks like – tired. We are exhausted.

It looks like – we all have loved ones we disagree with, either politically or otherwise, and it just doesn't matter that much anymore, not really.

It looks like – all that we really crave is:

> A hug
> To go home; to feel family
> To love and feel loved
> To laugh together
> Another hug
> To live a little, then to remember what joy feels like
> Freedom to be ___ (fill in your own blank)

By **surrender** I do not imply giving up. I imply letting go.

We are at that spot right now.

It is upon us to let go of every opinion and judgment and blaming voice we've believed mattered. There is no one to convince but ourselves.

It doesn't matter who you voted for in any election or any country. It doesn't matter what gender/sex you identify as.

It doesn't matter which god you worship or if you worship a god at all. It doesn't matter the color of your skin or the form of your clothing.

It doesn't matter if you enforce laws, educate children, repair machines or flip burgers.

There is only one thing that matters and it is your heart."

~

"It is the frequency of truth that enters now. It is the frequency of truth that exposes all —

All that you consider dark
And
All that you consider light
Right now.

The truth of what you are capable of arrives into your field at the same time that the truth of this fabricated reality does.

You are well-equipped for this.

Remember that."

~

Drops of Light

One had this to say on the June Solstice…

~

"So, welcome the frequency that enters today and breathe it in slowly. Allow it to surround the forth-coming announcements. You may be tempted to fall into despair right along with your fellow humans who are not forewarned.

Do not, as it will delay your progress and take you off course.

This is the beginning; it is not the end.

What you are witnessing, in these announcements of things and endings of things is akin to the ashes that form beneath the Phoenix as it rises.

You are here to transform a world.

It is done.

That is all.

Now the fun begins as you try your wings."

~

"I am assured that we are overturning these dark ones and that **there is a signal that initiates the ending**. Not the ending of us, the ending of this rule by corruption, deception, control and enslavement. I believe that the signal is our unified voice. Together we must stand up and say No."

~

"I asked the question a few days ago, "where are we in all of this?" (*meaning our "Ascension"*). I was told that there are **no precise time frames** for this, and that it was **difficult to describe** it to someone who has never done it before. Meaning, never freed a planet from its owners and ascended, while being human.

I said, we can feel this acceleration, yet, being human and entrenched in linear time, we'd like some sign-posts. It feels to be taking so very long… As we talked, it was suggested that I think of something few people have done.

I remembered my tandem jump (skydive). It is illustrative for several reasons:

It required an initial desire.

It was **a collective and personal experience that required an appointment.**

I **didn't lose either friends or family** at any point. **Some of us also jumped, others watched.**

There was a moment when the collective experience became my individual experience alone.

Drops of Light

There was no way to plan when that moment would happen.

I had to completely trust my tandem instructor, **let go and enjoy the ride**.

There was a necessary process and a guaranteed conclusion, even though some things went wrong at different points along the way (i.e., my goggles malfunctioned and I had a crash landing).

Once the metaphor was firmly established, I asked:

"So where are we in this process of Ascension/freeing the planet?"

"You haven't made the appointment."

"What?"

"You have desire. Yet **you have billions of humans who have to agree that it is time to schedule it, before that next step can be taken.** So, the appointment hasn't been scheduled yet." (At this writing there are 7,777,406,007 humans globally.)

There was a bit more discussion, yet at the end it was clear that the process could actually be scheduled and then occur within a very short time frame, as in "same day appointments available".

I did not sense, frankly, that it was believed, from their current point of view, that this would be the case here. I did sense that **there would be a precipitating event that would determine the timing and get folks ready to make the appointment. I have no idea what that event is, nor was I told.**"

~

And One continually kept us informed…

~

"Developments have reached a pivotal point and, quickly now, there will be full exposure. Full exposure of truth.

Full exposure of fact.

The darkness now moves into the light. The activities that have been conducted in the darkness now move into the light. Into the light of exposure, where more of the race will have access to them. Where more of the race will see them.

Everything changes with clarity, and the plan is destined to fail.

Literally consider what this will mean for the race. This is a time like no other. The light is bright, all gets exposed, there are legions of warriors and all of creation supporting and propelling this moment.

Drops of Light

The realization of it and full acclimation to it is solely yours however. As members of the race, you are embodying the horror as well as the brilliance.

It's taken quite a bit of "time".

It's taken quite a bit of intent.

You enjoy, and right now, the energy of creation behind you.

You will not do this quietly or alone.

It is to be spectacular."

~

"Your enlightenment occurs definitively, gradually and potentially instantly. You are preparing for a shift and doing so individually.

I tell you this. For your faith will remain unshakable when surrounded in darkness. It will be the light, sought by those without their own illumination. It will be the strength needed to proceed when it seems to be hopeless.

It will then be obvious as the truth; the One Light that remained while all else crumbled around it.

The light is other-worldly, perhaps, to those who know not their own.

For you are the Light of the World, my dear, dear human.

Once darkness initiates this final scene, **it will be you who bring the Light** – you who are the Light.

It will happen literally, viscerally, physically and absolutely.

Darkness to Light.

Deception to Truth.

Fear to Love.

This final act had to be opened on your timeline, and at your cue.

Just as soon as your light overtakes this darkness – it occurs.

Hold the Light."

~

> *Note* –

What came through but perhaps was not said was the intensely personal nature in the words **"dark to light"**. *It is not just that we are receiving truth about the world's deception in its leaders. It is that we are simultaneously uncovering and seeing the truth of who we are. Who we truly are. All false* *personality will be irrelevant and discarded now. All that you are, the truth that supplies your vitality and reason for being here at all, emerges now. As above so below.*

Rest easily with this, for **at your very center you are love, you are light, you are truth**. *All else is false.*

~

As August moved towards September…

~

"Here are a few things that I've been told:

The reason it's taking so long is because we want everyone to go with us on this journey. It was a collective decision made some time ago. We are living the consequences for it now. It was and is still, a great decision. (*even though it may not feel that way*) We wouldn't have it any other way, actually.

There have been stories of some folks leaving on ships first, while some folks stay here to live out their lives in a realm of polarity, and that there is, ultimately, a split between worlds (*2 earths*).

How it's been explained, and recently is that yes, some of us are leaving, and soon, due to desire, or for safety, or because our jobs are someplace else for a while. Personal choice dictates your location and you will be aware of your choice when the moment arrives.

There are some of us who have chosen to help the race adjust and create a new earth. That happens right here.

These humans will include some of you, and me. If you have some sort of recognition or feeling as you read this, it may be that you are included as well. It is not punishment and does not mean you are less evolved. It was and is personal choice.

We came to help transform a planet. All that we have prepped for, and known deeply throughout this lifetime, is happening right now. It won't be easy. You are skilled at this and will not leave until you have completed your mission."

~

"There are times that emblazon themselves on the notes of your memory, never to be lost. High noon today we stood over the Kennedy Expressway and poked flowers and balloons into the holes of a rusty chain link fence that also had an American Flag tied to it. We hugged, laughed, cried and waved at our fellow Chicagoans cruising below us at 70 MPH, many of them waving and honking. This morning, we didn't know each other. This afternoon, we have shared phone numbers and begun a plan. There were four of us.

We were all there because of Veronica Wolski. It was windy and hot, and not the place to be if heights bother you.

There is something about standing in the place where a movement was begun. Don't ever let them tell you that one person can't change the world.

One person did. Her name was Veronica Wolski. Today I stood on the place that she's been standing for years. **The People's Bridge.**

There are now other bridges in other towns, over other highways, and in some other countries because of Veronica Wolski.

I saw her standing above the Kennedy Expressway years ago, long before I knew her name. Eventually, I found her on Twitter. We exchanged a few messages and I purchased two shirts from her. I meant to get to that bridge someday...I never did. I am sorry we never met in person.

Yet today I felt her on that bridge. The full import of what it took for her to show up there day after day hit me. It took tenacity, belief in a purpose, fortitude, courage, bravery and independence; it took a deep love for humanity.

No one ever paid Veronica to do this. Yet eventually, it was clear that she was never going to stop.

We need to find each other, hug each other, support each other, love each other. This is why Veronica stood there day after day in rain and heat and wind and snow. She did it for us. So that we would one day stand up for ourselves. I am so very grateful that she did.

Fly high, our beloved Veronica. I am honored to have known you. You'll never be forgotten. Your light hasn't been doused completely – we'll carry it from here.

Godspeed Angel, Godspeed."

~

"This is the greatest show on earth, that we've all forgotten is just a show. We step out of the theater and debate/argue with one another over which actors/parts are true and which are false. They are neither. They are actors who are speaking lines and using props and movements to portray their point.

It's all a show.

The white hats are now in control of government. These wildly obvious movements and dictates are their lines and plot points. **They are trying to wake us up."**

~

Here's some conversations from the last months of 2021…

Drops of Light

~

"We are in the final moments of deep spiritual battle and now, the side holding the light and truth has entered the scene **consciously.**

Not everyone, no.

But those of you hearing these words, know the war of which I speak. Activate and let no person or event stop you. **All but the truth is illusion.**

Do not despair. In your darkest moment you will witness the brightest of lights.

These lights are you.
These lights are you.

Remember.
Remember.

Your most vital contribution to this moment now comes from the energy of your heart.

This is the calm before the storm.

The storm comes soon."

~

"When he (the Guardian) first showed up (in 2012), he said a few things that were surprising at the time, yet they are clarified with the lens of 2021. Here are some of them:

"You are being controlled by government that is against ways of One. "Satanic" worshippers of goat of Mendes, also star of Sirius. Enemies of One, or "criminals" in your words."

"We decided that your race will be able to change its destiny by your collective choice. Our arrival was unexpected, we already changed some of your destiny. The rest is up to your kind."

After my reference to the Illuminati order as "Dark Ones", here was his reply:

"Not the "dark ones", but corrupted ones. There is still Good in them. It is important how beings were learned and programmed to exist."

"We would be able to activate a very powerful solar flare to aid you. Sun is the creator and only Supporter of your life. Only He holds the key to your ultimate destiny. He as well does not agree with methods of Illuminati Order. You will be aided by Him, once you prove, to wish and live, be free from lies, deception, death that Illuminati brings to you."

"Sun will not harm you. He will only switch off all the electronics on your planet...Sun will play a crucial moment in your planet's history, as it was long ago."

Drops of Light

When these words were written, we were in a different place indeed than we find ourselves today. The reason for sharing them now is because of how he mentioned from the get-go that the reason he was dropping in and offering so much information was because humanity had to make a choice that year (2012). That choice was what we were going to do about the controllers.

We were eventually told that we ultimately, in the Fall of that year, (2012) chose to take care of them ourselves. We did not ask for an outside race to drop in and do it for us, or lead us.

Move to October of 2021. The choice humanity made was a worthy one. We chose not only to do this ourselves, but also to bring everyone along with us. Every. Single. One.

This includes the "corrupted ones", as specified so clearly by the Guardian. What has been concerning me since last Fall, when One said that this entire operation was unfolding so that the "corrupted ones" could ask for redemption, was **how does this happen???** *How do they come out in the open and then surrender or change sides or seek forgiveness???*

It is not for punishment's sake that this is orchestrated and so seemingly lengthy. **It is for love's sake.** *It is a beautiful and wise finale that we, those of us who came to anchor the light, agreed to. It sounded perfect when we started and it remains so. It's hard to see that though, while our egos are crying and our minds are restless and our bodies are impatient.*

Yet knowing this truth, somehow reduces the anxiety felt about time and dates. Knowing this truth really resonates within and creates a heart song that nothing else could.

Agape. That is what this is about. We will embody Agape. While human. Wow. We really are the ones we've been waiting for."
~

"Your new world will exist in a frequency that holds too fast a resonance for slavery or control. There are some among you still, who need to complete their agreed upon contracts before leaving, before it's complete, before moving on. These are not the majority of the race, yet in some cases now they are pivotal to world events. These could be government leaders as well as family members, yet in every case the reason for the prolonged situation and relationship is the fulfilling of a contract.

Regardless of reasons or current situation — all contracts will be fulfilled. This means, my dear human, that your new world begins on an even ground."
~

""Timeline" is such an inaccurate way to express how things proceed. For time is perception and not really a thing to be measured. And, there is no such thing as a straight line (*in a timeline*). It is more of a continually blooming flower."
~

"Your love and your light are a force for peace and

truth. This offers stability to a place that will feel highly unstable in the coming days.

You are here to ground the energy of love, and to beam the light of what remains true always. Your light is powerful my dear ones, and it is only just being activated.

You will not miss this part.

It is, quite literally, darkness to light."
~

"The unknown element has entered the picture. It has been put there by you, by the race. It is here where the brilliance of humanity is discovered.

For the human is not only a combination of spirit, genetics and flesh. The human is the exponential spark that bears a unique and elemental signature. His mark is known throughout all of Creation for its brilliance, its passion, its unique and formless expression of love. The adaptable human. The loyal human. The creative genius human.

This signature arises once more and denies any and all attempts to define and/or limit it.

This means that **there is no way on heaven or on earth to foresee an accurate timeline. As the human has historically done, he will change this**

one. Not intentionally so, but collaboratively and absolutely so.

The human has sped up the journey.

The collective energy has combined with celestial and pre-ordained events in such a powerful way that there is the equivalent of rocket-fuel pushing you ahead.

Hang on. Hold on to who and what you love, and enjoy this ride. You are all at the wheel now, with no map but plenty of fuel; rocket-fuel. No more rest stops.

Humanity has, once again, surprised us all and exceeded every expectation. This is truly remarkable and a testament to your brilliant light.

All of Creation watches as you craft this perfect landing.

Well done, dear human, well done."

~

One closed out 2021 with these words...

~

"The old world has ended and the crumbling of it happens for months and even years. Your desire for release from it has guaranteed that this be so.

Drops of Light

Although you are not responsible for physically escorting these old-world controllers away – your light and intent have paved the path for others to do so.

They walk away now.

They will leave, are leaving and have left. It has been a process and it has been years in its completion.

You may not witness their exit, yet you will be informed of the truth of their manipulation, corruption and abuse.

The Matrix, built by them and for their enjoyment, disintegrates. It will one day be visible only in books and photos, records and recordings.

Do not fear or doubt the outcome. Although things may appear both fearful and doubtful, they are not.

Know that you are light.

Know that you are love.

These truths bring forth your enlightenment.

Legions of others applaud you & add their light to your own.

Very quickly now, this too becomes visible."

2022 began this way...

~

Kid Rock released "**We the People**" in January,[9] a song for revolution, (*with plenty of language*).

~

"Currently (*January 28th*), North America is mesmerized with the 2022 **Canadian Freedom Convoy** which right now heads into Ottawa. They arrive Saturday.

The populace awakens at its own rate, and within every sub-group. We've united, without agreeing on almost anything at all. **Australia's and Italy's truckers have taken a cue from the Canadians**, and head for their respective capitols.

How many additional country's government leaders, and/or city names are you aware of than you were back in 2012? This is how physical Oneness begins.

We stop seeing separators. A decade ago, they were all that we could see.

It's a simple thing to recognize the majority when tyrants are the obvious minority. We have crossed a threshold of sorts. We walk now, arm in arm, into the next phase.

This is the demolition phase. It is followed by the build-up."

Drops of Light

~

Many of us "met" Canadian Jean-Claude on you tube around that time, @ Beyond Mystic, as he filled us in on the Freedom Convoy first hand, in ways that Mainstream Media wasn't. It was thrilling to witness our northern neighbors, in the dead of winter, become a beacon for the world. They gave us hope and inspiration.

Here's one woman's story, as shared on Facebook…

~

"Yesterday I went to Ottawa…this is what I experienced…

Walking through the street on my way to The Hill, I heard more "Good mornings" and "How are you?" than I have heard in all of the last couple of years.

And the smiles! The big beautiful smiles!! They meant so much more than words. Then there were trucks! So many beautiful trucks! Walking by many of them, waving to the men and women occupying them, thanking them for what they are doing for us, collectively, as a country. Having them thank ME for being there! All were humble, and grateful and very, very determined!

The police presence was not what I expected. Yes, there were officers sitting in their vehicles scattered around the roads involved, and there was a handful of officers, on foot, around the walkways leading of the parliament buildings. I spoke to many of them. Every one of them was friendly, kind and relaxed. I thanked them for what they do, for keeping us safe.

And then there was the music and the dancing. From tiny little kids to old people (like me) all laughing and dancing together. At one point, I was standing by a stage, a lady was singing and I was watching... just taking in everything around me. Not going to lie, my eyes welled up with tears.

The emotion was absolutely overwhelming. I felt the weight of the last two years melting off of me. The fear, the stress, the anxiety, the depression and worst of all, the hopelessness that was consuming me, all washing away. As I stood there with tears in my eyes, a lady came up to me, she must of seen how I was feeling. She didn't say anything at first, she stood in front of me and opened her arms... without a second thought, I went in for the hug. She said to me, "It's ok, everything is going to be alright ". And for the first time in two years, I believed it.

A short moment later, there was an elderly man wearing a sign around his neck that read "Free hugs". I told him that I would take one of those. As he hugged me, he whispered, "These hugs are saving my life!" I whispered back, "Mine too".

~

The Mainstream media told us these things...

Drops of Light

~

Wildfires in Boulder, Colorado, force the evacuation of over 30,000 people in January.

Cost of Living Crisis – Inflation hit 9.1% in June in the US, and 11.1% in the UK in October.

Covid-19 had a new variant called **Omicron**.

Russia invaded the **Ukraine** on February 24th.

In May, 19 students and 2 teachers were killed by a gunman at **Robb Elementary School in Uvalde, Texas.**

The US Supreme Court **overturned Roe-vs-Wade**, ending a woman's constitutional right to abortion. The decision on that right, which had been "leaked" that May, was returned to individual states on June 24th.

Queen Elizabeth II died on September 8th. She was 96 and had reigned for 70 years.

Massive **flooding in Pakistan**, due to monsoons that summer, caused $30 billion in damage.

On November 15th, **the world's population exceeded 8 billion**. Our first billion was reached in 1803.

The **United Kingdom had 3 Prime Ministers** in 2 months. The last (and current) PM is Rishi Sunak.

Humanitarian Crisis – 32 million people worldwide are currently **refugees**, only partly due to the war in Ukraine. Unresolved situations in Syria, Afghanistan, South Sudan, Yemen and Haiti contribute.

A 22-year-old Iranian, Mahsa Amini, died in police custody in Tehran, after being arrested for failing to cover her hair properly. This sparked **pro-tests, "Women, Life, Freedom!"**, around the country as well as public executions of protesters by security forces.

In September, the head of **the WHO declared the end of the pandemic was "in sight".**

The travel industry reports a **return to pre-Covid numbers.**

The **US Southwest experienced a record drought** that led to diminished crop yields.

The US House Select Committee begins to hold **hearings on the "Capitol Riot" of January 6, 2021.**

Europe experienced record heat waves.

Hurricane Ian ravaged Florida.

Ketanji Brown Jackson becomes **the first black woman** to sit **on the US Supreme Court.**

A 4th of July shooting in Highland Park, Illinois, US leaves 7 people dead.

Elon Musk buys Twitter.

Monkeypox is declared a public health emergency by the WHO, in July.

Al Qaeda leader Ayman al-Zawahiri is killed by a CIA drone strike.

The US Attorney General announces **charges against 4 Kentucky police officers** for the acci-dental killing of **Breonna Taylor** in March of 2020.

Donald Trump's Mar-a-Lago, Florida home was **searched by the FBI.**

Drops of Light

Anthony Fauci steps down as the U.S. advisor to the President.

Paul Pelosi, Nancy Pelosi's husband, **is assaulted** by a "home intruder".

In **Moscow, Idaho**, 4 college students were murdered in their apartment.

In December, **the Taliban announced a ban on women's higher education**. Now, the highest a woman can get educated in Afghanistan is the 6th grade.

~

In July, **the Georgia Guidestones were blown up**. It was July 6th. Yet **none of the mainstream news sources listed it as "important" for 2022**. Here's how it felt that day…

"This is fantastic news. A message has been sent. **Humanity has spoken.** *The comments on Twitter show that most of us are jubilant and understand what this means.*

Last year, I was asked to find out if this should be something done (by a Light Warrior who was thinking about orchestrating it himself). The answer, from One, was, "Not now. It will be accomplished at the right time." Well, I guess today is the time!!"

~

Thanks to those Canadians, we started 2022 off on a high note, with plenty of enthusiasm…

~

"Against all odds, and after a really rough two years, we've emerged as a single force for Freedom. Nicely done!"

~

One had this to say in January…

~

"It is the One.

Here I had to pause to get readers. I don't usually need them when I'm writing, but things were sort of blurry today.

Sophia, your eyesight will improve as you adjust to the light. *(Meaning the incoming light)* You will not require glasses always.

Will my health improve also?

Somewhat, yes, it will. There are surprises in store for you and for everyone. All things are improved, once they adjust, in a higher, brighter frequency.

When?

This is ongoing. It happens now. Every now moment shows improvement and Mastery.

I'm not sure what "and Mastery" signifies?

It signifies your awakening."

~

"It is important to realize that your current way of relegating authority outside of your own self is not going to support your new world. It is not up to

419

someone else to decide what laws, rules and allowances should exist for a sovereign populace. You've already lived that story, and it did not go well or support your **personal agency**.

When you consider "spelling" and the "spell" it has cast on the population, it is but a brief peek into this intentional deception and corruption you'll have to unravel. The term **"agency"** has been used most broadly for government authoritarian bureaus and not for personal empowerment. It is this sort of confusion that is present now in the naming of things, particularly those things that are part of your government, religious, education and monetary systems. You've accepted these names without considering their meaning, and thus remain unaware of their full effect on your psyche."

*A full story accompanied this paragraph, around the term **"agency"**. I was reminded that until the most recent 2 or 3 years, it is not one I'd heard often when referencing self-authority. This was an intentional act. It's like the word **"agency"** was sort of hi-jacked, and placed before us solely as indication of government power, of an organization holding authority over us. This, so that we would not recognize our personal power, or use it to advocate for ourselves and our will to act on our own authority.*

As evidence for our evolution, the term **"personal agency"** *is seen in the dialogue more often now, and recognized as truth.*

~

"You will find out, and quickly now, that there are some who came willingly to torment the race in order to wake it up. Their corruption, in some cases to enormous effect, has been their gift to mankind.

They sacrificed themselves in order to give this gift. It is a gift of enlightenment.

This is not to say that they realize this now, as humans, and while they do what they do. This is to say that everyone is sourced from love, **everyone is love**, and on the same team.

It does not seem so now."

~

On February 13ᵗʰ I was woken up...

~

"At 3:04 (CST) this morning reinforcements landed on your shores"
One.

[Watch the water]
Visualization: The worries and problems, of control by the evil/corrupted ones, are cast aside like snow on the runners of a fast-moving sled.

Drops of Light

The impression felt with the words was that this was off-world help to liberate the planet. This has to come before anything else and it is largely unseen. We are not going to meet them right now. This is not disclosure, this is assistance. Assistance to remove the mechanism of control that runs earth's society.

~

March was an active month...

~

"I went to see a film last week, which was **the first time I'd been to a theater in at least 2 years**! If you can, you may enjoy seeing the film **"Everything, everywhere, all at once."** It was intense and challenging and thought provoking. I laughed and cried and was transported for 2.5 hours. It is impossible to describe, yet there are elements of the multi-verse and the purpose of life all intertwined in a wild, wild ride!"

~

Then, on March 13th...

~

"We moved the clocks ahead in Illinois at 2AM on March 13, 2022. At that moment 2AM magically becomes 3AM on all of our devices. Also at that moment, I was woken up. So, I am unclear on the time of that waking. Was it 2AM or was it 3AM?

When it happened, I asked if it was the One and was told "yes" and to "take note of this time, when something changed". I asked if more discussion was desired and was told, "no, just make note of the time".

I remember wondering what exactly had changed and I believe the words I heard were "the frequency".

Later that morning, I spoke to the usual group here and they added a bit more information. They said "Frequency is another word for Timeline. The Time-line changed then. That's all that we can say at this point."

I've spoken to the One since then and was told that the time noted was "a precise signal" that needed to be recorded."

~

On March 21st ...

~

"This morning, between midnight and 3:30 AM, I was woken up. Here's what happened...

Did someone wake me up?

It is the One.

What is going on?

Note the time.

Why? Has something happened?

423

Drops of Light

Yes. This will cause disruption.

The next thing I remember is waking up, this time with a start. I realized I had nodded off. I checked the time. It was 3:30 AM. I don't know how long I'd slept, so the time frame of between midnight and 3:30 AM is a best guess.

Later this morning I reached out for more information...

It is the One.

The time was noted and recorded so that you (*empirical*) see the progression and anticipate the acceleration.

It was given here as a signal to those here assisting the shift. Light workers, Light warriors, etc., will feel the switch internally. This is similar to other markers, and it tells you that **the time is here, that there is progress, and that a specific level of light has been attained.**"

~

"You are on the home stretch. Know that regardless of how prepared you think you are, it will be a jolt to come face-to-face with these non-terrestrial helpers.

Yet that is to happen eventually.

You'll not encounter harshness or negative intentions from them. But *(you will encounter)* very real differences in expression and relationship.

Not all beings emote the way humans do. In fact, most don't. You'll find this off-putting at first, even mechanical. Yet know that they will proceed with utmost caution and attempts at sensitivity. They do not wish to offend, and will avoid it at all costs."

~

"Those who hold destructive intentions are reaching now for whatever they feel will allow them more control, more power or more "food". Their favorite "food" is fear.

For this reason, expect some fearful dramas to continue for a bit. These will likely occur soon, and appear outlandish; almost like a science fiction novel. You'll recognize them by their desperation.

Potentially, these could involve an "alien invasion", an "alien germ/illness", a threat of nuclear war, a threat of an armed invasion by a foreign "enemy" — to name a few. It will be frightening.

Each exists now as a possible move that will delay the inevitability of loss of control held by the current controllers. **This is a massive operation, hundreds of years in the planning, that will now fail.**

Drops of Light

To tell you that the whole of Creation is watching is an understatement. **The whole of Creation is on the edge of their seats."**

~

"The Dark ones have fallen. You can be sure of that. It is this moment when the lightworkers and light warriors will arise. There are many still shielded and or blinded by society's narrative, who will be drowsy. Yet it is time for them to begin. It is time for you all to begin.

You become then, a beacon for your fellow man. The truth is abhorrent, and many, seeing the darkness that has taken hold here, will feel an absence of light. This is where you come in. You are the light they seek.

In this way, you fulfill your purpose and vast potential. You supplement the void of love that will be evident when so many crimes against humanity are exposed.

You supplement with **you.**

You supplement with your light."

~

In April, the film "Watch the Water" was discussed at length...

~

"It (*meaning the virus*) was released in China and much

of what happened there was hidden from your view.

Hold on, and before we go on, tell me how, if the "dark hats" have been stopped and if help has arrived from off-planet **two months ago***, this crime has not been stopped? Also, if the "white hats" knew, (which it looks as if they did, due to their use of the phrase "watch the water"* **years ago***) why has it been allowed to go on?*

Why has it not been stopped and proper, useful therapies dispensed? None of this is adding up.

Thank you.

Sophia, you are distraught.

I am horrified.

There are truths and misrepresentations embedded in all that you are aware of.

This is a process. A process that humanity chose to complete on its own. As this is a free-will Universe, this was permitted.

Also, help was allowed to offer an assist once **mankind reached the goal of universal desire for liberation on his own.** This has occurred. You've liberated yourselves and saved yourselves, and help has arrived to assist with the clean-up and removal of the remaining players. This is done out of sight. This has been an ongoing and continuous operation so that updates are not necessary. It will be many months before it is complete.

You are witnessing a reversal of an era. An era that continued on, uninterrupted for the most part, for thousands of years.

Thousands of years Sophia. **It will not be un-done in an afternoon, a single operation, or a few months.**"

~

Still in April…

~

"Two weeks ago, I experienced a lucid dream. In it, I was with a group of people who were returning from a mission of sorts – working to heal an area of the planet and/or a group of people. We were in a train depot. All of us were saying goodbye as we went our separate ways.

The station was made of glass and white metal. I didn't see the trains, but envisioned them fast and light and silent.

One of the members of our group had to wait to be picked up and I waited with him. His parents showed up to meet him. They introduced themselves and his father said "I am blind, so I can't see you. But I'd like to know you, as you work with my son." I said "No problem, I'll tell you about myself."

He said "No, just hold this next to your eyes." He handed me a red/orange cloth or scarf. He then took the other end and held it to the side of his own eyes. Immediately, I felt I knew who he was, and that he knew me. It was a transference of our core selves and it was sent telepathically. The scarf as a vehicle for it wasn't actually necessary, yet it gave us both something to focus on, similar to a crystal ball. He "saw" me and I "saw" him. After a moment, he smiled, satisfied. He indicated that he approved of and felt better about the group that his son was traveling and working with.

It was a beautiful connection and one I'll never forget. I've been told that the cloth wasn't really necessary except as a vehicle to get things started. (*I guess we were newbies!*) Also, that our new earth has all that and more! It was incredible. We are going to love it."

~

"We are freeing ourselves, and some of us are choosing to do that in ways that seem counter-intuitive. Some of us are playing the role of darkness. This, so that others of us can play the role of light.

Who is who can sometimes be tough to parcel out, yet that is where the real juicy stuff happens. The human stuff; name calling, polarizing, accusing and judging. That's where all the action is. It's where we learn and grow and get stuck. It's what makes humanity so darn fun.

Because it is fun, you know. Although this is a really rough patch, there is no place more emotionally rich and passionately vibrant. Earth is creation's playground, and we, all of us humans, have always held the artist's brushes here. We just didn't know it.

We've collectively gathered to create our opus, and all of us will contribute to its brilliance. That is why it is taking so long. We have to sort out who paints which section with what color. It's sort of a mess right now, because we're having so much fun trying out each shade and paintbrush.

One of the more important components in a work of art is shading; shadow and light. These components give the piece depth and realism. Both black and white are necessary; darkness and brilliance.

Some of us chose the really dark portions. Others of us didn't.

Up until now, the earth has held a hidden and devastating amount of darkness. This means, now that we're aware of that truth, that it's time to replace that dark. Replace it with light. Our light. Your purpose will have something to do with that.

Before we can replace it, we'll have to identify it; identify the darkest part. This is what this post is about. Identifying the dark. It is not something you'll want to do, and not something most people will really want to witness. It's so dark that you may fear getting lost in there and being unable to get out. Yet there is a way, and it is worth the effort.

The dark is not someone holding a different opinion than yours or belonging to an opposing political party or someone who is rude. The dark is not someone who is richer than you, or a specific skin color. The dark is the opposite of light, period. Dark is defined as "being less light in color than other substances **of the same kind**".

Did you read that last part? **"Of the same kind"**. The dark, who are very much here now and seemingly in abundance, are **"of the same kind"** as you. Human, but with less light.

They chose to be dark, **so that we'd notice our light**. This is what is necessary for us to complete our opus. Real contrast, a display of polarization, good versus evil, dark to light. They (*the dark ones*) are so entrenched in destruction, destruction of life, that it blocked their light. They have to be stopped. In order to stop them, they have to be seen. Seen and identified visibly.

This darkness, once it is brought out, seen and eradicated, will complete our opus. Once our opus is complete, we can move on.

Spoiler alert: our opus holds all of us, many whom we don't agree with, some who we don't like and who may even have hurt our feelings. Our opus is us."

~

A few words about the Pleiadians/Pods that spring…

~

"I have not seen a pod physically. There have been a few false starts where I expected to do so, but did not. At this point it's been years (*since 2016*) and frankly, I question whether they'll ever pull it off. We'll all find out together on that score.

What I can share is an experience that my partner has had. I've reported on some of his happenings before. He is a deep trance channel, and a lot of "unusual" things occur. He has a clear recall of being in one (*a medical pod*), and that includes a visual. They are clear/transparent very large seats/chairs (*not beds*). There is something white behind the back of the chair. These chairs are really comfortable! That's what he has said about them. He remembers being on a ship when he was in one. He remembers the attendants who were in the room with him. They were male."

Here are some quotes from conversations that took place with the Pleiadians around that time:

"Every faction of health and help is about to be transformed on Earth. Every single aspect of life."

"Our goal is to assist and it is a cooperative one. We negotiate with earth humans now."

"There will come a time when you will meet more of us.

The entry into the human sphere and on the earth will occur in the near future, and in a coordinated fashion with other races. For now, our beds and technicians may "pass" as humans and human tech, in order to assist with the healing of the children."

"Trust that there is progress, a plan and an intention for the beds to arrive and assist the race."

"At this time, we have no specific time estimates for a general arrival. All of this is not under our control. It is a coordinated effort with multiple races involved, and components to consider. First it is (*and this has to take precedence*) the children."

~

Drops of Light

And One added this to our conversation…

~

"You build now a New World. It is structured from Love instead of fear. This Love includes inter-species harmony.

These changes are evident, even now, in 2022, in your sightings and recordings of numerous unusual animal friendships and peaceful interactions. In these, what you are witnessing are the misrepresentations of conflict and fear laid bare. The animals themselves are no longer in fear of a supposed "enemy" or "predator", because the current energy is not fear based – but Love based. These **animals are the least-susceptible to programming and so cooperation is witnessed here first.**

Prepare yourself to change the way you consider the world in which you live. All of its inhabitants will change with you. Thus, your New World is birthed."

~

In June there was a different sort of conversation…

~

"There are a few of us here, Sophia.

We all appreciate the chance to engage, once again, with the human race.

We watch and we marvel at the progress made here. It is not as if you have had an instruction manual or much physical assistance. Yet, here you are, freeing yourselves from control.

Who are you? Please introduce yourselves.

We are Galactic neighbors and there are three of us collaborating/combining our thoughts to reach you now. We reside near to, but not within, your Milky Galaxy.

Hello! How would you like to be addressed?

(*Warm, smiling eyes*) You have such an unusual style of communication. You confirm for us the notion of a gentle heart, so typical of the human.

However you (*choose to*) address us will not offend (*us*). Our "names" would be difficult to spell, so why not call us your Galactic Brothers?

You are male.

Yes, we felt you knew that.

Yes, I was just confirming.

What would you like to say to us today?

Drops of Light

That you are being cheered on by many more than you could possibly imagine. Some of the energy you are feeling comes from your supporters.

There are races who still suffer under the strong arm of this controlling group which you are extricating. Those especially, are enthusiastically waiting to witness your freedom.

Without knowing it, the humans have been illustrating "how it's done". **You've been writing a sort of instruction manual for throwing off this aggressive reptilian race that has controlled you and many others.** It is an outstanding achievement. We are eagerly anticipating true interaction with your race, once you complete this process of freeing yourselves!

We'd like to plant a seed. This could be called a seed of expectation. What we see is that many of you expect contact. Also, that the expectation for contact comes, in many cases, (*described/pictured/visualized*) from the same sources of media that lie to you regularly.

What we'd like this seed to do instead, is introduce the thought of wide-spread and far-reaching differences. These encompass body type, method of movement, style of communication, color, voice and pattern of life. None of these indicate negative intent or harm. They represent the expanse and possibility of life forms.

Intent is individually and uniquely determined. It will be felt. As you utilize your intuitive and telepathic senses, you will find yourself knowing on a deeper level the intent of the individual with whom you engage. It's a natural process.

This is why we answered today! (*Warm, smiling eyes*)

Great! Thanks, you guys! It is a pleasure to speak with you.

The pleasure is ours. We hope to soon engage in person!

Okay! Until then.

Until then. (*There is a sense of waving here, yet I am not sure that I saw hands… it was interesting*)"

~

    In July, "**A Re-Imagination ~ Handbook for the Many of One**" *was released. It is "a handbook of considerations for re-structuring this once-captured society."*

~

    And One had this to say…

~

"Others will seek your strength now. Know that all storms pass over and once they do, a rainbow is seen. Believe in the rainbow. Its presence assures you that

Drops of Light

regardless of the strength and destruction of the storm, light remains.

It is your light that breaks through every dark moment and it is your light that brought you here now, for this moment on earth.

Hold your truth. It is a beacon for those in need of it now."

~

"Let us speak now of what the light brings. For these are things that you'll consider "wonderful".

One of the first is clarity. Think of the image used to illustrate a good idea. It is a light bulb. This image signifies intelligence.

It is light that removes the darkness. It is light that provides clarity of direction.

When you are unable to identify something, light offers a clear picture as an assist.

Light is necessary for growth.

Light is your core truth.

And right now, there is more light bathing your world than there has ever been. You are all receiving and allowing the light.

The dark needed to be extreme in order for this shift to take place. The cry from humanity had to be loud enough to drown out those who prefer to operate in darkness. It was, and **now the light is here**. It increases daily."

~

As we proceeded through August & September, a Love Quest was held once more, in an effort to find what had been shattered the last 2+ years. Here was its introduction...

~

"For almost three years now we've all been in the process of loss. What we've lost is our innocence.

Before 2020, we held some deep-seated beliefs that no longer work. These were unquestioned. They were so embedded in our world view that they were part of the cloth itself. They'd become invisible.

Since 2020 there's been a gradual fraying of the fabric holding us together. Strand by strand our biases, beliefs and idiosyncrasies pulled away and showed themselves. In full color and separate now they can't help but be noticed. If not by us, then by someone close to us.

This fraying and noticing asks us to self-examine. If we are lucky and aware of what is happening, this will propel us into growth. **Growth, after all, is why we're here**."

~

Drops of Light

"It's 2022. A full decade has moved in between the last "ending of an age" (*2012*), and this one.

So, what's changed? Have we shifted?

Do we reside in a world of love, abundance, blue-birds, angels and bliss?

Are the off-worlders here?

This may sound silly, yet how many of us held out hope back then for the same things we wish for to-day? Did you think it was right around the corner then? Do you still believe it is right around the corner now?

If this decade has proven anything at all, then top of that list would have to be that those of us following blogs like this one, maintain a constant force of opti-mism. It is unstoppable. You might even say it's our calling card.

As we sit on the cusp of the final months of 2022, let's give ourselves a break. We've done some incredi-ble stuff!

The world **is** waking up.

Consciousness **is** shifting.

Our New World **is** being built. It's a vastly more unified populace that it was ten years ago. **This is because of you.**

This is due to your light, your love and your consistent belief in us and what we are capable of."

~

"We have been through times that have challenged every part of us, and we are still here! **Our purpose is to maintain the light** as we travel through this next part. Don't doubt your strength. It's real. It was one of the qualifications needed to incarnate right now.

It's time for us to recognize that everyone here has decided to stay for a reason, and that **everyone we encounter will benefit from our love and our light in some way.**"

~

One was still speaking to us regularly…

~

"It is suggested that you prepare for the coming storm.

You who read words like this are beacons for those who will be lost when it arrives; **Beacons in the Storm.**"

~

"For indeed, the tenacity and desire to live is so extreme within the (*earth-human*) race, that it simply cannot be doused. If one of you gives up, another of you pops up to reinforce his or her enthusiasm, and the will to live persists.

It is this insistence on life at all costs that once and finally ended the controller's dark plans. Their ultimate goal was doomed to failure from the start.

What has dragged it out this long is yet another un-planned characteristic of the race; your desire to in-clude everyone. This togetherness was your idea. The emotion that was felt when it was decided was one of not wanting anyone to miss the party. An idea that it was all of you who signed up to experience the suc-cessful conclusion for the race – so all of you should be together to celebrate it.

This is visceral unity, although not all of you are aware of its presence in your everyday. **You love each other. This, my dear human, is your calling card.**

Mankind made a decision to end this when as many as possible would be on board.

The slavery was ended. There were still members of the race who had not been given enough information to choose to join the party.

The final scene was postponed in order to awaken more of the race.

It will come as a huge shock to many more people than you know when the final scene is played. Not everyone is playing the same strategy and not everyone playing understands who invented the game.

It is Creation's game.

In this experiment, which is about to end, humanity has declared with absolute finality that Love wins. Love cannot be erased. Love's light refuses to be doused. Dear human, your essence has been confirmed in this experiment.

This, my dear, dear ones, was Creation's purpose. It was created, sanctioned and completed by the One, the Many, the All. Love is proven unrelenting, indestructible and absolute in the physical expression of humanity.

For you have stood side by side and against an onslaught of efforts to destroy you – and withstood them all. There is no unhappy ending or partial victory. Indeed, it is a victory unlike any other. In this game there are no real losers. It is Love that wins and this is a bonus for Creation itself.

Drops of Light

When you comprehend the vastness of what you have done my dear, dear human, you will rejoice. For certainly there are none but you who could have pulled off such a feat, and the ones after you will have learned this from you.

There is a seamless Unity to the way it occurred. You organically joined hearts and recognized your glory. In that state, you saw the essence of all souls and declared that they be honored.

It is in the honoring and allowing each soul to progress at his or her own rate that prolongs this game, this experiment that has already been concluded. It is Love."

~

In late October, One shared this...

~

"Events transpire for you on your planet right now, that will alter the course of your life.

Things like free access to energy and highly advanced medical technology are only a start. Methods for food preparation are available that will guarantee an end to hunger. There are advances in virtually every aspect of society.

These will astound the senses and uplift as well as simplify your existence. Much has been kept from you, dear human.

You've been raised and bred to be work animals for a non-human species. This is the awful truth of it.

Once you accept it as truth, everything that you've suffered through makes sense.

Religion was a tool used to instill in the population a reason for "suffering". Many teach the fact that you are born with sin as part of your soul. You are marked before you are able to hold a conscious thought, and this contributes to the way you have accepted the conditions of your slavery. You are taught, very early on, that you are not worthy.

This life has been a stimulus to a remembering. You are here to remember your truth and to realize your core. **You are the most brilliant of lights, favored in all of Creation.**"

~

We were now in November...

~

"We will speak today of light and its increase in your skies. This was not possible under prior conditions, and it is so now. It is not such a difficult search online to find recent

photos and videos of light craft, light ships, rainbows of light, light beams and pillars of light.

Drops of Light

Consider these to be concrete evidence that the light has increased.

What this means is that the frequency "allows" it to be seen. You are essentially moving fast enough to be in concert with the light. You accept these phenomena of light within your visual field.

You see them.

Consider this to be evidence of your progression. The race moves towards the light and does not hide the light.

And what does light do?

It raises the visual ability and it eliminates the dark.

This entire process has been one of rapidly increasing light. It increases in area, and it increases in brilliance. Light is now seen in places where it was never seen before.

Light is now present as a constant.

Light emanates from the enlightened ones, and from the awakened ones.

Light appears in your skies.

The light, your light, has been here always. Yet it remained shrouded in the preponderance of darkness here. No longer.

The light has overtaken the darkness.

Be assured that the light has won."
~

"There will be shocks for all. Those who have kept themselves shielded from the truth are also here to Awaken and to assist in this Awakening. Many surprises await you all, and there will be unlikely turnarounds and disclosures. Nothing is as it seems. You would be well advised to keep your mind and your heart **wide-open**.

Trust that you will be told the truth. Believe in the best of humanity. For it is that best that has carried you so far. A decade ago, you insisted that **everyone comes along and makes it to the finish line."**
~

"An onslaught of change rolls forward, engulfing reality as you know it. The purpose of our (*Sophia &* *One*) contact is to record the change and validate its meaning. This will yield vast reservoirs of comfort in future times. It will provide clarity where there is mostly confusion.

There are specific alterations that approach the fabric of your world/your reality. These are changes to what you see and know. They will, at first, feel shocking to you. This is because you have accepted your current "reality" as true.

You have had no reason not to, until now. The things you are learning/uncovering/exposing about those people and those institutions that run things here, provide plenty of reasons. You are realizing that things are not as they seem.

What you don't fully realize is just how many things are illusions and/or delusions. You know or suspect that you've been deceived. Yet you are not privy to the extent of that deception. It is almost complete.

The magnitude of falsehoods to which you assign credence is quite unimaginable. Almost all of what you've accepted as true – is not. The reality in which you reside was intentionally constructed. This, so that the race could be most readily contained within it.

Each element had a purpose. Your controllers have done this before.

What you need to know is that there are now more humans feeling this desperation as their fortunes, family members and livelihoods are threatened. Many do not know the deepest, darkest actions of the ones controlling the puppet strings.

They fell for the bait – hook, line and sinker. They wanted fame and/or glory and/or wealth and/or power. They did not fully comprehend the depravity beneath the presentation of those goals.

These are the most asleep.

It is for these lost souls that the awakening is drawn out. It is lengthened by their refusal to accept responsibility for anything other than "desire to get ahead" or "succeed" or "win the competition of life".

These folks are your fellow humans. These are the minds that are in most need of a jump-start to awaken.

You may liken it to an alarm. Some of you prefer soft music or bird-song to arouse you at the proper time. Yet, not all of you. Others of you require something loud and sudden to wake you up.

You've reached the point when loud and sudden is the only option remaining. Although this may sound abrasive and surprising to those of you already awake, it will not be shocking.

Those asleep and complicit in propelling the illusion will be stunned. It is then when you who are prepared already will be most needed."

~

Drops of Light

The Pleiadians had this to say in November. This is the last conversation we had that year. There has been no contact in 2023…

~

"Hello Sophia. How can we help you?

Hello and thanks. I am not getting a visual, which is unusual. Can you provide me with one or explain why? Thanks.

We are shielded. We are not the usual group to whom it is that you speak. We are an observing group. We assess the "Help the Human Race" project for different reasons.

Do you sense/see anything at all?

Yes. Dark, a wall of some kind that you are reaching out from behind. It is odd for me. I've always seen you or parts of the group.

Well, this is the way we've chosen for now. We are closer than you think.

What is it that you wanted contact for today?

It's been three months. I was told that I'd be updated by about this time. Thank you.

We can say this. Our technology has been and is currently being utilized on your earth. It is in the form of a spray, if you will. Your feedback at your last contact moment was instrumental in its adjustment and fine tuning.

It would appear to be having the desired effect where possible. There is a connection between calmness and health. In many cases health has been maintained or restored or encouraged. This, of course, happens invisibly and without recognition of its source. This is by design.

As far as the pods go, the plan remains. The timing is, as ever, fluid. Our delivery method has been perfected and improved so that it can happen on a moment's notice.

In some places, the pods are in full operation already. You would consider these places to be casualties of the crimes against the children and adults who have been abused, trafficked, tortured. These places are out of your sight.

Members of the Alliance work with technicians from our ships who know how these pods work and where they can be the most effective. Few, if any, questions are asked about the source of these, due to the severity of the need and the secrecy necessary to protect the humans. Again, these are in remote areas, out of your sight.

Drops of Light

There is so much you don't know. One of the reasons for today's wall is to maintain the secrecy. When it is appropriate you will see all and know all.

Be aware that contact will be initiated by us if and when there are either questions or announcements.

We are extremely busy. The time approaches when we'll be busier still, and you'll be aware when that time is here.

Are the "Healing Trails" continuing until then?

Yes. They will continue as your planet proceeds through the coming seasons and for several years. As we see there is great benefit to the population and no harm or fear. Quite the opposite. It is our mission to help the race and in any way that we can, we will continue to do so.

Now, is there something else?

No, there is not. Thank you for answering my questions today.

You are welcome, Sophia. Goodbye.

(This felt like a single male and it was not someone I've spoken to before. I felt the secrecy had something to do with his location; almost as if he was on the earth. That was a feeling

only, as he felt so very close. I was not shown or told any-thing.)"

~

The last month of 2022 ended with these words from One...

~

"These days you walk now will have you encountering further hardship. There will be awful truths.

As you do, you'll discover strength you didn't know you possessed and realize in what it is you truly believe.

For regardless of what you are told or not told – you will know your strength in Love. And regardless of what the day presents to you, **your Light will illuminate Truth**.

For Truth cannot be eradicated, although it can be hidden.

More powerful words than True ones do not exist. **Truth carries the Light of a billion stars.** There is no force greater.

As the Light of Truth blazes forth, Love erupts within and around it.

For Truth is Love and both are illuminated with your Light."

Drops of Light

~

"I come to you today to offer comfort.

Hear these words, for they echo Truth. Truth is what you have not had access to these many generations.

You are the bravest of the brave.

You are the strongest of the strong.

Your Light! Oh! Your Light is that of ten thousand brilliant bulbs! It not only emits from your very essence; it radiates throughout your being and is felt viscerally by anyone who is fortunate enough to be within range.

And what a range it is!

My dear, dear humble human. You have trudged and crawled through the murkiest, darkest times, only to emerge unscathed. For regardless of any attempt made to assault your spirit – you remain radiant.

You are not defeated, my dear ones, you are exalted. It is in your exaltation that this/your world is raised up. It is placed among realms of peace, glory and absolute agape.

For above all – you are Love.

Despite all – you are Love.

Throughout all – you are Love.

This Love that you are echoes through each event and every story.

Your Light will not be dimmed.

Your Light has not been dimmed.

Focus now on what you have felt and known always but have not been told by your society's mechanisms.

Focus now on your Truth.

You are Love.
You are Light.
You are Truth.

Your nature is one of loyalty, compassion, joy and abundance.

You desire consensus because you embody Oneness, and anything other than that feels foreign to you.

Consensus is not replication of the details. Consensus is agreement on the highest and best outcome for all concerned. Simply put, consensus is Unconditional Universal Love.

Drops of Light

This Love that you are emerges viscerally now in contrast to what is being exposed. Do not despair in what you see exposed. For **this is the wound that must see the Light in order to heal**.

And heal it will, my dear, beloved human. You would have it no other way.

Such is your Light.

Such is your Love.

Such is your Truth; that what you are capable of exceeds your current imaginings.

Yet, I tell you that you have not imagined the sheer wonder of who it is that you are. Feel this. Your Love resonates throughout your body and emerges in all that you see and do and think and feel and are.

You are magnificent and it is the raw power of your true Love Essence that makes you so.

Nothing and no one will stop your emergence or limit your radiance. The time for your cohesion is upon you and you are ready.

Remember who you are.

Feel the Truth of your Essence, and Love will surround and astound you each day.

This is your New World my dear human. It is not my doing, it is yours.

Remember.

That is all.

Thank you.

(Such emotion came through here! Tears, heartfelt and deep admiration for us. A proclamation of pure love. I cried throughout this transmission. It was so very deeply felt.)"

Drops of Light

Chapter 7
Becoming the Light
(2023~)

Oneness is now absolute.
Nothing that occurs for you now
feels separate from you.
You begin now to see yourself
as a Source of Light.
What began as a drop is now a flood;
a Flood of Light.

Drops of Light

One started this year (2023) with these words…

~

"So, my dear, dear human. This year may be both quieter and more raucous than the previous one.

You are weary. There is widespread agreement on that.

To offer a stimulant then, something to help keep you uplifted and moving forward, is the purpose of our conversation today.

This is a process. The race chose to take its time and have everyone along for the conclusion. It did so out of Love, trust and unity. It did so without conscious thought as to how long and challenging that decision was. It did so out of Love.

You may use the term "tough love" now to define the result of that choice. For you are an impatient be-ing. Yet more so you are a loving one. You will choose unity every time.

The coming year will expose the blatant corruption and control built into the current systems of govern-ment, commerce, education and medicine. Some will recognize these early and immediately know what they mean. Not all, and not the majority.

As truths are told and corruption is exposed, do not assume that it will initiate an "obvious" conclusion for everyone. Conclusions will be reached individually and in people's own time.

It is not important that any one human was aware before any other human. You are One. Now is the process of becoming consciously unified.

In your not-so-distant past, your unification was constructed and intended by an outside controlling force – the ones who assumed ownership here.

You are now in the process of Conscious Unity that emerges from within, from self-knowing, from inner Truth, from Love. **This is a beautiful, gradual emergence that will be, at a certain point, instantaneous and glorious.**

You cannot get there alone and in fact came here now to participate in a Global Awakening that springs from within each individual.

Know that regardless of what you say or don't say, your presence, your Light and your Love is what propels this Global Shift.

Everything speeds up because of your Light."

~

Drops of Light

Here's just some of what mainstream news reports so far this year, by month (today is October 10th) ...

~

January: Croatia replaced the kuna with the euro.
NFL Buffalo Bills Player **Damar Hamlin** collapses on the field due to cardiac arrest.
A US **teacher in Virgina** is shot by her 6-year-old student.
It takes 15 ballots to elect Republican **Kevin McCarthy** as Speaker of the US House of Representatives, the most since 1860.
Brazilian supporters of former president Jair Bolsonaro attack Government buildings in protest; 1500 are later arrested.
Attorney General Merrick Garland appoints a special counsel to **investigate Joe Biden**'s handling of classified documents.
Cyclone Cheneso makes landfall in Madagascar, leaving about 40,000 people homeless.
New Zealand Prime Minister Jacinda Ardern resigns. Chris Hipkins is sworn in.
China's northernmost city, Mohe, reports **record low temperatures** -53C (-63F).
Both America & Germany announce plans to send powerful battle tanks to **Ukraine**.
A suicide bomb blast at a mosque in **Peshawar, Pakistan** kills 100 and injures 157 people.
The **doomsday clock** was set to 90 seconds to midnight, which is the closest it's been since it was created in 1947.

February: A 7.8 magnitude **earthquake struck Turkey & Syria**, causing more than 59,000 deaths.

US records coldest wind-chill ever at Mount Washington University, New Hampshire (-108F)

A **train** carrying toxic chemicals de-rails in **East Palestine**, Ohio; starting a fire & leading to an intentional burn-off.

US Fighter jets shoot down a Chinese surveillance balloon off the eastern seaboard.

Scottish First Minister, Nikola Sturgeon, **resigns**.

US President "surprise" visits **Ukraine** and pledges aid.

The land **Armenian-Turkish border opened** for the first time in 35 years.

The FBI publicly confirmed that they believe **Covid-19 originated from a lab in Wuhan, China**.

Puffin, publisher of **Roald Dahl books**, says they'll publish both his original works as well as their recently edited ones. This, after widespread criticism.

March: The US record industry said that **vinyl record sales exceed CD sales** for the first time since 1987.

Tik-Tok announces a 60-minute **daily use limit** for people under the age of 18.

Leaked US DOD documents from the **Ukraine** war appear on Discord, associated with the online game Minecraft.

OpenAI released **GPT-4**, an upgraded version of their AI Chatbot.

Russia begins a missile attack on Ukrainian

infrastructure & cities.

Italy banned the use of OpenAI's ChatGPT over security concerns.

Iran & Saudi Arabia agree to re-establish diplomatic ties after talks in Beijing.

California's **Silicon Valley Bank collapses**; the largest US bank fail since 2008.

Xi Jinping appointed to historic 3rd term as president of China.

The US, UK & Australia announce the **AUKUS** deal for a nuclear-powered submarine fleet in the Indo-Pacific region to counter Chinese military build-up.

South Korea & Japan hold their first talks since 2011, in Tokyo.

Switzerland's largest bank, UBS, agrees to buy Credit Suisse for $3.2 billion to **stem global financial panic**.

Uganda passes an anti-homosexuality bill.

April: NASA announced the astronauts for a fly-by **mission to the moon**. It's the first one in over 50 years.

Finland joined NATO.

SpaceX's starship rocket exploded on its first full flight test.

The **Dalai Lama** apologizes for a video of him asking a boy to suck his tongue.

Germany closes its last 3 nuclear power plants.

Fox news settled a lawsuit with **Dominion** Voting Systems over the 2020 US Presidential election for $787.5 million.

US Supreme Court rules that the **abortion pill** mifepristone can remain widely available.

India surpasses China as the world's most populous country, with 1,425,775,850 people.

US President **Joe Biden** announces he'll run for a 2nd term.

May: Geoffrey Hinton, (the "**Godfather of AI**") resigned from Google to help spread the word about the dangers of this emerging technology.

Elon Musk received the go-ahead from the FDA to trial his **Neuralink** brain implants on humans.

WHO declares **Covid-19 over** as a global health emergency.

Canadian province **Alberta** declares a **state of emergency** due to wildfires; 25,000 people are evacuated.

King Charles III (Queen Camilla) is coronated; the first UK monarch crowned in 70 years.

Former Pakistani Prime Minister Imran Khan is arrested.

Donald Trump found guilty of sexually abusing E. Jean Carroll.

Heavy air attacks between **Palestinian & Israeli militants** leave more than 20 people dead in Gaza.

Elon Musk announces that his replacement CEO at Twitter is Linda Yaccarino from NBCUniversal.

Title 42 expires. It was a US pandemic-era policy that expelled most migrants.

Cyclone Mocha reaches the coast of **Myanmar**; at least 400 people die.

Montana becomes the first US state to **ban TikTok**.

Drops of Light

The final **"Indiana Jones"** film, still with Harrison Ford, premieres.

Illinois Attorney General's office reports that 451 **Catholic clergy sexually abused** over 2,000 children over 70 years.

Oath Keepers founder Stewart Rhodes is sentenced to 18 years for his part in the January 6, 2021 **Capitol attack**.

Fighting in **Sudan** caused the deaths of 828 civilians.

Turkey's President Recep Tayyip Erdoğan is re-elected.

400 **leading AI industry experts** sign a letter warning of the **"risk of extinction from AI"**; they say it should be a global priority.

June: A **3-train collision** in **India**'s Balasore district, Odisha state, leave 288 dead and thousands injured.

Mike Pence declares his **candidacy** for the Republican Presidential nomination.

A **dam collapse** at Nova Kakhovka, **Ukraine** leads to the evacuation of thousands of people.

Smoke from **Canadian wildfires** cause NY's air quality to reach 218aqi, the world's lowest.

Former UK Prime Minister **Boris Johnson** resigns as an MP.

Volodymyr Zelensky announced that the **Ukrainian counteroffensive** has begun.

An overcrowded **fishing boat capsizes** south of Greece, leaving 79 refugees & migrants dead, with more missing.

Fossils bones found in Tam Pà Ling (Cave of the

Monkeys), Laos, dated to 86,000 years, are the **oldest known examples of Homo sapiens** in South-East Asia.

Donald Trump was formally accused of mishandling classified documents.

Cyclone Biparjoy hits India's Gujarat coast; 180,000 people from India & Pakistan are evacuated from its path.

A **dengue fever** outbreak in **Peru** caused 248 deaths and 146,000 cases; health minister Rosa Gutiérrez resigns.

Rules for Grammy Awards were updated. They now restrict **AI-generated songs**.

Islamic state-linked militants attack a secondary school in Mpondwe, **Uganda**, killing 40 students there.

UK & Israel scientific team claims to have grown **synthetic human embryos** the equivalent of 14-day old natural ones.

Oceangate's **Titan submersible imploded** during an expedition to the wreckage of the Titanic; everyone onboard perished.

US approves its first **lab-grown meat**; chicken made from animal cells.

Kenya, Nairobi; **earliest possible evidence of cannibalism** found in 1.5-million-year-old fossilized hominin leg bones with cut marks made by stone tools.

US Supreme Court rules that college race-based admission programs to increase **diversity** are **illegal**, and **graphic artists can refuse work** from same-sex couples, and that President **Biden overstepped his authority** with a student debt forgiveness plan for 40-million students.

July: Yakutia region, **Siberia** declares a state of emergency as **forest fires** rage across 61,000 hectares of land.

Hottest average global temperatures ever are recorded for 3 consecutive days (17.18C/62.92F).

Meta launches **Threads**, Instagram's new public conversations app, & with 30 million downloads it becomes the most rapidly downloaded app ever.

World's first **robot-human press conference** held in Geneva, Switzerland.

British singer-song writer Elton John completes his final tour, **"Farewell Yellow Brick Road"**, in Sweden.

The **Dutch government**, led by PM Mark Rutte, collapses.

India launches its 3rd moon mission.

Iran's Persian Gulf International Airport hit a **heat index of 152F/66.7C**.

Typhoon Talim makes landfall in China's Guandong coast; 230,000+ people are evacuated.

Phoenix, Arizona has **31 consecutive days** with temperatures **at or above 110°F (43.3°C)**, breaking a 50 yr. record.

Cambodia's Authoritarian **Prime Minister** Hun Sen **resigns**; the office passes to his son.

For the first time, **fruit flies are genetically**

engineered to reproduce without a male.

Two films, "**Barbie**" and "**Oppenheimer**" opened in cinemas. "Barbie" passed 1 billion at the global box office.

Good Vibes festival, an annual music festival in Malaysia, was **canceled** after the lead singer kissed his bandmate on stage to protest Malaysia's anti-LGBTQ+ laws.

Niger President Mohamed Bazoum was removed by a **military coup**.

NASA lists July as the **warmest month** in 174 years.

August: **Donald Trump** is indicted on charges of conspiring to defraud the country and prevent a peaceful transfer of power.

Maui, Hawaii suffers massive damage from **wildfires**. **Lahaina** is destroyed. The death toll starts at 97, while many are unaccounted for.

San Francisco, CA gave approval to 2 **driverless taxi** companies (robo-taxis) to run 24/7, after a year of testing.

Russia Space Agency's Luna 25 lunar lander crash landed on the moon. It was Russia's first attempt since the 1970's.

Canada's NW Territory & British Columbia call a state of emergency due to **wildfires**. More than 50,000 people are evacuated as a result.

The **US 30-year fixed mortgage rate** rises **above 7%** for the first time in 21 years.

Ecuador votes against drilling for oil in Yasuni

Drops of Light

National Park, which is inhabited by indigenous groups in the Amazon.

India's Chandrayaan-3 lunar mission is the first to land at the **moon's southern pole** successfully.

Greece's wildfires claim the lives of 20 people, including migrants crossing the border from Turkey.

In an attempt to balance global power, **BRICS** invites 6 new nations to join.

Donald Trump gets a mug shot at Fulton County jail in Georgia.

September: Typhoon Haikui reaches Tawain, forcing the evacuation of 400,000 people.

Enrique Tarrio, (**Proud Boys** chairman) is sentenced to 22 years in prison for his role in the **2021 US Capitol attack**.

Mexico's Supreme Court **de-criminalizes abortion** nationwide.

Intense **flooding** in **Hong Kong, Shenzhen & southern Chinese cities** is caused by the heaviest rainfall in 140 years.

A **6.8 magnitude earthquake in Morrocco** caused the deaths of over 2,000 people.

Two dams collapse in Derna, Libya, & leave thousands missing.

Earliest record of humans building with wood discovered in Zambia, at nearly half a million years old.

US Homeland Security grants special status to 472,000 Venezuelans already in the country, allowing them to work.

Rupert Murdoch retires from the Boards of Fox & News corporation, leaving his son, Lachlan, in charge.

NY City is flooded due to historic levels of rainfall.

October: Kevin McCarthy becomes the first Speaker of the US House of Representatives to be **ousted** by his own party.

23,000 old fossil footprints are confirmed as possibly the oldest evidence of humans in the Americas.

Two 6.8 magnitude **earthquakes** strike **Afghanistan**, leaving more than 800 people dead.

On October 7th, **Hamas launches an air & land attack on Israel from Gaza**, killing hundreds & taking hostages. **Israel**'s Prime Minister Benjamin Netanyahu **declares war** the following day.

Robert F. Kennedy Jr. launches an independent bid for the **US Presidency**.

Tina Turner, Lisa Marie Presley, Sinéad O'Connor, Jimmy Buffet, Michael Gambon, and Dianne Feinstein have died so far this year.

Last bit of news, which is an attempt to be on a "lighter" note, but actually isn't. The **world's record** was set this week for the **heaviest pumpkin** in Anoka, Minnesota, US: a 2,749-pound jack-o'-lantern gourd. Humans are amazing. Our ability to interject a consistent flow of enthusiasm for life, despite everything else, is the best thing about us.

~

Drops of Light

2023 has been an unexpectedly challenging year. This book has been written throughout this personal triage. We'll finish our story now, primarily with words from One; a beneficial constant in all of the chaos...

~

"What happens now is that the Light takes hold, and with this increased illumination the dark is exposed. It is seen clearly.

You enter a new phase of Acceptance now, as what has been previously accepted as True, and for the good of mankind is questioned on every front.

It will not take too long for the Shift to proceed. **Humanity seeks always common ground, something it can relate to, associate what it sees, hears, smells, tastes and touches with, and ultimately – believe in.**

This will not be easy or simply accomplished. The increased Light illuminates it all to assist and ease the process. The disruptions in your sleep and other regulatory patterns are due to the increased Light and rapid frequency.

It is recommended that you buckle up, and settle in for the ride. It promises to be a wild one."

~

"As you build up your inner light, your discernment strengthens, and formulating a decision about what you are hearing gets easier. The importance of your inner fortitude cannot be over-stated. This is the reason you are here.

Be conscious and remain steadfast in your knowing of who you are. You are some of the bravest of the brave, the strongest of the strong and the most brilliant lights. You are so very necessary to the current unfolding on your planet."

~

"You are meant for this time you now walk in. You are the strongest and surest of lights, here to not only weather the storm, but also to lead others to safety when they find themselves lost.

You are not alone.

All of this is chosen in complete harmony with many, many others. They stand beside you now and urge you on. They can see the end, and it is glorious.[10]"

~

"To be human is to live a life of extremes. To be human is an exquisite combination of profound loss and exquisite pleasure, alongside extreme passion. To be human is the ultimate thrill-ride. And you wanted it all.

So now, as the end stage of this casting-off is initiated – you shall have it all. It will be a mess; a difficult, glorious, spectacle of Man discovering both the best and the worst about what he is.

It will be a challenge to avert your eyes. You will have to though, in order to maintain a steady flow of your true power.

It becomes imperative that you access and broadcast your true essence. That of Love. That of Light. This will hold you steady through the mayhem, and stabilize many others as well.

You are a beacon, and your Light is necessary. For in many ways and places it will appear to be dark, very dark. Do not avoid these dark places. Go there ready with full illumination.

Remember that at the end, when all is said and all is done, there will be people still. There will be community still. There will be a society. **Those who are left standing among the ruins of the collapsed society will be the re-builders. They will be enlightened by the beacons who never dimmed their light, and they will be fortified by that constant illumination."**

~

"In the days ahead of you there will be reference to "The Builders". These Builders are you.

These Builders are the Great Ones who saw first,

and continued to see possibilities for change.

These are the Masters who collected themselves from far and wide in order to facilitate the Shift in Consciousness.

For make no mistake my dear, dear humans. This happens now because you are here. It happens because you have deemed it so. It happens because you are persistent and with that capacity you have seen, and not ever given up on, a New Earth.

Your New Earth has been introduced and is now seen by many. These humans will carry on because you've shown them what is possible. You've done so with your Light.

There will be many who come after you. They will continue the process. They will enter a different world than you have entered. It will be a world that holds a solid vision of Unity and Global Restoration. This is the world you have created. This exists because of you.

You are the Builders."

~

"You are Light Bearers. You are Love Conduits. Your presence, once activated and accepted by you as valid, is meant to act as a field of acceptance, a cushion of Love, a wave of calm, a moment of Peace.

Drops of Light

Once felt, those who share your place will begin their own process of healing. Their process may or may not include asking questions of you, and that doesn't matter. The fact that their process has begun is enough. It is why you are spread out all over the globe.

Be where you are in full. **It is time for you to recognize your true purpose. It is to provide a safe place, indeed to build a field, for this Global Awakening."**

*Here I saw a sort of **global light grid**. It was both powerful, and beautiful.*

~

At the end of May, this happened…

~

I was woken in the early morning hours. The following conversation took place:

"It is the One.

Things have happened. We will discuss them now. **The controllers have been defeated.** Their direct influence here is over. **Their reign is finished.**

What happens next is anyone's guess. The human players of their games may or may not know of their defeat. What they do know however, is that they have everything to lose once they are discovered and outed. It's up to Man to determine what will be done now. For the major force of the controllers is just gone.

You will see, and quite clearly now, who is promoting fear and division still. These will be humans who see no problem in capitalizing on fear; i.e., taking advantage of it to make money.

What will play out now will be most telling. What you should see, if you are to believe in the fact that there is an Alliance for "good" in charge – are major disclosures of all kinds.

The cabal is no longer a threat. The War has been won.

What happens now will be rapid and it will be a grand unveiling. Much will be apparent to those who know the Truth.

You will quickly discern each player's loyalty, and see who or what is propelling them. It will be obvious.

This story plays out for years. Yet now, the motivation and desire of each one of you will be what is driving your life.

The battle is over. The light has won.

Drops of Light

You are now "held down" only by those humans who sold their souls for profit and who have only their own protection and benefit as a driving force. Watch carefully. The playbook is about to get interesting."

~

"Your "light body" is another term for your "core essence". It is that part of you that is not imagined. It is the part of you that remains, regardless of how many imaginings you have from it. It is your core Truth.

It is the you that emanates from the everything, and encompasses the everything. It is Truth. It is the you that remains when all else falls away.

The term "light body" may be giving a false or erroneous impression. Because it is not necessarily a body in the form you know of as a body; with a head, torso, two arms and two legs.

Your light body is not to be confused with your soul. What we will do to explore the subject is to start at the beginning.

For initially there was nothing but pure potential. As this was the potential for everything, what followed immediately was the manifestation; the manifestation of life.

Now life initially was without form. What it needed in order to have form was intent.

For once life was initiated the questions followed.

Questions of shape, size, sound, purpose, sensation were some of the initial queries. With infinite potential came endless possibilities. A management system of some sort was developed with intent.

For creation to know itself, it had to frame itself around a possibility. It had to answer its own question. The question was "Who am I?"

And here is where intelligence responded and birthed infinite answers. Each answer a component of the whole – complete unto itself yet significant in its unique response.

Not a clone (identical) or a puppet (controlled) but **a segment of the everything with its own fingerprints**.

This segment, this fragment of creation itself has imagined itself countless ways. Today it imagines itself to be you who reads these words right now.

This you, who is imagining the you who reads these words, is what you refer to as your "light

body".

You may think of this component as an over-seer.
You may think of this aspect as a watcher. It holds
only your best interests for you. It will not alter your
plan for your day or your life, yet will assist if asked.

It knows why you are here. It will not interfere with
your free will choice to do whatever it is that you are
in the act of choosing. It is the purest form of source
you hold, and it is right here with you always.

Mostly you will know it as your closest friend.
Generally, you will know it as your "higher self",
although there is no "higher" or "lower" in creation.
Specifically in that unique portion of creation that is
known as you.

**So, your light body is your core. It is pure love,
pure light, pure energy. It is the first emission
from pure potential – the spark that imagined
you.**

There is a misunderstanding around the term and the
purpose for "light body". There is a supposition that
to achieve the "light body" state is the ultimate in
human spiritual evolution.

This supposition leaves out the gift and brilliance that
is the human body. It is the marriage of both that

results in expansion and energizes personal spiritual evolution.

The light body is your core.

In order for you to be here at all, your light body has to be accessible. For there is not ever an incarnate soul without a solid foundation and pure intent. Your foundation is your light body. It is your core from which all of you springs.

Your light body is you in pure form. It is the you that sees the ego body and knows every reason why each nuance was created. **Your light body is your closest companion.**"

~

"**Your world is filled with Masters.** They are scattered on every continent, in every age group and belief system. A Master is a term that defines a soul who incarnates into a life that he or she has experienced already.

The warriors and enlightened ones here now are coming into full acknowledgement so that two things can be accomplished. One is that they come from a place of full immersion into the human physical experience and head into an experience of a multi-faceted self with complete awareness of every part.

The second thing is that because of that fully

481

immersed personality – the rest of their family, friends and associates will identify with them. **In this way**, absorption happens, learning occurs and **the Light expands**."

~

"There are a series of sky events that transpire for you here on earth. No one will miss these.

It will be as if the sky is sending a message, and this sight will be visible everywhere. The timing for this cannot be precisely measured or given. It is on your horizon and close to what you consider "right now".

Although the awakening has been happening for such a long time, this event will feel like an activation. Once it occurs there will be no doubts.

What it is, is an equalizer. It will occur for the entire race on earth and will in that way erase your differences.

What this event signifies is the rapid onslaught of Gaia's response. It tells you the change-over has happened. It introduces New Earth."

~

"The matrix is no longer functioning.

You have moved mountains to make way for the New Earth. It is you who have done this, dear human.

Remember who the Builders are."

~

"In this the year of 2023 you enter your active stage of participation. You are not meant to retreat into the shadows. You are here to light them up.

This is what you do naturally, and it is why you do not see it so readily. Light naturally emanates from you and no special effort is required for it to do so.

You are the Light Bringers.

You are the Builders.

Trust that there is a beneficial all-encompassing moment and it arrives quickly now. The worst of things build, reach a crescendo and then collapse under their own weight. All changes then. There is a reversal.

It is your Light that illuminates this next part. It is your Light that introduces the possibility of it at all."

~

"You are here to increase the level of Light on the planet. It matters not who believes what you are saying and who doesn't. **Your illumination is why you are here**, not your beliefs.

Drops of Light

The knowing of your own Light is enough. It doesn't matter if those closest to you recognize it or even see it. What matters, in every case, is that they feel it.

You are here to increase the Light on planet Earth. It is because of your Light that the Great Awakening occurs at all. You, as part of the Collective, have initiated this Awakening. If you think on this, you'll see the changes that occur continually. Awareness is spreading.

As it does, the Light Quotient here increases, and Earth becomes a more comfortable place for you to reside. More Light helps you as well, to see and actualize your abilities. This will happen gradually and seamlessly.

Your world becomes a place of greater acceptance for the Light."

~

"**You approach the singularity.**

You will experience a moment – a zero-point moment of pure potential.

Once you traverse through that moment you will have accessed pure potential. After that moment, your world changes.

It is at this moment when your composure and Light will be so very much needed. It is the moment when you'll sense an energetic opportunity, and a pulse. You'll know then why you are here. You will recognize it. **It will be like the starting sound before a race."**

~

"Many times, have you been told the truth of your being. Yet have you seen this truth with your own eyes? The eyes you use now to read these words?

On most days, you have not. Such is the power of the illusion, and the control matrix that has been used to create it.

For you do not **know** your greatness in the same way you feel your struggles. The convincing has been a thorough one.

Your churches tell you to obey. Your doctors tell you that you are ill. Your banks tell you that you are broke. You must "work" to "earn" the right to live. Your schools segregate you and teach blatant conformity. There are no instances of "authority" that validate your wonder.

This is why it is said "The meek shall inherit the earth". You are the meek, of whom is spoken here. You have come in droves to remind each other and tell the world. You are so much more than you've been "allowed" to "imagine".

You are the Essence of Creation itself.

You hold within, every power and attribute that you think of as "Enlightened". Yet you have isolated these to fantasy and fairy tales, and thus restricted your access to Truth.

As your New World emerges and arises, so do you. It is your Light that illuminates what has been hidden. This hidden nature will show itself once you accept it as valid.

Your imagination will have to be seen as a tool rather than a child's plaything. It is your key to full actual-ization of your skills. It offers you insight. Insight to Truth. Insight into your power. Insight into the gifts you have, the light you hold, your Truth.

Allow it to guide you, dear one. See it as a road map to hidden treasure.

~

> *So, we'll end here, knowing that our story is still being written. Remember back in the summer of 2021 when this conversation happened? (see Chapter 6)*

~

"So where are we in this process of Ascension/freeing the planet?"

"You haven't made the appointment."

"What?"

~

Well, on **October 7, 2023***, I asked once more:*

"Where are we today?

"You've made the appointment, and you're now in the waiting room."

~

Nicely done humanity, nicely done.

Drops of Light

End Notes

[1] (January 1, 2012) **Message to Off World Beings**:

"2012 looks to be the Year of the Channel. Dozens of prophecies, from as many off-world beings, repeatedly speak to us, through us, and about us.
We are listening, with varying degrees of belief and enthusiasm. We are infusing these sources with divinity, and placing a whole lot of weight and power on each statement. At times, there is even anger expressed when things don't turn out exactly as prophesied.
It is time to channel the only source with the power to accurately predict our future. It is time to speak for ourselves.
Perhaps these beings have a broader vantage point, more advanced technology or a longer lifespan, yet they are not human. They, are watching us.
They cannot create in this reality, but we can. Let's introduce ourselves to them.

Hello, to all of you Off World Beings! We're enjoying your messages and would them to be more conversational. Here's a place to start –
As humans, being, we are insatiable. We are eternally hopeful. We never let go of our belief that there is something better possible. We're experts at second chances, do-overs, and trying again. There is a reason we were chosen to be here at this time, and it is deep within every one of us. It is our heart. Our ability to feel what we are and express what we are is what makes us uniquely suited to this task.
Although the Truth has been hidden from us these many years, it has not stopped us. You have watched us progress and witnessed our tenacity. We may not have known how we were expanding, but against all odds, this slave race of subservient beings has evolved to take command and intentionally create a future that benefits not some of us, but all of us.
This is because of our Light and our Power. We are sourced from the essence of creation and we can feel that Source.
Who we are is Love personified. We feel each other in each smile and every glance.
We will risk our lives to save each other; and join hands, hearts, and bodies across enemy lines, racial differences, borders and nationalities.
We are One, and although we have not used these words until now, our hearts have felt them always.
This is what you don't know about us, and even these words can't portray the full extent of our divinity.
It has to be felt, and in order to feel it, you must be human.

We do what we do, and will always be capable of doing more because we love each other. We live what we are, and what we are – is Love.
Our task now is to take this love we feel so deeply for each other, into ourselves. We do not love ourselves without condition, yet. But we will.

This shift we are undergoing is taking time, not because we are slow but because we want everyone on board when it happens.
We want it to be seamless and easily done for all of us. Our unity is something we understand deeply and feel in our every pore. We feel the Truth of our Oneness and know that together we can accomplish anything.
It is our heart that motivates and empowers us, and this is something that we know and we feel. Every one of us understands passion at a core level. Our feelings are the fuel of our magnificence. What is happening for us is that we are waking up to the brilliance of our own Truth. In every moment we are Love, and as we shake off the dust of oppression, we see just how expanding and all-encompassing we actually are.
We will get there as One because we believe that we will, and we are actualizing our very essence. There is no doubt in our hearts, and there resides our greatest strength. Our hearts hold the Source of Creation, and they beat as One.
We are the Ones we are waiting for.
Thank you."

[2] (January 20, 2012) **Response to Off World Beings II**

"Hello again all you off world beings!
Let me explain a few more things about us humans. We are really suspicious of voices in our heads. Telepathic communication is something we've heard about, but we are not used to it. Historically, we've been locked up and put away for talking to invisible people, and these memories make us a bit skittish.
We are creatures of habit. So much so that when something brand new is introduced to us, we may not even see it at first. Your presence will eradicate much of the history we've learned, and our memories are associative.
A gradual introduction will have to take place. It will give us something to hang onto as we shift. We've seen your ships. Depending on who you talk to, that's either a good thing or a bad thing.
We've seen artist's renderings of what some of you are supposed to look like, but we have not yet spoken face to face.

So, to whomever is listening, I'm sorry I missed you last week. But maybe this helps to explain a bit about why I did.

For the rest of you, you tube reaches much further than we thought. Here's what happened:

At 12:20 AM I was woken up. There were no sounds, no lights, my family was asleep. I thought to myself "What woke me up?" and I heard "We did!"
"Where are you?" I replied.
"Come take a look out back!", I heard.
Well, it was cold. I was cozy and sleepy and I responded "Look, if I get up out of this warm bed and you aren't there? I'm going to be really pissed!"

"Come on!" I heard again. "Just come check."
"This is stupid" I responded. And I rolled over, and went back to sleep.

The next morning, I ran out back to check. No note. No imprint in the snow. "Shoot".
I told my partner and he said "Are you kidding me? They come from half-way across the galaxy, wake you up, and you won't even walk into the next room to talk to them? What are you, nuts?"

Well, I was afraid I was nuts, and that's why I didn't get up. Look, the only ones who seem to have an understanding of you are the government and the military. They do not represent the people, and there are seven billion of us. With a little patience, we'd like to take disclosure into our own hands, talk to you ourselves, and get to know you. Without any "spin" from the media, the military or the government.
We suspect you're just like us, only with much cooler rides!
Thanks for listening. Next time, I'll get up."

[3] "For storms shall rage and oceans roar
When Gabriel stands on sea and shore,
And he **blows his wondrous horn**."

by Ursula Southeil (c. 1488–1561) aka Mother Shipton

[4] **"If you close your eyes"**

What is happening now is extraordinary. In this fictional arena called time we are becoming One. It transcends language so hang in there as a telling is attempted.

Yesterday polarity roared, gasping for breath. There was a moment of confusion. Within reach and in plain sight were the oxygen tanks; familiar and easy to operate. Yet nearby, something else insisted; something new and untested.

It was not reached for as much as it arrived, right on time. In one bold moment of unity, agape arrived. It said "I know you. I have seen you. There is nothing you can do to change the way I feel for you. You are no parts distasteful, hateful, repulsive or disappointing. You are me. How can I hurt or hate that which I

491

understand? I am you."

This answer came clothed as a human. Another who knew the question without sound or words; who felt it and responded. Oneness. The oxygen tanks remain unused, we are breathing new air.

Oneness transforms everything. It is not taught so much as recognized; learned so much as remembered. The precise moment in which you realize that God has always been within
you, you know truth. You are God. As God, there is no other. None to judge. None to

blame. None to fight. None to harm. None lesser or greater. Just One. One to love.

Yesterday life played its songs and stories, reminding us of what we are doing. We are closing not just a door, but a plot line. Its recurring roles and lives and struggles were lived so that we'd understand completely. We do. We can walk as One now. We can trust each other. We are One, in real time.

The walls must fall. It's the only way. *Acceptance of love erases any risk.* We must be willingly, unconditionally ourselves. All the walls were glass anyway. We just pretended they were either mirrors or bricks. We've moved past the need for pretense.

Oneness breathes only love. When you meet another who breathes that air, joy sort of melts from their pores. Look around, it is happening in surprising faces. You can see it in their eyes; agape.

If you close your eyes, you can feel it. You've been here before. Remember. You are the One you've been waiting for.

[5] **"The Ultimate Addiction"**

You are human. Gloriously, exuberantly, perfectly human. *There is no better version of you.* Let go of your "higher" self. You are multi-faceted. You have lots of parts. There is one version of you, the one with an expanded view, who has decided to watch you now, joining this life you are living. Your life. The messy one. The one with you in it.

What is going to emerge at the other end of all of this is another version of us. Call it what you want, time is an illusion and Oneness is truth. This means that we didn't "start" anywhere and there are no "higher" parts of ourselves holding wisdom we don't yet have. It's all you, all the time.

What we need are new words. Words to unleash the creativity of a world full of multi-billionaire light beings. What does a world with no restraints feel like? Can you imagine life without financial, spiritual, mental or physical limitation? Can you even visualize ten billion dollars? It is a one, followed by ten zeros. Those zeros, that seem to have all the power, are just a whole lotta nothing. It is the One in front of them that makes it all happen. That One would be you, the force of creation, here now to craft a world without limits.

The whole point seems to have been to drive ourselves to the edge of insanity, waiting, wondering and miserable; only to realize no one is coming. It is done.

There are no ascended masters, galactic saviors or "higher" versions of ourselves on the way to save us. This is our planet and we love her. We are the Masters, the ones here to shift with her.

This was the trip you came for. You have everything you need. No extra attachments are required to utilize the power here. The power source is you – you've just forgotten how to turn yourself on. You've done this before. Today you are here to do it as a human. You chose and were chosen to do this. You are not alone.

We knew before we came that we'd have to get to this breaking point before we realized the truth:

The only answer is us.

The only place to be is here.

The only time is now.

The only ones to do it knew that they could, and that when the moment arrived, they would.

It is upon us now to find the new. We need words and tools that never were. That 90% of unused stuff in your brain is getting itchy. Your ability to create is legion. It's why you were chosen. Take the crayons out of the box. Work some magic.

Start happening. Imagine eternal vitality, relentless abundance, pervasive peace and wild joy, right alongside no traffic, great parking spots, good hair days and free concerts. Hold happy. Breathe music. Whisper trees. The vision you are holding is the life you are molding.

We are addicted to ourselves and there is not a 12-step program. We wouldn't join one if there were. Humanity is the hottest game in town. Everyone is watching and wants to join in. We are passionately unhappy, dramatically ecstatic and violently loving. We create things just to tear them down from boredom. We run too fast, hide in corners, sing off key and gossip. The human condition is us, and we love every inch and nuance. We excite ourselves.

There is no better version to become. We are here to harness our innate essence. While every single channel we listen to tells us how cool we are, we continue to believe we're supposed to be something else. These voices are reminders, nothing more or less, *and we put them there*. This entire life is our creation.

We were never supposed to change. The answer is not outside of ourselves. We planned to fall desperately in love – with us. We've hidden our magnificence in gold, in others and in promises of more. We've blamed our failure on lack, on others and on outside limitation.

There's no place else to go with this. We've reached part 2 – self-emergence. Your emotions are the trigger and the best part of you; they fuel the human experience and create worlds. Enjoy them and watch what happens.

You love to emote, to feel and to push beyond. The angst of your heart is the subject of every song, each story and all of your favorite movies. To dream is your birthright. You've grown up inside institutions and ideas that said looking out the window was wrong, wasteful even. This attempt to systematically erase your core truth has failed. You are bigger than any method of thought.

Embrace your humanity. Your emotions are key to your power. You only need desire and it is done. Love who you are, see what you want and don't stop until amazing happens. Contrast fuels creation.

We do that for each other. We supply contrast. We give each other sparks. We are the Masters and the answer to every prayer. We know what to do. The reason we haven't seen it yet or heard it yet is because we haven't done it yet. We've been waiting.

We are the Ones we've been waiting for.

[6] "Sea of Chains"

You are swimming in a sea of chains. There are so many and they are so thick, you cannot tell what yours are attached to – but yes, you are shackled. It is not as if your very life depends on what's at the end of that shackle – *it is that you believe that it does.* It is that belief that keeps you bound. Keeps you moving to wherever it drags you. Keeps you asking to be released.

It is your belief that holds you, your mind that binds you.

The effort to control you focuses on a constant stream of programming as well as entertainment and food, to keep you fat and happy, mesmerized and asleep. You know this and yet you continue to search beyond yourself for the keys to your release.

There is only one person who can release the hold slavery has on your life. There is only one way it can occur.

The way is entirely self-motivated, self-sustained and springs from self-awareness. There are no unknowns that depend on another to be known. Self-reliant, self-propelled and self-conscious – these are the attributes of a sovereign being.

Your slavery has reached down to your core – it sits so deeply in your thinking that it is cloaked in familiarity. It will not be comfortable to dig it out and look at it. Your society puts on you pressure to conform. You are tired. You'd like to have someone take care of this for you – to fix it so that you can live without the chains, requirements, debt and dependence.

Freedom is a full-time job. You cannot be partially free. As the details of deception and corruption are unearthed, you become gradually horrified at its scope. Once your eyes are open, they will not easily be shut.

Ask "Who is served by this?" before undertaking any thought, word or action. Let the answer direct your movements. The system of slavery is only upheld if we participate. Non-compliance means you answer to no one. The guns of our governments and spaceships of those off planet do not, in truth, signify control or ownership. We are, each of us, equal and sovereign beings. The only thing you can be sure about in any interaction is that your perception is informing your opinion.

The desire for bliss or to be numbed to the harsh realities of the day to day keep us staring at our electronic devices and stagnant. This is not an accident. Nothing changes until and unless we change it. We signed up for this, confident we'd pull it off. A fully conscious, sovereign being experiences joy and fulfillment in deeply satisfying moments. We will get there.

Perseverance, determination and tenacity are demanded of us. We knew this was a part of it and that the payoff, when it came, would be that much sweeter because we did it ourselves. We are the ones we are waiting for.

[7] **This was written 8 years ago.**

Drops of Light

It's 2023, and the conversation around choosing a non-specific gender on a medical form has escalated into "trans-wars"; with secret alternative sexual identities available and hidden in school closets and/or online for middle school-aged children without parental knowledge. It was recognized initially as this generation's "bra-burning" moment; a refusal, by a sexually mature individual, to be categorized by a word on a form. What the culture is facing today around trans-sexual identity is potentially more permanent and harmful for those youngest and most impressionable; surgery. It is a divisive, sensitive and difficult issue we now struggle to come to terms with as a people.

[8] **"What about Us?" Pink**

We are searchlights, we can see in the dark
We are rockets, pointed up at the stars
We are billions of beautiful hearts

And you sold us down the river too far
What about us?
What about all the times you said you had the
answers?
What about us?
What about all the broken happy ever afters?
What about us?
What about all the plans that ended in disaster?
What about love? What about trust?
What about us?
We are problems that want to be solved
We are children that need to be loved
We were willin', we came when you called
But man, you fooled us, enough is enough, oh
What about us?
What about all the times you said you had the answers?
What about us?
What about all the broken happy ever afters?
Oh, what about us?
What about all the plans that ended in disaster?
Oh, what about love? What about trust?
What about us?
Oh, what about us?
What about all the plans that ended in disaster?
What about love? What about trust?
What about us?
Sticks and stones, they may break these bones
But then I'll be ready, are you ready?
It's the start of us, waking up come on

Are you ready? I'll be ready
I don't want control; I want to let go
Are you ready? I'll be ready
'Cause now it's time to let them know
We are ready, what about us?
What about us?
What about all the times you said you had the
answers?
So what about us?
What about all the broken happy ever afters?
Oh, what about us?
What about all the plans that ended in disaster?
Oh, what about love? What about trust?
What about us?
What about us?
What about us?
What about us?
What about us?
What about us?
What about us?

[9] "We the People" Kid Rock

We the people in all we do
Reserve the right to scream "F*ck you"
(Hey-yeah) Ow
(Hey-yeah) Huh
"Wear your mask, take your pills"
Now a whole generation's mentally ill
(Hey-yeah) Man, f*ck Fauci
(Hey-yeah)

But COVID's near, it's coming to town
We gotta act quick, shut our borders down
Joe Biden does, the media embraces
Big Don does it and they call him racist

We the people (woo, let's go Brandon)
We the people (woo, let's go Brandon)
We the people (woo, let's go Brandon)
We the people

F*ck Facebook, f*ck Twitter too
And the mainstream media, f*ck you too, too, too
(Woo) Yeah, you

Drops of Light

We the people (ooh, yeah)
We the people

Inflation's up, like the minimum wage
So it's all the same, and ain't a damn thing changed
(Hey-yeah)
(Hey-yeah)
You piece of shit, I don't see color
"Black lives matter", no shit, motherfucker
(Hey-yeah)
(Hey-yeah)

But we gotta keep fighting for the right to be free
And every human being doesn't have to agree
We all bleed red, brother, listen to me
It's time for love and unity

We the people (woo, let's go Brandon)
We the people (woo, let's go Brandon)
We the people (woo, let's go Brandon)
We the people

F*ck CNN, f*ck TMZ
And you social media trolls, y'all can suck on deez (deez)
Deez nuts, that's what's up

We the people (ha-ha)

If you're down with love and wanna make things better
All we gotta do is just come together
Weather the storm, and take my hand
Then follow my lead to the promised land
'Cause we the people, we gotta unite
To follow that good time guiding light
Climb aboard this love boat
And rock that bitch up and down the coast

In order to form a more perfect union
Do ordain and establish this constitution for the United States of America

We the people (woo, let's go Brandon)
We the people (woo, let's go Brandon)
We the people (woo, let's go Brandon)
We the people

Standing up, and standing tall
'Cause it's all for one and it's one for all
All, all, all
We the people (woo)
We the people

(Let's go Brandon)
(Let's go Brandon)
(Let's go Brandon)
(Let's go Brandon)

[10] **Here there was a vision, and it is one I also saw and recorded for Words of One,**
Volume II. It is this:

"The visuals were so very powerful and numerous.
The force, or push, from our Ancestors was seen as a wide swath of people, smiling, all glowing brightly from the other side and nodding.
All forms of humanity were there – the facial structures and colors and variations were vast.
I was reminded of versions seen only in museums of our Ancestors, they were alive and grinning and sort of holding fast the force that was pushing us forward, the correction we are making for what happened here. So much love…"

The End

or maybe the beginning.

Made in United States
Troutdale, OR
12/15/2023

15894961R00279